# Urban Spaces in Nineteenth-Century Ireland

EDITED BY GEORGINA LARAGY,
OLWEN PURDUE AND
JONATHAN JEFFREY WRIGHT

LIVERPOOL UNIVERSITY PRESS

First published 2018 by
Liverpool University Press
4 Cambridge Street
Liverpool
L69 7ZU

Copyright © 2018 Liverpool University Press

The right of Georgina Laragy, Olwen Purdue and Jonathan Jeffrey Wright to be identified as the editors of this book has been asserted by them in accordance with the Copyright, Designs and Patents Act 1988.

All rights reserved. No part of this book may be reproduced, stored in a retrieval system, or transmitted, in any form or by any means, electronic, mechanical, photocopying, recording, or otherwise, without the prior written permission of the publisher.

British Library Cataloguing-in-Publication data
A British Library CIP record is available

ISBN 978-1-78694-152-7

Typeset by Carnegie Book Production, Lancaster
Printed and bound by TJ International Ltd, Padstow, Cornwall, PL28 8RW

# Urban Spaces
in Nineteenth-Century Ireland

The Society for the Study of Nineteenth-Century Ireland

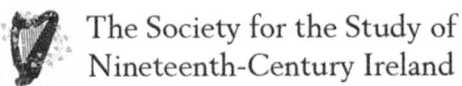 The Society for the Study of
Nineteenth-Century Ireland

The purpose of the Society is to promote research into nineteenth-century Ireland, and membership is open to scholars both from Ireland and other countries. The Society welcomes members from a wide range of disciplines: literature, history, economics, geography, sociology, anthropology, theology, women's studies, fine arts, etc. It thus seeks to foster an inter-disciplinary approach to nineteenth-century Irish studies.

Series editors: Laurence M. Geary & Ciara Breathnach

# Contents

*List of Figures* vii

*List of Tables* ix

Introduction 1
    *Olwen Purdue and Jonathan Jeffrey Wright*

1 'The Royal Paragon': Setting Out Suburban Space in Nineteenth-Century Dublin 13
    *Laura Johnstone*

2 Municipal Social Housing in Ireland, 1866–1914 42
    *Matthew Potter*

3 'The Donegalls' Backside': Donegall Place, the White Linen Hall and the Development of Space and Place in Nineteenth-Century Belfast 61
    *Jonathan Jeffrey Wright*

4 The School and the Home: Constructing Childhood and Space in Dublin Boarding Schools 84
    *Mary Hatfield*

5 'High Walls and Locked Doors': Contested Spaces in the Belfast Workhouse, 1880–1905 106
    *Olwen Purdue*

6 Levelling Up the Lower Deeps: Rural and Suburban Spaces at an Edwardian Asylum 125
    *Gillian Allmond*

7 Locating Investigations into Suicidal Deaths in Urban Ireland, 1901–1915 144
  *Georgina Laragy*

8 Visualising the City: Images of Ireland's Urban World, c.1790–1820 162
  *Mary Jane Boland*

9 Forging a Shared Identity: Irish Migrants and Steel Cities, 1850–1900 183
  *Oliver Betts*

*Index* 201

# Figures

1.1 and 1.2 [surveyor unknown], 'Survey of the Estate of Monkstown with the Town of Dunleary in the County of Dublin' (1792) (Pakenham papers, private collection, Tullynally Castle, Castlepollard, Co. Westmeath, T/3763/Q9. Courtesy of Thomas Pakenham) 16–17

1.3 and 1.4 Sherrard, Brassington & Greene, 'Survey of the Town of Dunleary and Royal Paragon in the County of Dublin', Estate map (1813) (Pakenham papers, private collection, Tullynally Castle, Castlepollard, Co. Westmeath, T/3763/Q9. Courtesy of Thomas Pakenham) 20–21

1.5 John Hill, 'Plan and survey of part of the Town of Dunleary the Property of Lords Longford and de Vesci', Estate map (1816) (Pakenham papers, private collection, Tullynally Castle, Castlepollard, Co. Westmeath, T/3763/Q9. Courtesy of Thomas Pakenham) 24

1.6 First edition Ordnance Survey map of Dublin, scale 1:10,560 (6 inches to 1 mile), sheet no. 23 (Dublin, 1843) (Courtesy of the board of Trinity College Dublin) 25

1.7 Author, Monkstown Crescent, Monkstown, Co. Dublin, photograph, April 2014 26

1.8 Author, Longford Terrace, Monkstown, Co. Dublin, photograph, April 2014 31

1.9 Ordnance Survey map of Monkstown, scale 1:1,056 (5 feet to 1 mile), sheet no. 23/45 (Dublin, 1866) (Courtesy of the board of Trinity College Dublin) 37

4.1 Building and grounds of Loreto House, Rathfarnham, Dublin (c.1900) (Institute of the Blessed Virgin Mary (Loreto), Institute and Irish Province Archives) 92

4.2 Decimus Burton's ground plan of proposed farm buildings for
the Royal Hibernian Military School, January 1836
(Office of Public Works, National Archive of Ireland,
OPW/5HC/2/65–68. Thanks to the Director of the National
Archives for permission to reproduce the image)   98

6.1 District Lunatic Asylums in Ireland and their distances from
nearest urban centres
(List of asylums and dates of opening taken from Markus
Reuber, 'State and private lunatic asylums in Ireland: medics,
fools and maniacs (1600–1900)', Ph.D. thesis, University of
Cologne, 1994. Linear distances obtained from Google Maps)   130

6.2 Bird's-eye view of Purdysburn villa colony (detail)
(Belfast District Lunatic Asylum annual report, 1921)   135

6.3 Ground-, first- and attic-floor plans of Purdysburn villa for
chronic/recovering patients
(redrawn from original plans)   136

6.4 Elevation and cross-section of Purdysburn villa showing
fireplaces and flues.
(Estates Department, Knockbracken Healthcare Park)   138

8.1 Nathaniel (the Elder) Grogan (c.1740–1808), *North Gate Bridge*
(c.1794), etching, 35.5 cm × 27 cm
(Crawford Art Gallery, Cork)   164

8.2 Nathaniel (the Elder) Grogan (c.1740–1808), *Patrick's Bridge*
(c.1796), aquatint, 36 cm × 46 cm
(private collection)   169

8.3 Nathaniel (the Elder) Grogan (c.1740–1808), *Boats on the River
Lee below Tivoli* (c.1790), oil on canvas, 94.3 cm × 168 cm
(National Gallery of Ireland, NGI 4074)   170

8.4 William Turner de Lond (*fl.* 1820–26), *Market Place and
Courthouse at Ennis* (c.1821), oil on canvas, 75.6 cm × 106 cm
(Merrion Hotel, Dublin)   175

8.5 William Turner de Lond (*fl.* 1820–26), *George IV, King of
England, entering Dublin* (c.1821), oil on canvas, 171 cm × 279 cm
(National Gallery of Ireland, NGI 1148)   178

8.6 William Turner de Lond (*fl.* 1820–26), *The Chairing of Thomas
Spring Rice* (c.1821), oil on canvas
(Limerick Chamber of Commerce)   180

# Tables

2.1  Social housing legislation in Ireland, 1866–1914                48
2.2  Number of housing units in a sample group of eleven municipal
     authorities by 1914                                             51
2.3  Percentages of families in Irish urban areas by class
     of accommodation, 1881                                          53
2.4  Rateable valuation in Irish urban areas per head of population,
     1881–85                                                         54

# Introduction

*Olwen Purdue and Jonathan Jeffrey Wright*

That urban history has developed slowly in Ireland has long been acknowledged. Writing in 1981, David Harkness and Mary O'Dowd remarked that '[t]he study of the town in Ireland has too long been neglected' and in a wide-ranging historiographical survey, published some five years later, Mary E. Daly made a similar point, highlighting a 'past neglect of urban history' in Ireland.[1] For Daly, this 'neglect' was attributable to causes both scholarly and cultural. These included Irish historians' tendency to focus on politics and the 'struggle for national independence', and 'the popular belief that towns were somehow alien to Irish culture'.[2] It should, however, be noted that a tendency to overlook the history of Ireland's urban centres was by no means unique to the twentieth century. Indeed, as Rosemary Sweet has demonstrated, while the eighteenth and early nineteenth centuries were marked, in England, by an 'abundance of descriptive urban literature', reflecting the 'flourishing condition of English towns', such literature was limited in Ireland. There, its production was hampered by a fragile 'civic tradition' and the hangovers of Ireland's troubled seventeenth century, which 'left the eighteenth-century urban inhabitants a legacy of contested history' that provided 'a powerful check on the expression of communal sentiment'.[3]

---

1 David Harkness and Mary O'Dowd, 'Introduction' in David Harkness and Mary O'Dowd (eds), *The town in Ireland* (Belfast, 1981), pp 1–5 at 1; Mary E. Daly, 'Irish urban history: a survey' in *Urban History*, xiii (1986), pp 61–72 at 61.
2 Daly, 'Irish urban history', p. 61.
3 Rosemary Sweet, 'Provincial culture and urban histories in England and Ireland during the long eighteenth century' in Peter Borsay and Lindsay Proudfoot (eds), *Provincial towns in early modern England and Ireland: change, convergence and divergence* (Oxford, 2002), pp 223–39 at 223, 224, 231 and 234. See also, for the writing of Irish urban history in the late eighteenth and early nineteenth centuries, and more recent scholarly and cultural 'anti-urbanism', David Dickson, 'Town and city' in Eugenio F. Biagini and Mary E. Daly, *The Cambridge social history of modern Ireland* (Cambridge, 2017), pp 112–28 at 112–15.

Whatever the causes, immediate or long-term, of the 'neglect' of urban history in Ireland, it appeared by the late 1980s that things were beginning to change: 'the history of Irish towns and cities is being explored with an unprecedentedly high level of attention', Daly observed in her 1986 survey, though this increased attention was not sufficient to prevent the conclusion that the study of urban history in Ireland remained at 'an early stage'.[4] In the intervening period, further development has taken place, though whether Irish urban history has today reached a point of full maturity is open to debate. Much work remains to be done and comparing Irish urban history with its British counterpart proves revealing, for in Ireland, as David Dickson has observed, 'the pursuit of urban history has in recent decades been far weaker than in the neighbouring island'.[5] Yet if we might conclude that Irish urban history continues to develop slowly, it is important to note that it *has* continued to develop. Whatever may be said of the speed of its development, urban history remains a fixture on the Irish historiographical scene and has recently shown encouraging signs of growth.

A brief glance at recent publications and scholarly developments illustrates the point. As might be expected, Ireland's largest and most closely studied urban centres – Belfast and Dublin – have continued to attract attention.[6] Indeed, the past five years alone have witnessed the appearance of landmark publications on each, in the form of *Belfast 400: people, place and history* (2012), edited by Sean Connolly, and *Dublin: the making of a capital city* (2014), authored by David Dickson.[7] Looking beyond Belfast and Dublin, Dickson has also contributed a major volume on Cork and its hinterland, and new work has appeared which sheds light – directly in some instances, indirectly in others – on other urban centres, including Derry, Galway,

---

4 Daly, 'Irish urban history', pp 61, 68.
5 David Dickson, 'The state of Dublin's history' in *Éire-Ireland*, xlv, nos. 1 and 2 (2010), pp 198–212 at 204.
6 See, for recent work on Dublin, ibid. In addition to Connolly's work, cited below, recent publications on aspects of Belfast's history include Raymond Gillespie, *Early Belfast: the origins and growth of an Ulster town to 1750* (Belfast, 2007); A.C. Hepburn, *Catholic Belfast and nationalist Ireland in the era of Joe Devlin, 1871–1934* (Oxford, 2008); John Bew, *The glory of being Britons: civic unionism in nineteenth-century Belfast* (Dublin, 2009); Mark Doyle, *Fighting like the Devil for the sake of God: Protestants, Catholics and the origins of violence in Victorian Belfast* (Manchester, 2009); W.A. Maguire, *Belfast: a history* (Lancaster, 2009); Stephen A. Royle, *Portrait of an industrial city: 'clanging Belfast', 1750–1914* (Belfast, 2011); Olwen Purdue (ed.), *Belfast, the emerging city: 1850–1914* (Dublin, 2012); Jonathan Jeffrey Wright, *The 'natural leaders' and their world: politics, culture and society in Belfast, c.1801–1832* (Liverpool, 2012); and Kyle Hughes, *The Scots in Victorian and Edwardian Belfast: a study in elite migration* (Edinburgh, 2013).
7 S.J. Connolly (ed.), *Belfast 400: people, place and history* (Liverpool 2012); David Dickson, *Dublin: the making of a capital city* (London, 2014).

Kilkenny, Limerick and Sligo.[8] Likewise, new work has appeared on urban settlements in medieval Ireland, while attempts have been made to study the provincial towns of early modern Ireland alongside their English counterparts, and much needed light had been shed on urban government and municipal politics.[9] In addition, an Irish Modern Urban History Group, 'concerned with the history of the development and function of cities and towns in Ireland, and of the political, social and cultural history of urban spaces they contain', has recently been established, and scholars of Ireland's urban history now have an invaluable and ever-expanding resource in the Royal Irish Academy's *Irish historic towns atlas*.[10] To date, atlas fascicles have been produced for Armagh, Athlone, Bandon, Belfast, Bray, Carlingford, Carrickfergus, Derry, Downpatrick, Dublin, Dundalk, Ennis, Fethard, Galway, Kells, Kildare, Kilkenny, Limerick, Longford, Maynooth, Mullingar, Sligo, Trim, Tuam and Youghal, while those for Ballyshannon, Cahir, Carlow, Cashel, Cavan, Clonmel, Cork, Drogheda, Dungannon, Loughrea, Naas, Newry, Roscommon, Tralee, Tullamore and Waterford are in preparation.[11] Significant works of scholarship in their own right, these fascicles are of immense value in drawing together information which may be used to chart the growth of individual urban settlements and, as John Bradley has demonstrated, to undertake comparative research on the development of Ireland's towns.[12]

---

8 John Cunningham, *A town tormented by the sea: Galway, 1790–1914* (Dublin, 2004); David Dickson, *Old world colony: Cork and South Munster 1630–1830* (Cork, 2005); Matthew Potter, *The government and the people of Limerick: the history of Limerick Corporation/City Council, 1197–2006* (Limerick, 2006); Robert Gavin, William P. Kelly and Dolores O'Reilly, *Atlantic gateway: the port and city of Londonderry since 1700* (Dublin, 2009); John Bradley and Michael O'Dwyer (eds), *Kilkenny through the centuries: chapters in the history of an Irish city* (Kilkenny, 2009); D.A. Fleming, *Politics and provincial people: Sligo and Limerick, 1691–1761* (Manchester, 2010).

9 Recent publications on urban development in medieval Ireland include Michael Potterton, *Medieval Trim: history and archaeology* (Dublin, 2005); John Bradley, Anngret Simms and Alan J. Fletcher (eds), *Dublin in the medieval world: studies in honour of Howard B. Clarke* (Dublin, 2009); Michael Potterton and Matthew Seaver (eds), *Uncovering medieval Trim: archaeological excavations in and around Trim, Co. Meath* (Dublin, 2009); Margaret Murphy and Michael Potterton (eds), *The Dublin region in the middle ages: settlement, land-use and economy* (Dublin, 2010); Sparky Booker and Cherie N. Peters (eds), *Tales of medieval Dublin* (Dublin, 2014). For early modern towns, see Borsay and Proudfoot, *Provincial town in early modern England and Ireland*, and for urban governance, see Gerald Hall, *Ulster liberalism, 1778–1876: the middle path* (Dublin, 2011), pp 99–124 and Matthew Potter, *The municipal revolution in Ireland: a handbook of urban government in Ireland since 1800* (Dublin, 2011).

10 Irish Modern Urban History Group, available at https://irishurbanhistory.wordpress.com/2014/07/28/about-us/ (accessed 5 July 2016).

11 Irish Historic Towns Atlas Publications, available at https://www.ria.ie/research-projects/irish-historic-towns-atlas/about-publications (accessed 4 Oct. 2017).

12 John Bradley, 'The Irish Historic Towns Atlas as a source for urban history' in

Taking all of this into account, it appears that, notwithstanding its late emergence and somewhat halting development, there are grounds for some optimism regarding the future of Irish urban history, and it is hoped that the present volume, which has its origins in the 2014 conference of the Society for the Study for Nineteenth Century Ireland, will serve to demonstrate still further the vitality and potential of the field. More particularly, however, it is hoped that it will make a new and quite distinct contribution to the literature on Ireland's towns and cities. Chiefly penned by early career researchers, the chapters that follow vary widely in terms of subject matter and methodology but are united by an effort to engage with the concept of urban space. To put this another way, this is a volume which is not simply concerned with people who happened to live, or events that happened to occur, in Ireland's urban spaces, but a volume which takes as its focus the spaces themselves.

Those familiar with the development of urban history in Ireland might object that there is nothing particularly new in focusing specifically on urban space. A close scrutiny of the shape and spatial development of urban settlements has long been a characteristic of Irish urban history, leading Vanessa Harding to identify 'attention to morphology' as a 'distinctive aspect of Irish urban history'.[13] However, while the study of urban space can, and in some of the following chapters does, involve the examination of the ways in which a town or city has developed, it can also involve rather more, for in recent years, under the influence of a 'spatial turn', the concept of space has emerged as a significant focus for cultural and historical inquiry.[14] The roots of this 'spatial turn' lie in

Howard B. Clarke, Jacinta Prunty and Mark Hennessy (eds), *Surveying Ireland's past: multidisciplinary essays in honour of Anngret Simms* (Dublin, 2004), pp 727–46. See also Dickson, 'The state of Dublin's history', p. 201.

13 Harding sees 'the achievements of the *Irish Historic Towns Atlas*' as illustrative of this morphological focus. Vanessa Harding, Review of Peter C. Clark and Raymond Gillespie (eds), *Two capitals: London and Dublin, 1500–1840* (Oxford, 2001) and Peter Borsay and Lindsay Proudfoot (eds), *Provincial towns in early modern England and Ireland: change, convergence, and divergence* (Oxford, 2002) in *English Historical Review*, cxviii, no. 477 (2003), pp 715–17 at 717.

14 Simon Gunn, 'The spatial turn: changing histories of space and place' in Simon Gunn and Robert J. Morris (eds), *Identities in Space: contested terrains in the Western City since 1850* (Aldershot, 2001), pp 1–14 at 1. For further discussion of the 'spatial turn', see Diarmid A. Finnegan, 'The spatial turn: geographical approaches in the history of science' in *Journal of the History of Biology*, xli, no. 2 (2008), pp 369–88; Ralph Kingston, 'Mind over matter? History and the spatial turn' in *Cultural and Social History*, vii, no. 1 (2010), pp 111–21; Jo Guldi, 'Landscape and place' in Simon Gunn and Lucy Faire (eds), *Research methods for history* (Edinburgh, 2011), pp 66–80; Katrina Navickas, '"Why I am tired of turning": a theoretical interlude', seminar paper delivered at the Institute of Historical Research in December 2011, available at www.historyworkingpapers.org/?page_id=225 (accessed 7 July 2016); Beat Kumin and Cornelie Usborne, 'At home and in the workplace: a historical introduction to the "spatial turn"' in *History and Theory*, lii, no. 3 (2013), pp 305–18.

the work of a range of sociologists, historians and geographers, including Michel Foucault, Edward Soja, Michel de Certau, Henri Lefebvre and David Harvey.[15] In simple terms, however, the 'spatial turn' might be said to reflect an awareness that space is not 'neutral'. The historical geographer David N. Livingstone has made precisely this point, observing that 'space is far from a "neutral container" in which life is transacted … Rather, it is itself constitutive of systems of human interaction. At every scale from the international to the domestic, we inhabit locations that at once enable and constrain routine social relations'.[16] Likewise, in an early historiographic intervention, Simon Gunn demonstrated that the idea of space as 'neutral dimension' had been called into question, asserting that 'space is increasingly seen as produced by material and symbolic forces in different forms' and that 'following Foucault, there is a growing recognition that "space is fundamental in any exercise of power"', while Katrina Navickas, reflecting on the 'spatial turn' more recently, has explained that space, once 'treated as a neutral, abstract and uniform medium in which action and social relations operated', is 'now defined as a social construction, formed by culture and in itself forming culture, shaping power and enabling agency'.[17]

Described thus, the spatial turn can be seen to have an obvious relevance to the study of history and it has, unsurprisingly, informed historical scholarship on a wide range of themes. Historians of British radicalism in the late eighteenth and early nineteenth centuries have engaged with the spatial.[18] So, too, have historians of science and, most significantly in the current context, historians of urban space.[19] However, engaging with space is not without its potential pitfalls. Scholars such as Navickas and Leif Jerram have highlighted conceptual imprecision and a tendency to overlook space's materiality and to conflate it with place as particular problems of historical scholarship informed by the 'spatial turn'.[20] Among other things, Jerram has complained that 'the

---

15  Guldi, 'Landscape and place', p. 66; Gunn, 'The spatial turn', pp 1, 3, 4, 9, 10; Kingston, 'Mind over matter?', pp 112, 114, 115; Navickas, '"Why I am tired of turning"'; Katrina Navickas, *Protest and the politics of space and place, 1789–1848* (Manchester, 2016), pp 14–16.
16  David N. Livingstone, *Putting science in its place: geographies of scientific knowledge* (Chicago, 2003), p. 7.
17  Gunn, 'The spatial turn', pp 2, 9; Navickas, *Protest and the politics of space and place*, pp 13, 14.
18  Navickas, '"Why I am tired of turning"'; Jonathan Jeffrey Wright, 'An Anglo-Irish radical in the late Georgian metropolis: Peter Finnerty and the politics of contempt' in *Journal of British Studies*, liii, no. 3 (2014), pp 660–84 at 668.
19  Finnegan, 'The spatial turn'; Gunn, 'The spatial turn', p. 10; Fiona Williamson, 'The spatial turn of social and cultural history: a review of the current field' in *European History Quarterly*, xliv, no. 4 (2014), 703–17.
20  Navickas, *Protest and the politics of space and place*, pp 15–16; Leif Jerram, 'Space: a useless category for historical analysis?' in *History and Theory*, lii, no. 3 (2013), pp 400–19.

profitable attention to place (when it has been offered) has ... functioned to make it harder to talk about space, because the word "space" has also been used interchangeably with place to refer to values, symbols, beliefs, actions, and performances'.[21] Similarly, Navickas has complained that 'the historical spatial turn often confuses the meaning of space with place'. Drawing on Jerram's arguments, she insists that 'space shapes physical action by its materiality not by its symbolism' and argues for a clear distinction between the two.[22]

Engaging with space thus requires a degree of conceptual precision and a recognition that space is not place. Yet if there are conceptual pitfalls to avoid, a spatial approach to historical analysis nevertheless offers much. Indeed, while cautioning that 'it is essential to retain a critical perspective on the literature that has gathered around the "spatial turn" as well as on postmodernism', Gunn has suggested that 'the principal insights of the "spatial turn" remain of central importance to historians, and perhaps especially to urban historians'.[23] The idea, already discussed, that space is not 'neutral', but 'is itself constitutive of systems of interaction', might be identified as one key insight.[24] Gunn, however, suggests three more, namely: 'that social processes require to be analyzed in space as well as through time; that issues of the ownership and meanings of space are often deeply embedded in historical conflicts and processes; and that, in a more radical sense than has applied hitherto, histories of people require to be integrated with histories of place'.[25]

From all of this, it is clear that focusing specifically on the concept of urban space involves more than morphology alone. Engaging with space opens up a range of questions which might shed light on the histories of Ireland's towns and cities. How were spaces constructed within Irish towns and cities and how, in turn, did a town or city's spaces shape its character? Put another way, how did urban spaces shape the behaviour of those who lived within them, and in what ways did they reflect power relationships? What, moreover, was the relationship between space and place? How did spaces, understood in material terms, become places? Illustrating the potential of a spatially focused approach to the study of Irish towns and cities, the chapters that follow address such questions in a variety of ways and focus on a range of Irish urban spaces, including individual buildings, areas within cities and, indeed, entire cities, viewed in comparative perspective. That being said, three broad approaches to urban space and place have been employed in the chapters that follow. The first group of chapters explores the morphology of a variety of

---

21 Jerram, 'Space: a useless category for historical analysis?', p. 418.
22 Navickas, *Protest and the politics of space and place*, p. 15.
23 Gunn, 'The spatial turn', p. 11.
24 Livingstone, *Putting science in its place*, p. 7.
25 Gunn, 'The spatial turn', p. 11.

Irish urban spaces, looking both at the factors and the agents that influenced their development throughout the nineteenth century and at the ways that these spaces became places and their meanings and functions developed over time. A second group of chapters goes on to focus on specific urban spaces, exploring how they were used and understood by different social groups and how they facilitated social interaction and the exertion, or subversion, of knowledge, authority and control. Finally, the last two chapters examine the ways in which people moved around within and between these urban spaces, and the ways in which other spaces globally impacted on the lives of those Irish people who came to live in them and took on a significance of their own as Irish 'places'.

The opening chapter by Laura Johnstone raises the question of what actually constitutes urban space through its study of that liminal space between urban and rural – the suburban. By examining the role of landlords in the nineteenth-century morphology of Monkstown, Dublin, from a rural seaside resort into an urban residential extension of the city, the chapter provides an insight into the uncertain identity of early suburbs such as this – neither fully rural nor urban, but an in-between peripheral edge, separate from but inextricably linked to the urban core. The chapter demonstrates the extent to which the De Vesci and Pakenham families, joint owners of the landed estate which encompassed Monkstown, were involved in envisioning, planning and executing the construction of those architectural set pieces which would make up the new residential area. Using leases to control the form and architectural style of the new developments, these largely rural landlords played a central role in the design and planning of urban spaces, highlighting the tensions in our understanding of these spaces as being at once part of the rural estate landscape and an essential part of the city.

The development of these residential areas was also driven by the Victorian preoccupation with escaping the physical and moral contamination of the urban core, a theme that runs through several chapters in this volume. Johnstone's chapter directly addresses this, exploring the way in which this space between rural and urban was transformed by twin notions of health and leisure during the eighteenth and nineteenth centuries. The role of the seaside town as a temporary place of health-giving relief from the city is well documented; however, here we see the very early recognition that the proximity of Monkstown to the urban core allowed for it to become a very attractive place of permanent residence which was at once urban and rural. Not just the location, but the physical organisation of the planned houses and infrastructure, strongly influenced by the grand urban architectural set pieces of Bath in England, spoke of this as a distinctly urban development of permanent residences, yet one that was free from the tight planning constraints of Dublin's urban core.

The theme of urban planning is picked up in Matthew Potter's chapter on the role of the state in providing and regulating domestic space for the labouring classes through the development of social housing. While the deplorable conditions of housing in many Irish towns and cities are well known, this chapter demonstrates that by the end of the nineteenth century Ireland had one of the largest social housing programmes in the world. The Housing of the Working Classes Act 1890, probably the most significant housing act of the period under review, led to the transformation of existing urban spaces and the creation of new ones as local authorities were empowered not merely to replace slums, but to build new houses on greenfield sites to meet general housing needs. Before its enactment, Irish municipal authorities had constructed a total of some 570 social housing units, compared with around 4,400 in the two decades following. While this Act provided an important framework for improvement, Potter argues that the enthusiasm for building projects was driven not so much by social concern as by political expediency: the need of the Irish Parliamentary Party to control the threat of organised labour and the desire of the state to 'kill Home Rule with kindness'. Thus, urban spaces have the potential to become a tool in the hands of political elites who can alter and adapt them in order to further particular agendas.

Jonathan Wright examines the role of elites in the transformation of a different type of urban landscape through his 'spatial microhistory' of the area around Donegall Square in Belfast. This quarter of the town was dominated by the White Linen Hall until the building was demolished to make way for Belfast City Hall in 1896. As the heart of the north's linen trade, and funded by public subscription, the White Linen Hall was significant as a thriving commercial space and, due to its use as a venue for a range of cultural activities, as an important cultural space for the town's wealthy elites. As a *place*, it symbolised the self-sufficiency and wealth of the town's leading citizens, and the radical political tradition with which they had been associated in the closing years of the eighteenth century. As with Monkstown in Dublin, the physical development of this quarter, and its role as a genteel residential area, was strongly influenced by the area's leading landlords, the marquises of Donegall, who both granted the land for the construction of the White Linen Hall and controlled the development of the residential streetscape that surrounded it. Encouraged by this landed intervention, and in common with towns across Britain, this part of Belfast experienced something of an urban renaissance, the White Linen Hall and the residential streets surrounding it combining to create an impressive residential urban space befitting the increasingly significant town.

Despite the initial aim of the Donegalls to create a salubrious residential area around the White Linen Hall, however, this central quarter of Belfast gradually followed the natural evolution of other British urban cores and, as its wealthy upper middle classes decamped to the suburbs, increasingly became associated with trade and commerce. As the use of these spaces changed from residential, recreational and cultural to commercial, so the symbolic association of these places with radical politics and the civic leadership of Belfast's linen elites gradually gave way to the desire to represent the emergence of Belfast as a thriving industrial city at the heart of the British Empire. Through this study of the changing functions and meaning of one small part of the city, Wright's chapter explores the very complex relationship between place, space and the changing social, economic and political contexts within which these spaces (and places) develop.

Shifting the focus from the development of residential areas within towns and cities, the following three chapters turn their attention to specific institutional spaces, each of them exploring the ways in which different institutional spaces within towns and cities acted as ways of enforcing, and in some cases resisting, both physical and social control. In Mary Hatfield's chapter on educational spaces and Olwen Purdue's on spaces of welfare, we see the physical structures of these institutions being designed in such a way as to segregate along lines of class, gender, age and perceived moral status. The language of 'protection' is used frequently, generally the protection of those deemed innocent from moral contagion or from the gaze of others. Walls of Dublin boarding schools were built extra high in order to protect pupils from the gaze of those outside and from the physical and moral dangers of the city, just as the walls of the workhouse were built high to protect those outside from exposure to the paupers within. Internal divisions were also used as ways of constructing private and public spaces and controlling the movements of those within them. As Hatfield demonstrates, the spatial policies that shaped the construction of schools varied depending on issues of gender and class. The two boarding schools under consideration, the Royal Hibernian Military School, located in Phoenix Park, and the Loreto convent school, Rathfarnham, were very different in terms of their educational goals and pedagogical strategies. The former, established to offer an education for military orphans, provided a general education and skills training for Protestant boys and girls; the latter, founded by the Loreto order, was a secondary school for girls of wealthy Catholic families. These differences were reflected in the physical layouts of the schools and their choice of location; yet in each case spaces were used to segregate and to reinforce hierarchies along lines of class, gender and perceived moral status, thus indicating dominant ideologies about childhood and the city in early-nineteenth-century Ireland.

Spaces were similarly constructed in order to reinforce hierarchies and exert control within Irish workhouses, those austere buildings that dominated the landscapes of so many large Irish towns. Through an exploration of Belfast city workhouse, Purdue demonstrates how strict segregation along lines of age, gender, physical health and moral status was enforced through the physical layout of these buildings, each of which was built to a common design, with segregation and separation representing key functions. The use of space within workhouses was intended to be closely prescribed and strictly enforced in order to prevent physical contagion of the healthy by the diseased, and the moral by the immoral. Children were to be kept strictly apart from adults and men from women; separate buildings were erected for those with fever; and those deemed prostitutes or women with illegitimate children were to be kept in 'separation wards'. Spaces were constructed to facilitate supervision and control of the inmates, and to reform them through education and punishment. While space was used by those in authority to control and to reform, however, it was also used by the poor to subvert the underlying principles of the Poor Law and to exert a degree of agency over how they experienced welfare provision. The very wall of the workhouse itself became a space where core ideas about how the Poor Law should be administered were not just subverted but openly challenged by the poor.

Gillian Allmond also explores the ways in which spaces were used to enforce physical separation, remove patients from the physical and moral contagion of the city and 'level up the lower deeps of social life' to the middle-class ideal, in her chapter on the development of Purdysburn Lunatic Asylum to the south of Belfast. Purdysburn was a prime example of the 'Colony' asylums for the insane poor which were being constructed at the turn of the twentieth century in Ireland and Scotland and which would eventually become the model for new asylum building across Britain. These sites were designed to provide therapeutic spaces for the poor, removing them from the evils of the inner city and affording contrasting spaces constructed to resemble the light and airy nature of a middle-class environment thought necessary for healing and well-being. A theme that emerges from several of the chapters in this volume is that an elevated site outside the city was regarded as the ideal location to which to remove those in need of care, the physical elevation contrasting with the depths of physical and moral degradation represented by the inner urban core. This attitude was reflected in contemporary medical texts which dwelt heavily on the impact on mental and physical health of the darkness, dirt, odour and lack of air associated with urban living. Allmond's chapter demonstrates how asylums such as Purdysburn were materially constituted in opposition to the darkness, dirt and immorality of the urban slum and argues that location, architecture, construction and interior spaces were all employed to create light, air and space, providing a hygienic environment that was not only more healthy physically but mentally and morally as well. The physical spaces and materiality of the asylum, it argues, present us with a cultural signpost for contemporary bourgeois fears of the decline and degeneration that were thought to be fostered by unhealthy urban environments.

Georgina Laragy's chapter on turn-of-the-century Dublin explores the relationship between urban space and death by suicide. Taking a sample of suicides across a 15-year period, it examines the ways in which a knowledge of and familiarity with the spaces in which the victim lived and died facilitated the official examination of death and furthered an understanding of the events that may have led to the death. Challenging Durkheim's assertions that the anonymity of urban life was itself a contributory factor in suicide, Laragy uses coroners' reports to demonstrate the extent to which those who died were known by their neighbours. The close proximity of urban dwellers, particularly in the urban core where families and individuals lived cheek-by-jowl, rendered it all but impossible for someone to live their life in privacy. Social isolation, therefore, while possibly contributing to some suicides, was certainly not the cause of them all. The scientific investigation of sudden death by suicide also had an increasingly spatial dimension to it, particularly towards the end of the nineteenth century as the drive for greater understanding of the exact nature of death led to the creation of spaces for scientific inquiry, while the desirability of keeping the dead physically separate from the living was also becoming ever more apparent. As Laragy shows, the opening of the new city morgue in 1902 to replace the earlier one on Marlborough Street reflected the strong sense of the need to keep the dead spatially separate from the living, while the uses of space within the morgue now formed an important part of the investigative processes.

While many of the chapters in this volume highlight the very negative way in which the Victorian middle classes regarded the city, particularly the streets and alleys of its inner core, the chapter which follows, in contrast, explores visual representation of urban space as a trope through which artists expressed ideas of social order and civic improvement. Mary Jane Boland's exploration of the work of Cork-born artist Nathaniel Grogan (c.1740–1808) and Turner de Lond, a Scottish artist who lived in Ireland from c.1818 to c.1822, contrasts the negative ways in which the urban was represented in English paintings of the late eighteenth and early nineteenth centuries with the representation of social cohesion and ordered urban space seen in the works of these artists of Ireland. The urban world they portrayed is energised and expanding, in stark contrast to the Hogarthian misery and urban decay familiar from representations of the urban at this time. Boland argues that this almost idealised representation of the urban was actually a reflection of the values of the society for which it was intended rather than an actual representation of the somewhat more harsh realities of urban life. In a country that was overwhelmingly rural, backward and fractured by agrarian unrest, these paintings provide a fascinating insight into the aspirations of those living within the metropolitan landscape and interacting with its citizens, who saw the city as a civilised, and civilising, space. Boland concludes that those who viewed these representations of Irish urban spaces could take pride in the progress and modernity of the social system they represented.

The relationship between urban spaces and identity is the central theme of Oliver Betts's chapter, which takes the focus away from Ireland itself to examine an important part of the Irish urban experience – Irish communities in cities outside of Ireland. The chapter looks at the ways in which Irish migrants and their descendants adapted to life in three steel cities – Middlesbrough, Coatbridge and Pittsburgh – in the latter half of the nineteenth century and argues that, despite the challenges and limitations presented by these environments, Irish communities were able to utilise the newly created civic spaces to advance their own cultural and religious identities. Not only did the streets of these cities provide spaces within which various identities could be enacted, they themselves were also actors in the construction of these identities. These harsh industrial landscapes changed the living patterns of those who migrated from rural Ireland. Many of the men, for example, had arrived with little or no experience of heavy industry; yet, as Betts demonstrates, by the start of the twentieth century they had established themselves as the hard men of steel production in all three cities. The nature of these cities, with their emphasis on male-dominated heavy industry, also reinforced gender divisions within migrant communities. While the steel works provided a masculine space that fostered a communality among labourers, and the public and civic spaces an arena within which Irish masculinity manifested itself through violence linked to political, cultural and religious traditions, the experience of women, relegated as they were to the more marginal spaces of these cities, was quite different. For women and children, the more domestic spaces of the home, the street and the church were the arenas within which cultural identity was formed and fostered, an identity firmly based on family and religion. As Betts concludes, the particular spaces of these steel cities facilitated the development of a cohesive Irish identity – these were spaces within which the identities of the migrant Irish were both moulded and displayed.

From the conceptualising of different urban spaces to the lived experience of them and the reality of how they acted upon or were used by different social groups, these chapters bring important new insights on the working of urban space in nineteenth-century Ireland. If, as has been asserted, Irish urban history is still in its early stages, this collection represents an important step forward, bringing new ideas to bear on what now looks to be a vibrant expanding area.

# 1
# 'The Royal Paragon': Setting Out Suburban Space in Nineteenth-Century Dublin

*Laura Johnstone*

Monkstown and Salthill, located approximately six miles from Dublin City, was transformed in the early nineteenth century from a rural fishing village and seasonal resort into a fashionable residential suburb for the emerging middle classes. The transformation of the area in the early nineteenth century created a place which was neither fully rural nor urban but an in-between, peripheral space. This was evident in D'Alton's description of Monkstown in 1838 as 'a locality, not perhaps in itself either town or village, but surrounded by elegant villas, noble demesnes, and tasteful bathing lodges'.[1] The juxtaposition of rural idyll and fashionable suburbia created a new territory in Monkstown and Salthill. A new suburban landscape emerged which was defined by streets, rows of terraced houses, detached and semi-detached villas and gardens.

The idealised notion of the 'private, healthy, quasi-rural existence that lies at the heart of English suburbs'[2] has been examined by J.W.R. Whitehand, Christine Carr, Robert Fishman, F.M.L. Thompson, H.J. Dyos, David Cannadine, Elizabeth McKellar and Gillian Darley among others.[3] The creation of the maritime suburb of Monkstown embodied the key concepts

---

1 John D'Alton, *The history of the County of Dublin* (Dublin, 1838), p. 864.
2 J.W.R. Whitehand and Christine M.H. Carr, 'England's garden suburbs: development and change' in Richard Harris and Peter J. Larkham (eds), *Changing suburbs: foundation, form and function* (London, 1999), p. 78.
3 For discussion of early suburbs, see Robert Fishman, *Bourgeois utopias: the rise and fall of suburbia* (New York, 1987); F.M.L. Thompson, *The rise of suburbia* (Leicester, 1982); David Cannadine, *Lords and landlords: the aristocracy and the towns, 1774–1967* (Leicester, 1980); Robert Fishman, *Bourgeois utopias: the rise and fall of suburbia* (New York, 1987).

of suburban space as defined by Fishman, which included the separation of home from workplace, middle from working class and the rise of romantic and religious beliefs promoting the natural and the rural.[4] Neither city nor country, the emerging nineteenth-century suburb of Monkstown was part of the fragmentary and scattered nature of the changing coastal landscape. It was difficult to define these spaces when the terms 'rural' and 'suburb', 'centre' and 'periphery' were neither stable nor absolute. The clear boundaries between town and country, and between classes and cultures, were becoming blurred by the rapidity of suburban growth in the early nineteenth century.

Monkstown was part of the 420 acre Dublin estate jointly inherited by Thomas Vesey, 1st Viscount de Vesci, and Edward Michael Pakenham, 2nd Baron Longford in 1778.[5] Their heirs John Vesey, 2nd Viscount de Vesci (1771–1855) and Thomas Pakenham, 2nd Earl of Longford (1774–1835)[6] oversaw the rapid development of the area in the first half of the nineteenth century.[7] The changing nature of these spaces from rural resort landscapes to suburban residential areas was influenced by the ground landlords, the agents for the estate and speculative developers.

Monkstown, which was also known as Dunleary, began to expand from the beginning of the eighteenth century. As the approach to Dublin port had become hazardous, ships often had to await favourable tides off Dunleary and passengers were brought into the village by boat and then continued by road to the city. This led to the establishment of a coffee house, the first piece of leisure infrastructure in the area, situated on an outcrop overlooking Dunleary Creek.[8] The area was also developing as a summer resort, with sea bathing becoming popular as early as 1710.[9] It continued to grow in importance as both a resort and landing place for ships, and in 1767 a

---

4 Fishman, *Bourgeois utopias*, p. 239.
5 Charles Dunbar, who died without issue, bequeathed part of his estate to Lords Longford and de Vesci. Dunbar stated in his will that his intention was 'to continue his real estate in the family and blood of the late Primate Boyle'. Lords Longford and de Vesci were descendants through marriage of Archbishop Boyle.
6 John Vesey born in 1771, became the 2nd Viscount de Vesci on the death of his father in 1804. Thomas Pakenham, born in 1774, inherited the title 2nd Earl of Longford on the death of his father in 1792.
7 This unusual situation of two distant relatives jointly inheriting and managing a large estate resulted in an extensive amount of correspondence between the two ground landlords and their agents, Stewart and Kincaid. This correspondence, in conjunction with estate surveys and proposed plans, provides a valuable source for analysing the development of the area.
8 Peter Pearson, *Between the mountains and the sea: Dun Laoghaire Rathdown County* (Dublin, 2007), p. 194.
9 Weston St John Joyce, *The neighbourhood of Dublin: its topography, antiquities and historical association* (Dublin, 1913), p. 44.

new pier was completed which became the departure point for the English packet ships.[10]

Changing attitudes to health and leisure played an important part in coastal suburban development in the nineteenth century. Alain Corbin details how the negative perception of the sea as unknowable and dangerous changed between 1750 and 1840 as an 'irresistible rise of a collective desire for the shore became evident in representations of the sea in art and literature'.[11] He describes how cure-takers began visiting the seashore to 'combat melancholy and spleen', and from 1750 onwards crowds went to Brighton to enjoy the pleasures and health benefits of sea bathing.[12] From its outset the residential development of coastal suburbs was bound up with seasonal leisure resorts, with many examples in England including Brighton, Leamington Spa and Hove.[13] Brighton's success as a resort resulted in the construction of squares, crescents and terraces, which produced 'one of the great sequences of Regency and early Victorian town planning in England'.[14] The seafront terraces of Brighton were a source of inspiration to the Longford de Vesci estate when they planned development in Monkstown.

When Lords Longford and de Vesci inherited the Monkstown Estate in 1778, it was still a predominantly rural landscape with some substantial villas dotted around the area. Cooper described Dunleary in 1780 as 'a very small inconsiderable Village remarkable only for a handsome semi-circular Harbour whose banks are very high all around'.[15] G.T. Stokes described how 'about 1780, Seapoint and the adjoining streets and squares and roads was a perfectly rural district'.[16] The area was still fields where cows grazed and provided milk for the Dublin market. It was an alternative environment to the congested city, but it was still dependent upon the urban core. Research in Britain highlights a need for further investigation of peripheral areas of cities. As McKellar argues regarding the suburbs of London, 'we need to redefine and extend our concept of "the urban" to incorporate the periphery as well as the centre'.[17]

In the late eighteenth and early nineteenth centuries the Longford de Vesci

10  This pier survives today as the inner coal harbour pier.
11  Alain Corbin, *The lure of the sea: the discovery of the seaside in the western world 1750–1840* (Cambridge, 1994), p. 53.
12  Ibid., p. 163.
13  A.M. Stern, David Fishman and Jacob Tilove, *Paradise planned: the garden suburb and the modern city* (New York, 2013), p. 295.
14  Ibid., p. 27.
15  Austin Cooper, cited in Kevin Murray, 'Old Dunleary harbour' in *Dublin Historical Record*, vii, no. 4 (Dublin, 1945), p. 151.
16  G.T. Stokes, 'The antiquities from Kingstown to Dublin (continued)' in *Journal of the Royal Society of Antiquaries of Ireland*, 5th ser., v, no. 1 (Mar. 1895), p. 6.
17  Elizabeth McKellar, 'Peripheral visions: alternative aspects and rural presences in mid-eighteenth-century London' in *Art History*, xxii, no. 4 (Nov. 1999), p. 495.

estate commissioned numerous surveys and proposed plans for Monkstown. Periodical surveys were an essential estate management tool as they set out the boundaries of the estate, provided an overview of how leases stood and could be used to plan development. They were particularly useful for John Vesey and Thomas Pakenham as neither landlord lived on their Dublin estates.[18] The 1792 *Survey of Monkstown with the town of Dunleary* (Figure 1.1) documents a changing landscape beyond the outskirts of the city which was neither urban nor rural. The picturesque setting had encouraged the construction of some

18 Vesey's main residence was at Abbeyleix in County Laois, while Pakenham resided at Pakenham Hall at Castlepollard in County Westmeath.

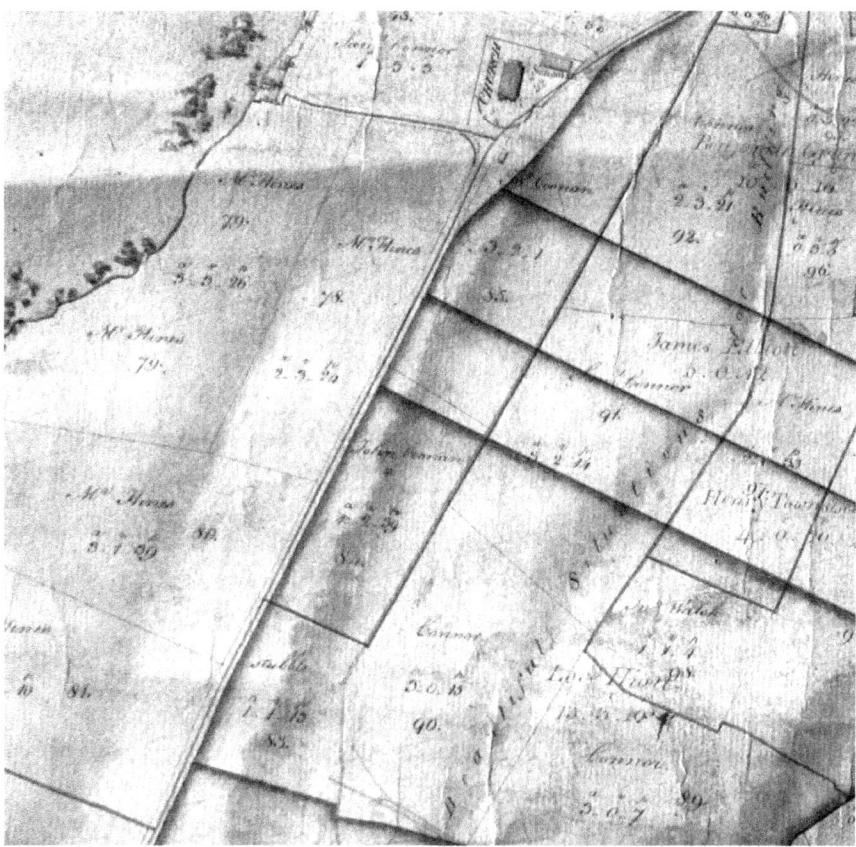

1.1 and 1.2   [surveyor unknown], 'Survey of the Estate of Monkstown with the Town of Dunleary in the County of Dublin' (1792) (Pakenham papers, private collection, Tullynally Castle, Castlepollard, Co. Westmeath, T/3763/Q9. Courtesy of Thomas Pakenham)

fine country detached villa residences, all within riding distance of the city. Most of these villas were summer retreats, but some had become permanent residences.

The survey shows Monkstown Church, a simple rectangular church with a square tower built in 1789, and a schoolhouse built adjacent to it in 1791, on a site granted for ever by the ground landlords to the church wardens for the nominal sum of £29 in July 1785.[19] The location of the church at the bottom of Monkstown Avenue, which was then called 'the road from

---

19   Etain Murphy, *A glorious extravaganza: the history of Monkstown Parish Church* (Bray, 2003), p. 30.

Dublin by the Black Rock', established a pleasing new vista as the traveller approached Monkstown and the village of Dunleary from the direction of the city. The construction of the church changed the character of the landscape and marked the beginning of a shift from rural to semi-urban. It is likely that the estate granted this prominent site for the church to encourage residential development in the area. The imposing approach route to the church created a focal point for future development. Andrew Saint emphasises the importance of the estate church in the creation of London's suburbs, stating that the church 'is a guarantee of respectability and order', and that it 'helps to ensure that the rental from the surrounding property stays high'.[20] In 1818, Warburton described Monkstown church as 'perhaps one of the largest and finest edifices erected for a country congregation in Ireland'.[21] However, by 1823, this 'country congregation' was expanding and it was decided that a new, larger church was required. In 1831, John Semple designed a total transformation of the original modest Georgian church, rebuilding it in the gothic style and increasing the capacity of the church to 800. The need for this much larger church was due to rapid residential development of the area in the early nineteenth century.

The 1792 map depicts Dunleary as a very small village of small labourers' cottages, located along the old road to Dunleary. Salt Hill House, a large three-storey building, was located overlooking Dunleary harbour.[22] The identification of part of the coastline beside Salt Hill House as a 'Sea Bathing Place' demonstrates the importance of Dunleary as a leisure space and a seasonal escape from the city. Beyond Salt Hill House the cottages continued as far as the coffee house. The existing house types varied in scale between the small, terraced, single-storey buildings close to the pier and the bigger, detached, villa-style houses on large plots of land in the surrounding area. However, the potential of the area for significant residential development had already been identified by the ground landlords. The plots of land to the south of Monkstown Road were described as 'Beautiful Situations for Building' in a handwritten note which was added to the survey (Figure 1.2). The function of the landscape would change from rural and agricultural with a seasonal resort and leisure aspect in the eighteenth century to predominantly suburban and residential in the early nineteenth century.

By 1802, the potential for suburban residential development was becoming more widely recognised. The area was marketed in *Walker's Hibernian*

---

20 Andrew Saint, 'The quality of the London suburb' in *London Suburbs* (London, 1999), p. 16.
21 J. Warburton, J. Whitelaw and R. Walsh, *The history of the city of Dublin: from the earliest accounts to the present time* (2 vols, London, 1818), ii, p. 1272.
22 Salthill House was incorporated into the Salthill Hotel, which was bought by the Dublin to Kingstown Railway Company in 1833.

*Magazine* as a summer resort and place of 'rural retirement' from 'the noise dust and vulgar confusion' of the urban core.[23] The article idealised the seaside rural setting and the amusements to be enjoyed by residents at this fashionable resort. It noted the key attractions of the area as its proximity to sea-bathing and its rural vistas.[24] The shift in perception of the landscape as suitable for year-round residence rather than simply as a place of summer resort is evident:

> there are other parts of this ground, on which are erected neat bathing villas, constructed with taste and convenience; several of them inhabited by people of property, and respectability; others ready for immediate occupation – so that on these grounds above there now exists a society to be envied, so much so that many of its inhabitants reside there the whole year.[25]

This recognition of the area as a suitable place for permanent residence for the wealthy and emerging middle classes was a key turning point in its development. Fishman describes how this shift disassociated home and work environments by creating 'neighbourhoods based both on the idea of a single class and on that of a single (domestic) function'.[26]

The estate's surveys and design proposals show that the suburban landscape was increasingly spatially regulated in the nineteenth century. The 1813 proposed plan for the Royal Paragon introduced a radical change in scale, house type and lifestyle to the existing character of the area. The estate introduced an urban house type (long terraces of houses set out on regular plots) in a rural seaside setting that had not previously experienced large-scale planned development.

The 1813 plan by the surveyors Sherrard, Brassington & Greene (Figure 1.3) was described as a 'survey' but is in fact a combination of a survey of the existing built fabric and an ambitious proposed plan for a formal crescent facing the seafront and urban plots along the main street. This dual role of surveyor and urban planner was not unusual and some of the other proposed schemes on the Longford de Vesci estate were similarly prepared by surveyors rather than architects.

The survey shows the newly laid out street adjacent to Monkstown Church. This new street, which is present-day Monkstown Road, effectively cut off old Dunleary village and created a new improved route. To the east of Monkstown Church, the plots which were developed as Monkstown Crescent were set out

---

23 'Monkstown, Dublin' in *Walker's Hibernian Magazine* (Feb. 1802).
24 Ibid.
25 Ibid.
26 Fishman, *Bourgeois utopias*, p. 25.

1.3 and 1.4 Sherrard, Brassington & Greene, 'Survey of the Town of Dunleary and Royal Paragon in the County of Dublin', Estate map (1813) (Pakenham papers, private collection, Tullynally Castle, Castlepollard, Co. Westmeath, T/3763/Q9. Courtesy of Thomas Pakenham)

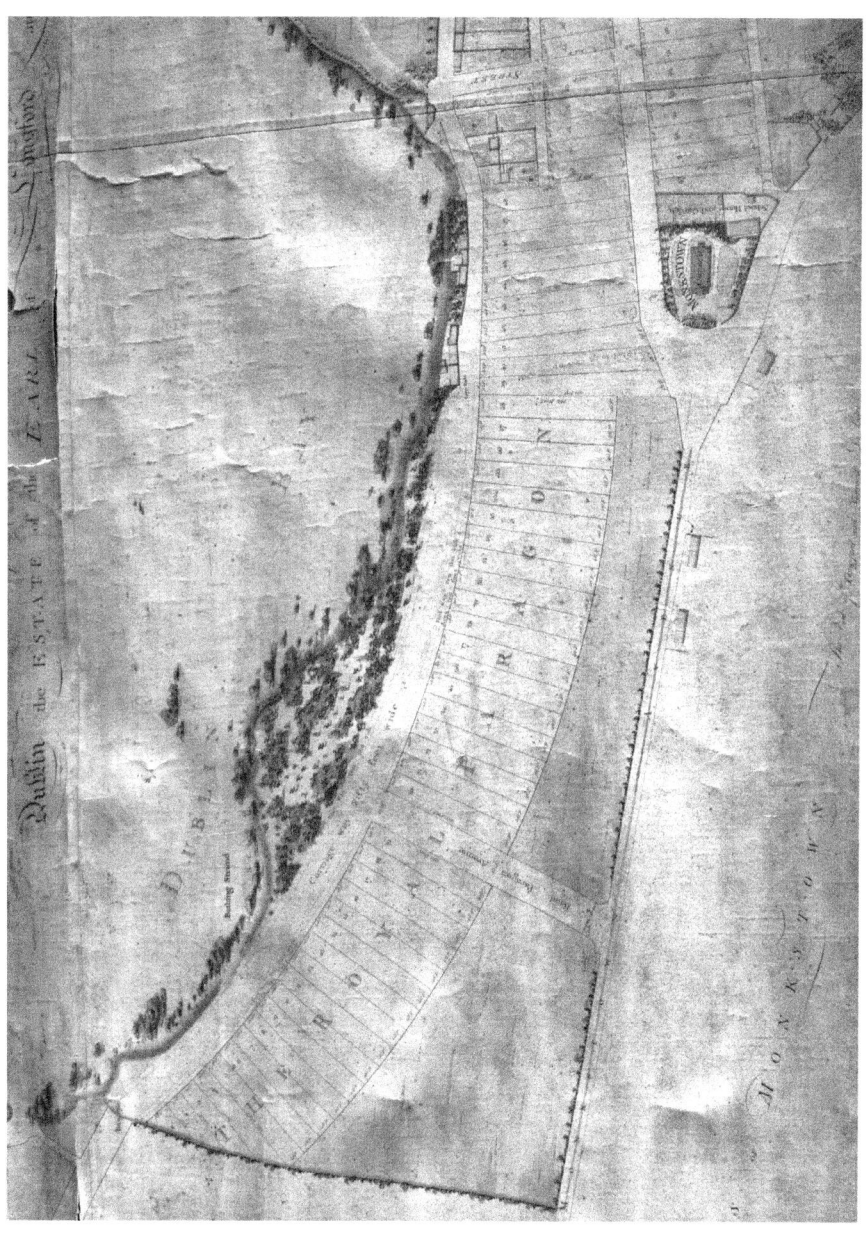

in a regular pattern all 40 feet wide. The plots, numbered 81–97, were 200 feet deep and had a lane to the rear, which allowed for the construction of stables at the end of the gardens. All the plots on the north side of the new street were also 40 feet wide, suggesting that the estate considered this the ideal standard width of plot. The pre-existing eighteenth-century cottages in old Dunleary village appeared haphazard in layout compared with the new regular geometry; the new regularity helped to 'suburbanise' the landscape. The estate also set out a proposed new road further inland, to the south-east of Monkstown Church, which is now known as Pakenham Road.

The proposed plan for the Royal Paragon (Figure 1.4) represents a radical shift in the character of the space, particularly in how it was viewed by its owners. It shows the ground landlords' ambition to build urban architectural set pieces on a grand scale. Like the Paragon on the new Kent Road in the east end of London (1787–91) and the Paragon at Blackheath (1794–1807), both designed by the surveyor Michael Searles, the Royal Paragon scheme had its formal origins in the Royal Crescent in Bath.[27] The Royal Crescent, designed by John Wood the younger, was built between 1767 and 1775. John Archer describes how the townhouse terrace of 30 houses in a semi-elliptical form turned its back on the town of Bath, 'facing instead the distant horizon and bringing the landscape into visual context with the houses'.[28] In a similar way, the Royal Paragon was designed to turn its back on the main street of Monkstown, and instead to face towards the sea, prioritising a visual and spatial relationship with the coastline over a formal facade facing onto the main thoroughfare.

The proposed Royal Paragon was a very ambitious scheme of 48 houses. The plan specified that a carriageway would be built along the seafront 50 feet wide, with a footway 10 feet wide to either side. This footpath would provide an exclusive seaside promenade for the residents. The seafront carriageway was envisaged as a private road with access only from Royal Paragon Avenue in the centre with turnstiles at each end to restrict access. This private route indicated that the estate wanted to develop this area with exclusive high-end housing. The building plots at 46 feet wide and 260 feet long were larger than the plots set out along Monkstown Road.

The ground landlords intended to use the same development process as was common in Dublin City, setting out the terraces in building plots to lease to speculative builders who would construct the houses in accordance with the terms of the lease. Most speculative builders would build on two or three

27 Chris Miele, 'From aristocratic ideal to middle-class idyll: 1690–1840' in *London Suburbs* (London, 1999), p. 49.
28 John Archer, *Architecture and suburbia: from English villa to American dream house, 1690–2000* (Minneapolis, Minn., 2005), p. 209.

plots at a time. When the lease expired, the plot and house would revert to the ground landlord. This method of procurement transferred the financial risk of development onto the developer and ensured the ground landlords maintained control of the estate.

The proposed scheme was too ambitious for its time and did not proceed in the form shown on the 1813 plan. In its place the more modest schemes of Clifton and Longford Terraces were built in the 1830s, 40s and 50s. These schemes achieved many of the aims of the Royal Paragon vision, by building extensive terraces with sea views on long plots which allowed for generous rear gardens and stables. The provision of private rear gardens was essential to encourage the middle classes to move out from the city centre. These gardens provided an illusion of countryside that linked familiar spaces to a new suburban environment. The front gardens of these terraces inserted a new space between the street and the house, an intermediate space between public and private domains.

In 1816, the commencement of construction of the new asylum harbour half a mile east of the coffee house at old Dunleary, moved the commercial centre of the area eastwards. George IV departed from the new asylum harbour in 1821, and the growing town was renamed Kingstown in his honour.[29] 'Kingstown owes its present condition, name, and indeed existence to the visit of George IV in 1821, since which time it has become a fashionable watering-place. Previously, it was the little fishing village of Dunleary'.[30]

Some plots close to the asylum harbour which had been let on 99-year leases in 1804 and 1812 were subdivided and sublet through middlemen and developed in a haphazard manner as labourers' cottages and courts to provide accommodation for the workers constructing the harbour. Monkstown and Salthill remained a residential and leisure landscape, removed from the increasing commercial activity at the new harbour. The continued importance of the seaside as a healthy seasonal escape for urban dwellers is evident in Warburton's description from 1818; 'The whole population of Dublin seem to crowd to the water in the summer months, and all ranks and ages think bathing a specific for the preservation of health or the cure of distemper'.[31]

The estate's plans for the area continued with John Hill's *A plan and survey of part of the Town of Dunleary* in 1816.[32] Hill set out Monkstown Crescent, to the east of Monkstown Church, as a slightly curved row of pairs of semi-detached villa-style houses. The proposal consisted of eight pairs

29 Arnold Horner, 'Dun Laoghaire's Great Harbour' in *History Ireland*, xxi, no. 5 (Oct. 2013), p. 26.
30 W.F. Wakeman, *Dublin: what's to be seen and how to see it, with excursions to the country and suburbs* (Dublin, 1853), p. 146.
31 Warburton, Whitelaw and Walsh, *History of the city of Dublin*, ii, p. 1173.
32 Ibid.

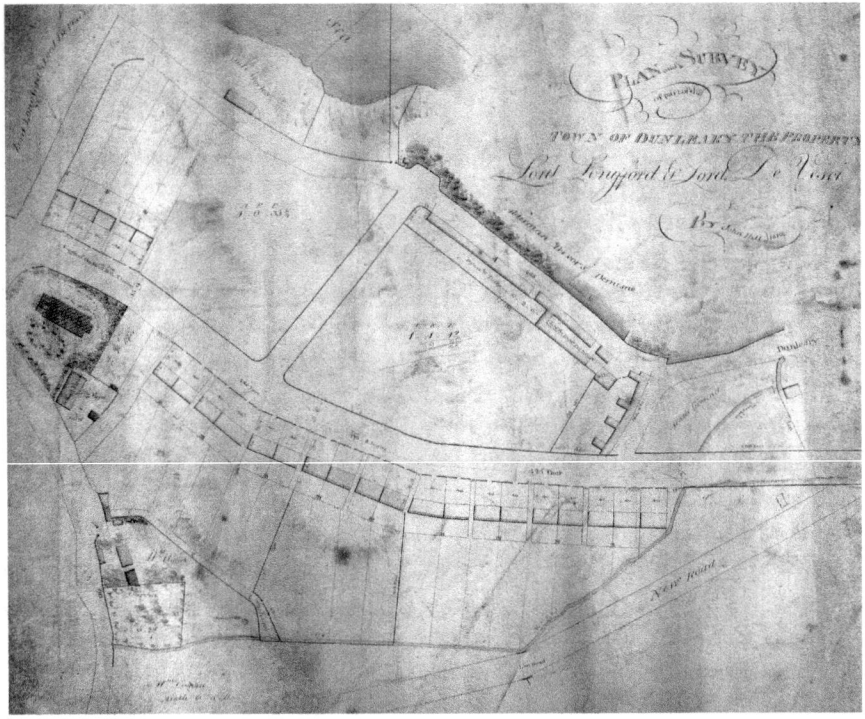

1.5. John Hill, 'Plan and survey of part of the Town of Dunleary the Property of Lords Longford and de Vesci', Estate map (1816) (Pakenham papers, private collection, Tullynally Castle, Castlepollard, Co. Westmeath, T/3763/Q9. Courtesy of Thomas Pakenham)

of semi-detached houses and a final group of three houses at the eastern end of the row (Figure 1.5). It is significant that Hill's plan was for modest semi-detached houses rather than grand terraced houses, like the plans for terraces facing onto the seafront. This indicates a shift towards a more suburban house type.

Monkstown Crescent was in fact built as a villa terrace of five houses, a central pair of semi-detached houses and a further terrace of eight houses as shown on the first edition Ordnance Survey map (Figure 1.6). The houses are a mixture of single-storey and single-storey-over-basement, three-bays-wide houses. The facades were stucco finished, with sliding sash windows, painted granite sills and central fan-lighted panelled doors with side lights (Figure 1.7). All the houses except the last house, No. 16, are three bays wide with a central front door and reception rooms to either side of a central hallway. No. 16, closest to Monkstown Church, was added much later in the 1850s and is two bays wide and two storeys over basement. Nos. 1–3 were originally built

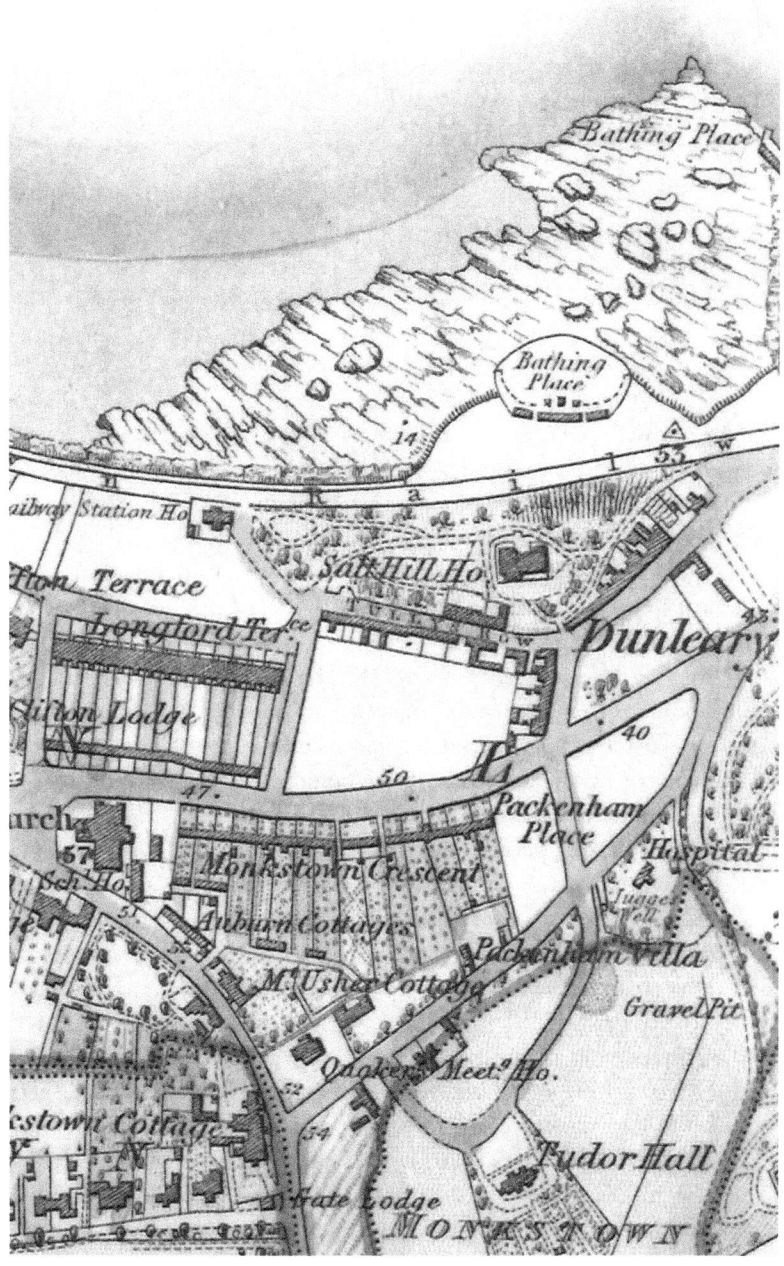

1.6. First edition Ordnance Survey map of Dublin,
scale 1:10,560 (6 inches to 1 mile), sheet no. 23 (Dublin, 1843)
(Courtesy of the board of Trinity College Dublin)

1.7. Author, Monkstown Crescent, Monkstown, Co. Dublin, photograph, April 2014

in 1831 as a group of three houses, but by 1843 they were connected to the semi-detached villas Nos. 4 and 5 by an infill piece. Nos. 6 and 7 is another semi-detached pair of villas. Nos. 8–11, built in 1828, all display similar characteristics indicating they were by the same developer. Jeffrey Barcroft, a builder and speculative developer who also invested on Longford Terrace, built the last four houses, Nos. 12–15, and there is a notable change in style, with these houses rising higher out of the ground with a longer flight of granite steps leading up to the central doorcase. The location of the entrance and reception rooms at first-floor level, with the bedrooms below at semi-basement level, was to provide sea views from the reception rooms. However, these views would be blocked by the construction of Longford Terrace in the 1840s and 1850s. These villa-terrace houses were neither rural nor urban in architectural style. Their symmetrical facades were modelled on urban classicism, but they differed from their urban counterparts in their wider plan and lower profile, as they were only one storey over basement. Their relatively wide plot frontage and low profile were hallmarks of a suburban house type. They were described in 1837 as 'a row of very neat looking cottages south of the road leading from Blackrock to Kingstown'.[33]

Hill's scheme was an outline proposal for the development of the space rather than a rigid master plan. An overall masterplan for the area was not imposed by the estate. Instead, plans for parts of the estate were proposed, either by speculative developers or by surveyors commissioned by the estate, and these were assessed by the agents and ground landlords. Monkstown Crescent is an example of houses constructed by a number of different developers who built two, three or four houses at a time, with changes to the architectural character of the houses legible along the row as each developer built in a slightly different way. The plot widths and basic plan were consistent,

---

33  Ordnance Survey, *Field survey book Kingstown* (1837), p. 187.

but the doorcase, window and parapet design as well as the level of ornamentation varied along the crescent. On the more carefully controlled development of Longford Terrace it is impossible to read from the built form of the houses where one developer finished and another began because the estate insisted on total homogeneity along the facade.

William Duncan's 1825 survey plan and section entitled 'The ground intended for New Brighton' reveals the ground landlords' intention to develop the area in a similar way to an English seaside resort town.[34] The survey was prepared as part of an architectural competition for architects and engineers to design 'The New Brighton'. The area surveyed is present-day Belgrave Square, Seafield Avenue, Brighton Terrace, Albany Avenue and Clifton Terrace. The advertisement for the competition in the *Freeman's Journal* offered prize money to the three best schemes and listed Lords Longford and de Vesci as patrons of The New Brighton Company.[35] Participants were invited to view Duncan's survey plan and section at the offices of Stewart and Kincaid, the agents for the estate. A section through the sloping terrain was provided so that the proposed designs could take into account the sloping coastal topography and maximise sea views. The proposed sea-facing terraces on this site did not go ahead as planned, but the name of the scheme, 'New Brighton', and the stucco finish of the facades indicates that as early as the 1820s the estate was modelling its plans for Monkstown on English coastal towns, such as Brighton, where monumental stucco-rendered seafront terraces were fashionable. Kingstown and Salthill were directly compared with Brighton in contemporary guidebooks:

> There are other times when Kingstown and Salthill adjoining, shine with extraordinary brilliance … the fashionable crowds promenading on the pier during the summer evening will present as many specimens of beauty, blooming with nature's tints, as can be seen anywhere else in the world perhaps, not excepting the west pier at Brighton.[36]

Following the estate's various surveys and proposed schemes, the opening of the Dublin to Kingstown line in 1834 and the construction of Clifton Terrace, Longford Terrace, Brighton Terrace and Monkstown Crescent in the first half of the nineteenth century ensured the transformation of this resort setting to a more formal suburban geometry of streets and terraces.

---

34 William Duncan, 'Map of the ground intended for New Brighton' (map, 1825), Pakenham papers, T/3763/Q9.
35 'New Brighton company' in *Freeman's Journal* (5 Nov. 1825).
36 James Godkin and John Walker, *The new hand-book of Ireland, an illustrated guide for tourists and travellers* (Dublin, 1871), p. 151.

The Dublin to Kingstown Railway was Britain's first suburban railway line, opening almost two years ahead of London's Greenwich line.[37] Its construction created a new spatial environment as Dublin city reached out along the coast to its hinterlands. The railway company constructed oval 'elegant and spacious baths' in front of Salthill Hotel and offered reduced fares to encourage weekend day-trippers out from the city to these resort suburbs to enjoy the sea-baths, parks and promenades.[38] In 1837, the railway company's architect John Skipton Mulvany designed a new railway station to the west of Salthill Hotel to serve the baths, and the now expanding suburb of Monkstown. The baths and railway station can be seen on the first edition Ordnance Survey map (Figure 1.6). The importance of the baths as part of the leisure infrastructure was demonstrated in this description in 1857: 'The baths at Salthill, unquestionably superior to all others in the vicinity of Dublin, induce many people from different parts of Ireland to make the Hotel their temporary residence'.[39] Across Britain railway companies promoted the attractions of open sea-bathing, an activity which had generated the development of seaside resort towns.[40]

The construction of the Dublin to Kingstown Railway radically transformed the rocky coastline at Monkstown and created a new physical barrier for people who wished to access the sea on foot. Many of the ground landlords along the coast opposed the construction of the railway as it alienated their access to the sea and interfered with their views. Sir Harcourt Lees of Blackrock House and Lord Cloncurry of Maretimo to the west of Monkstown demanded compensation to allow construction of the railway through their land. Lord Cloncurry received the sum of £2,000 and a small private harbour and private footbridge so he would still have access to the sea.[41] This finely built footbridge with twin granite towers was designed by Mulvany. For Sir Harcourt Lees, the railway company was required to construct a tunnel for the railway through the demesne of Blackrock House to maintain the ground's connection with its seafront land.

The railway company bought Salthill Hotel in 1833 as they needed to run their railway line through its grounds and in 1836 Mulvany designed the extension of the hotel.[42] They cut back the cliffs at Salthill creating a steep

---

37 David Dickson, *Dublin: the making of a capital city* (London, 2014), p. 324.
38 Samuel Lewis, *A topographical dictionary of Ireland* (London, 1837), p. 227.
39 G.W. Irwin, *Irwin's Dublin guide: a descriptive guide to the Irish metropolis, its environs and the County of Wicklow* (Dublin, 1857), p. 105.
40 John K. Walton, *Wonderland by the waves: a history of the seaside resorts of Lancashire* (Preston, 1992), p. 2.
41 Pearson, *Between the mountains and the sea*, p. 256.
42 Frederick O'Dwyer, 'The architecture of John Skipton Mulvany' in *Irish Architectural and Decorative Studies*, iii (2000), p. 18.

slope. This ground inland of the new railway line would later be landscaped as pleasure grounds for the residents of Longford Terrace.

Unlike other ground landlords in the area such as Lord Cloncurry and Sir Harcourt Lees, Lords Longford and de Vesci cooperated with the transfer of the required land on their estate to facilitate the construction of the railway line. In April 1833, Stewart and Kincaid set out in a letter to the railway company the estate's claim for compensation for the land between 'The Strand and Sea Shore above low water mark from the Martello Tower to Salt Hill'. The ground landlords felt they had a right to compensation but were willing to waive this claim 'in consideration of the great benefit which they expect their Estate will derive from the Railway'.[43] Regarding 'A portion of ground in Salthill thro which the Railway passes', they were willing to forego compensation so long as the value of the area was not diminished by the works and the sea views were protected:

> Their Lordships expect that no material injury will be done to the place so as to lessen the amount of or affect the Security for the future Rent and that the Ground at the South west of the open Cutting will be sloped down in an Ornamental manner from the dwelling house to near the level of the Railway and the Ground north-east of said Cutting covered a few feet so as to improve and extend the marine view from the windows of the house.[44]

In general, the estate wanted to encourage the construction of the railway line, so long as the seafront, which would be drastically altered by the excavation of the cliffs, was landscaped to a high standard and suitable footpaths were provided for the public. Lords Longford and de Vesci believed that the railway would increase the value of their estate by encouraging residential development. They were influenced in this view by their agent Joseph Kincaid who was a director and investor in the Dublin to Kingstown Railway Company. Kincaid assured Lord de Vesci that his position did not pose a potential conflict of interest as he would put the interests of the Longford de Vesci estate first in carrying out his role on the board; 'If I should be director of the Company it will of course be my first duty to promote the interests of the Kingstown Estate. Every other duty must be subservient to that'.[45]

---

43 Stewart Kincaid to Lords Longford and de Vesci, Apr. 1833, National Library of Ireland, De Vesci papers, MS 38,955.
44 Ibid.
45 Joseph Kincaid to Lord de Vesci, Mar. 1845, National Library of Ireland, De Vesci papers, MS 38,956/3.

Due to objections from local residents and businessmen, the railway initially only ran as far as Salthill and did not extend to the new asylum harbour at Kingstown. Kincaid supported the extension of the railway beyond Salthill to Kingstown informing the ground landlords that 'the proposed extension will be of great value to the Kingstown Estate, establishing an immense trade at the Harbour which otherwise it could not have & increasing the value of Building Ground at Glenageary & other remote parts of the Estate'.[46] In 1836, work began on an extension of the railway to the Kingstown terminus.[47]

The development of Monkstown involved sophisticated suburban design strategies, negotiated leases and the collaboration of ground landlords, agents and speculative developers. These factors were crucial to the development of Longford Terrace on part of the land which had been set out for the Royal Paragon. The layout was very similar to the ambitious 1813 plan, and although the plots at 31 feet 6 inches wide were narrower than the proposed 46-foot-wide plots of the paragon they were the same length, at approximately 200 feet long. The first, western section was completed by 1843 and consisted of fifteen three-bay three-storey-over-basement houses. The second, eastern half of the terrace consisted of thirteen houses and was not completed until 1861, a delay which was due to the topography of the site, the need to provide a separate access road and negotiations between the estate and the developers about costs.

As Andrew Saint has noted in relation to London's suburbs, 'speculation and the suburb are indissoluble',[48] and the collaboration of speculative developers and the estate was essential to the construction of Longford Terrace. The estate laid out the roads, set out the building plots and provided a network of sewage drains. They commissioned an overall plan for the terrace which they showed to potential speculators so that they could imagine the completed streetscape. Each of the fifteen building plots on the western section of Longford Terrace was 31 feet 6 inches wide, set out with a front garden, a long back garden and stables to the rear, leased for 99 years at an annual rent of £15 5s. 0d. Thomas Bradley was essential to the success of the Longford Terrace scheme. He was one of the first developers to build on the western terrace in 1842 and built eight of the fifteen houses.[49] He also built five houses on the eastern terrace in 1856. He was a timber merchant and speculative developer who was also active on the Pembroke estate, building on

---

46 Stewart Kincaid to Lords Longford and de Vesci, Apr. 1833, National Library of Ireland, De Vesci papers, MS 38,955.
47 Jason Bolton et al., *The Martello towers of Dublin* (Dublin, 2012), p. 131.
48 Saint, 'The quality of the London suburb', p. 16.
49 Stewart Kincaid, Rental book for the Kingstown estate, 1856, Pakenham papers, T/3763/T/11/1.

1.8   Author, Longford Terrace, Monkstown, Co. Dublin, photograph, April 2014

Pembroke Road and Haddington Road in Ballsbridge.[50] The other speculative developers who invested in the initial western terrace of Longford Terrace were Jeffrey Barcroft, who built four houses, and William Moyers who built three houses.[51] The first lease for house No. 7 was granted in August 1842 to Jeffrey Barcroft, who had built four houses on Monkstown Crescent. A month later Barcroft leased three further building plots for houses Nos. 1, 2 and 3. William Moyers took a lease for Nos. 4, 5 and 6 and Bradley took a lease for Nos. 8, 9 and 10. William Moyers was an active builder on the estate, building houses on Vesey Place and laying drains to the rear of De Vesci Terrace on the estate's behalf. Having leased the first ten building plots in 1842, the final five building plots for Nos. 11–15 were leased two years later in May 1844 to Bradley, who successfully completed the construction of the western terrace. The completed western terrace is shown on the first edition Ordnance Survey map (Figure 1.6).

Although the western terrace was constructed by three different developers it gives the appearance of a perfectly homogenous row of identical houses (Figure 1.8). The regularity of the facade was due to the lease covenants which stipulated that the developers were required to agree plans and elevations with the estate before commencing construction. The estate carefully controlled development ensuring the houses were all built with the same three-bay-wide

---

50   Dickson, *Dublin: the making of a capital city*, p. 328.
51   Aug. 1842, no. 7 leased to Geoffrey Barcroft; Sept. 1842, nos. 1, 2, 3 to Geoffrey Barcroft; Sept. 1842, nos. 4, 5, 6 to William Moyers; Sept. 1842, nos. 8, 9, 10 to Thomas Bradley; May 1844, nos. 11, 12, 13, 14, 15 to Thomas Bradley.

three-storey-over-basement elevation, and did not allow variation in the window or doorcase design, or in the colour of the stucco finish. This results in an impressive set-piece of fifteen almost identical houses, with ruled and lined rendered basement walls to granite plinth course, rusticated rendered walls to ground floor and second floor, string course at sill level of second floor windows and simple rendered cornices and friezes to parapet walls. The servants' quarters were in the basement and the first-floor drawing room occupied the full width of the front of the house with three sliding sash timber windows making the most of the sea views. The coastal terraces of Monkstown were described in 1851 as 'residences approximating to or on the line of road to Kingstown, in beautiful aligned terraces [that] front the sea'.[52]

The residents of the western section of Longford Terrace were a mixture of military and professional gentlemen including Major James Harrison at No. 4, two barristers, Brindley Hone at No. 5 and John H. Lecky at No. 10, Charles Copeland of the Royal Bank of Ireland at No. 7 and John Busby, a magistrate, at No. 14.[53] James R. Stewart, the agent for the estate, lived at No. 11 until 1853.[54] These professionals commuted to the city centre for work, fully separating their workplace from their home and establishing their houses as fully suburban and residential in their function. Following the completion of the houses of the western terrace in 1844, a number of residents began corresponding with the estate regarding the landscaping of the pleasure ground to the front of the terrace and the condition of the roads. Charles Copeland was very keen to see the pleasure ground completed. He informed Stewart Kincaid that 'The Directors of the Kingstown railway have contributed £25 towards diffraying [sic] the cost of laying out the grounds in

---

52  Alexander Thom, *Thom's Dublin city & county street directory* (Dublin, 1851), p. 934.
53  Ibid. List of residents, Longford Terrace, no. 1: Hon. Mrs John Massy; no. 2: John Moore; no. 3: Mrs Steele; no. 4: Major James Harrison; no. 5: Brindley Hone, barrister, Brindley Hone jun., proctor; no. 7: Charles Copeland, Royal Bank; no. 8: Murdock Green; no. 9: John H. Lecky, barrister; no. 10: Richard Armit; no. 11: James Robert Stewart; no. 12: Mrs Dwyer; no. 13: Charles Bowen II; no. 14: John Busby; no. 15: Mrs. William.
54  The Stewart family had strong links to the Pakenham family and to the Monkstown estate in Dublin. Henry Stewart was married to Elizabeth Pakenham, a daughter of Lord Longford, was MP for Longford Borough and was the Pakenham family land agent and agent for the joint Longford/De Vesci estate from c.1790. Joseph Kincaid became Henry Stewart's business partner in 1827 and the name was changed to Stewart and Kincaid in 1829. Following Henry Stewart's death in 1840, the firm was continued by his son James Robert Stewart and Joseph Kincaid. James R. Stewart was one of the trustees of the Mariners church in Kingstown from its opening in 1837 to his death on 10 Dec. 1889 at the age of 84. From 1844, James R. Stewart resided in the newly built house no. 11 Longford Terrace, but this became too crowded as his family expanded. By 1853, the Stewart family, including 11 children, moved to the larger Monkstown House on Monkstown Avenue. In 1857, the Stewarts moved to Gortleitragh on Sloperton.

front of this Terrace being a full equal to your subscription on account of the Lords of the Soil, beyond which they did not think it right to go'.[55] Copeland requested that the estate increase their subscription to induce the railway company to do the same:

> the Directors might be willing to increase their subscription to Fifty pounds provided Lords De Vesci and Longford can be induced to do the same. As the contemplated improvement cannot be credibly carried out unless we get the increased contribution from the Railway Directors & yourselves, may I venture to hope that you will take the subject into your favourable consideration and provide me with an answer at your earliest convenience.[56]

The estate agreed and by May 1844 the landscaping work carried out by Jeffrey Barcroft, who had built houses Nos. 1, 2, 3 and 7, was almost finished and Copeland requested payment from the estate:

> Mr. Barcroft having informed me that the laying out of the Ground at Longford Terrace being near completed you were ready to pay My Lord's subscription towards the cost thereof. I take the liberty of enclosing you a receipt for the amount, for which perhaps you will favour me with a cheque.[57]

Copeland continued to correspond with the agents over a number of months regarding the 'very unsatisfactory condition of the Iron railing and grounds at Longford Terrace'.[58] He proposed a scheme for improvement whereby each house would contribute £15 and the estate and the developers who had built the houses would contribute £25 each.[59] This was agreed at a meeting of some of the gentlemen of Longford Terrace at Stewart Kincaid's offices. However, in spite of this agreement, Copeland complained that Thomas Bradley was refusing to pay his share, leaving the other subscribers to cover the shortfall: 'The extraordinary conduct of Mr. Bradley in refusing to pay up his subscription towards the improvements at Salt Hill has placed myself and the other contributors in an awkward position'.[60]

Another common theme of correspondence between the residents and the agents was the state of the roads in front of Clifton and Longford Terrace.

---

55 Charles Copeland to Stewart Kincaid, 25 Feb. 1844, Pakenham papers, T/3763/H/2K/6.
56 Ibid.
57 Charles Copeland to James R. Stewart, 21 May 1844, Pakenham papers, T/3763/H/2K/6.
58 Charles Copeland to Stewart Kincaid, 2 Oct. 1844, Pakenham papers, T/3763/H/2K/6.
59 Charles Copeland to Stewart Kincaid, 8 Mar. 1844, Pakenham papers, T/3763/H/2K/6.
60 Charles Copeland to Stewart Kincaid, 8 May 1844, Pakenham papers, T/3763/H/2K/6.

Major James Harrison, who lived at No. 4 Longford Terrace, also wrote on behalf of the residents to Stewart Kincaid, stating that they were willing to contribute to the cost of improving the road in front of the terrace:

> no public assistance could be obtained towards making the Road, and that the expense of so doing must therefore necessarily fall on the inhabitants, for it was considered that the Road would be perfectly impassable this winter if not previously formed and made, it was at the same time surmised that the Estate on which Longford Terrace is situated would probably bear part of the expense.[61]

By November 1845, the improvement works had been carried out. However, Major James Harrison complained that Bradley had not contributed his share and asked James R. Stewart to intervene:

> If you have any influence with Mr. Bradley perhaps you would see if it would have any effect in inducing him to pay for his Houses, he declines at present. I think he might be persuaded by you to make some arrangement with his tenants and get us out of debt if possible.[62]

Construction of the second, eastern section of Longford Terrace closer to old Dunleary was delayed until 1855 due to the physical constraints of the site and difficulty in finding speculative developers who were willing to invest in the scheme. This was partly due to the developers' objections to the design. The agents informed the ground landlords in June 1852 that 'The builders having raised considerable objections for the proposed plans for the continuation of Longford Terrace we have had several meetings with them and the architect and we cannot say that the matter is settled'.[63] The architect mentioned in this letter was John Skipton Mulvany, and another letter from the agents to the ground landlords in April 1852 that mentions 'the Plans made out by Mulvany for the arrangement of the new Terrace at Salt Hill' also confirms that Mulvany was the architect for the second, eastern terrace, at least.[64] Who was the architect for the eastern terrace was hitherto unclear and it had been attributed to either Mulvany or George Papworth on stylistic grounds.[65]

61 J. Harrison to Stewart Kincaid, 3 Nov. 1845, Pakenham papers, T/3763/H/2K/9.
62 J. Harrison to J. Stewart, 29 Nov. 1845, Pakenham papers, T/3763/H/2K/9.
63 Stewart Kincaid to Lord de Vesci, 28 June 1852, National Library of Ireland, De Vesci papers, MS 39,008/4–6.
64 Stewart Kincaid to Lords Longford and de Vesci, 20 Apr. 1852, National Library of Ireland, De Vesci papers, MS 39,006/7.
65 Frederick O'Dwyer, 'The architecture of John Skipton Mulvany' in *Irish Architectural and Decorative Studies*, iii (2000), p. 18. O'Dwyer states that John Skipton Mulvany certainly

Unfortunately, the architect for the earlier, western section is not clarified in the estate correspondence.[66]

Unlike in Edinburgh, Bath and London, where architects played a significant role in designing terraces of houses in the early nineteenth century, domestic building in Dublin was typically developer-led and constructed by artisan tradesmen without the involvement of architects at this time. The employment of John Skipton Mulvany to design the eastern terrace contributed to the homogenous form of the final terrace, which was composed as a coherent whole rather than being constructed in an ad hoc fashion: three of four adjoining houses were built one at a time by speculative developers. In 1854, the estate paid Mulvany £13 6s. 6d. for his design and also paid the surveyor Martin H. Carroll for 'marking out eight building plots at Salt Hill set to Mr. Bradley and Mr. Moyers'.[67] This estate investment in the architectural quality of the overall terrace is evident in its completed form today.

The road to Dunleary slopes downhill, and if the new, eastern section of Longford Terrace was built at road level it would have been much lower than the initial western section, which would have resulted in an unsatisfactory street-scape from an architectural point of view and less impressive sea views from the new eastern terrace. The ground landlords were very concerned with maintaining consistent parapet levels between the two terraces, which, in addition to the continuous decorative cornice, created strong horizontal emphasis in the elevations. This emphasis on a consistent parapet height along terraces to create a coherent harmonious facade, even where the ground level varied, was also evident in the design of De Vesci Terrace and Vesey Place.[68] To resolve the level difference, Kincaid proposed building a new private access road to the eastern terrace, higher than the existing road to old Dunleary.[69] A similar private access road had been constructed for Gresham Terrace in Kingstown, close to the asylum harbour:

> Raking the level of the New Terrace up to that of the present Terrace by having a second private road as at Gresham Terrace made out of the Dublin Road to Old Dunleary. You will observe the level of the two

---

designed the cut stone retaining wall to the front of the terrace and may have designed the houses themselves.

66 Pearson, *Between the mountains and the sea*, p. 226. Pearson attributes the design to George Papworth, who designed very similar houses at Gresham Terrace for Thomas Gresham.
67 Accounts of Longford/De Vesci Joint Estate, 1 May 1854, National Library of Ireland, De Vesci papers, MS 39,260/4.
68 Laura Johnstone, 'On one level to the eye: visions for suburbia on the Longford/De Vesci estate' in *Irish Architectural and Decorative Studies*, xvii (2015), p. 93.
69 J. Kincaid to Lords Longford and de Vesci, 20 Apr. 1852, National Library of Ireland, De Vesci papers, MS 39,006/7.

roads will vary very much at the lower end the public road falls towards the town. The entire Expenditure of these works would be £650 or £50 each on 13 houses, but that would save the Builders the cost of front filling in part each house & also dividing the several gardens in front of each house as on the Old terrace which would be fairly charged to the party taking the ground.[70]

In April 1852, the agents were already negotiating with Bradley regarding preparing the ground and building the private access road and said they 'should be pleased to get Mr. Bradley commenced as soon as possible & the works could go on along with the erection of houses'.[71] However, negotiations with the lead developers Bradley and Moyers regarding the design delayed the building of the houses. In July 1852, Stewart asked Mulvany to send the plans to Vesey, but they were still with Moyers:

> He sent to Mulvany the architect on Thursday to send you the Salt hill plans that evening & thought he had done so. I have again sent this though & it appears they are with Mr. Moyers the builder & he has been directed to send them to you forthwith. There are however no material alterations in them since you approved of them. Mr. Bradley and Mr. Moyers as tenants having withdrawn their objections to the plans.[72]

The estate paid £325, half the construction cost of the ground works, private road and granite retaining wall designed by Mulvany, and the rest of the cost was borne by the tenants: 'The tenants pay £25 a house for the cost of the terrace in front'.[73] The fact that the estate invested large amounts of money in preparing the ground and private road, demonstrates that they wanted to encourage a certain class of development. They were satisfied with the initial western terrace and were determined that the eastern terrace would be developed to the same high standard, providing houses with sea views in a unified terrace.

The challenging topography and the labour and expense involved in providing the new higher private road with its cut stone granite retaining wall contributed to the delayed commencement of the eastern section, started over a decade after the western section was completed. Kincaid expected in July 1852 'to have an agreement for the work & also agreements for 8 or 10

---

70 Ibid.
71 Ibid.
72 J. Kincaid to Thomas Vesey, 31 July 1852, National Library of Ireland, De Vesci papers, MS 39,008/4–6.
73 Ibid.

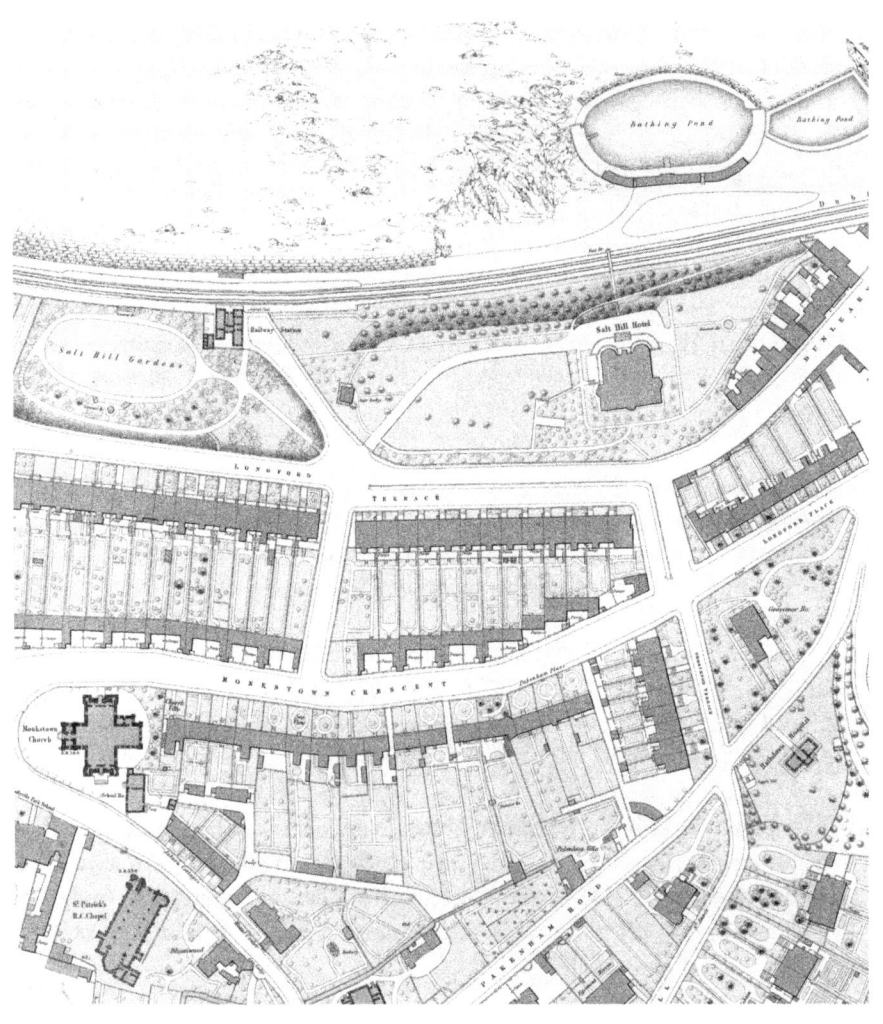

1.9   Ordnance Survey map of Monkstown,
scale 1:1,056 (5 feet to 1 mile), sheet no. 23/45 (Dublin, 1866)
(Courtesy of the board of Trinity College Dublin)

of the lots of the ground signed in a day or two'.[74] However, it was not until November 1855 that the first building plot, No. 16, was leased to Edward Rotherham. At 35 feet wide, it was slightly wider than the standard plot. Bradley was once again an influential investor leasing building plots for the next five houses, Nos. 17–21, in February 1856. William Moyers continued the eastern terrace, building No. 22 on a lease granted in 1858.

74   Ibid.

Similar to the earlier, western terrace, the first eight houses were built on plots 31 feet 6 inches wide and approximately 200 feet deep (long enough to accommodate back gardens and stables to the rear) and were leased for 99 years at an annual rent of £15 5s. 0d. However, the design of the front facade differed slightly as they were not set back behind front gardens due to the location of the private access road directly in front of the terrace, as shown on the Ordnance Survey map of 1866 (Figure 1.9).

It was very difficult to find investors for the final five building plots to complete the terrace and construction stalled once again. In August 1856, Stewart Kincaid wrote to Thomas Vesey, now 3rd Viscount de Vesci, informing him that William Moyers wanted to lease plots 24 and 25 for building:

> Mr. Moyers now offers to take 2 lots more on Longford Terrace as stated giving 7/6 p. foot in place of 10/- and not giving any contribution towards the Sewers & other works. The former lettings being at 10/- p. foot and £25 for each house towards sewerage.[75]

The difficulty in letting the ground was due to the reduced depth of the sites, which made it difficult to accommodate stables to the rear. Moyers was offered a reduced rent for each building plot and proposed to build the houses without any stables.[76]

> His plan would be to build the houses same as the others and not to build any stables in the first instance which would allow him to let the house considerably lower than those with stables. He might perhaps be induced to give 8/- p. foot but I think not more. This would still leave 3 lots to be disposed of.[77]

By this time the market for grand houses with private stables was decreasing and the proximity of Salthill train station reduced the need for private carriages. Less-expensive houses without stables could be let at a cheaper rent to members of the expanding professional classes who used the train to commute to the city centre. The ground landlords agreed to Moyers's terms and in January 1860 he built Nos. 24 and 25 on shallower plots which were cheaper, at £12 yearly rent, and slightly wider than the rest of the terrace at 33 feet wide. Letting the final plots to complete the terrace was a cause of great

---

75 J. Kincaid to 3rd Viscount de Vesci, 20 Aug. 1856, National Library of Ireland, De Vesci papers, MS 39,008/12.
76 Ibid.
77 Ibid.

concern for the estate. Kincaid suggested allowing the builders to construct stables on the other side of the road opposite the terrace:

> The origin of the alarm was that finding a great difficulty in letting the end of Longford Terrace, next Old Dunleary on account of the depth of the lots being reduced at the road from 250ft to 150ft leaving it scarcely profitable to build stables in the rere it occurred to me that we might with advantage allow the stables to be built exactly opposite each lot on the other side of the Public Road.[78]

These stables 'would have the same elevation as the ones constructed to the rear of the western part of Longford Terrace, and this façade would face onto the public road but be sufficiently distanced from the front of the houses of Longford Terrace, in order to minimise their impact'. Kincaid detailed how the coach houses 'would face the buildings of the parties to the minimum and would be at a point distanced from them'.[79] However, this proposal was not accepted by the ground landlords and instead they let the plots at reduced rents and allowed the builders to decide whether to put stables in the reduced rear gardens or not: 'letting the corner end as it stands allowing the Builders to choose for themselves whether they will build stables by encroaching on their own gardens or not have any'.[80] In 1861, the final two plots, No. 27 and 28, were let to George Moyers, William Moyers's son. These were the widest plots, 38 feet wide, and the cheapest at £10 yearly rent. The Ordnance Survey Map of 1865 (Figure 1.9) shows how the rear gardens reduce dramatically in length at the eastern end of the terrace. Nos. 27 and 28 do not have a proper coach house in the rear garden. The final house, No. 28, is L-shaped, as was specifically requested by Lord de Vesci, in order to present a pleasing facade to the side road: 'nothing but the gable you wished to be an L shape showing a good part to the Road'.[81] William Moyers and his son George were influential in the construction of Longford Terrace, building three of the houses of the first terrace and five of the second terrace.

The second, eastern terrace varied in some ways from the initial, western terrace. The houses don't have front gardens as the front of the plots were shortened by the private access road, and the terrace is also not as homogeneous as the initial, western terrace as the last five houses of the terrace are wider. However, overall, the streetscape is still remarkably homogeneous, and the overall effect is of two matching terraces.

78   Ibid.
79   Ibid.
80   Ibid.
81   Ibid.

Longford Terrace differed from its urban counterparts in Dublin city centre because the ground landlords insisted on consistency of fenestration, parapet level and materials. The diversity of fenestration and parapet height which was common in the Georgian squares of Dublin's city centre was not acceptable in these architect-designed nineteenth-century suburban terraces, which were more symmetrical and featured more decorative ornament. The formal symmetrical composition of Longford Terrace and other terraces on the Monkstown estate aimed to recreate the types of terraces popular in British cities, particularly in coastal resorts such as Bath and Brighton. As discussed earlier, the original idea of blocks of houses presented as one monumental unity derived from English examples such as the Royal Crescent in Bath.

The ground landlords' investment in commissioning surveys and proposed plans and employing architects such as John Skipton Mulvany to design terraces demonstrates their long-term strategy for sustained profit by protecting the character of parts of their estate. This was not the case on all parts of the estate, but Longford Terrace was an example of carefully planned, estate-controlled, development. The lease was the key tool in controlling development, and covenants in the lease protected sea views and ensured the regularity of the elevation.

Monkstown changed dramatically in the first half of the nineteenth century as a merchant middle class began occupying and urbanising what had been a rural landscape. In the early nineteenth century, the ground landlords and their agents were attempting to make the idea of permanently inhabiting this rocky coastal area attractive. They did this by surveying and identifying plots of land for development and setting out terraces, many of which faced the sea, making the most of the area's aesthetic and picturesque qualities. The ground landlords influenced the urban morphology of their estates by setting out the location of terraces, churches and infrastructure. The estate surveys are relevant in uncovering the priorities of the decision-makers at the time, which ultimately shaped the urban form, architectural design and character of these suburbs.

By the nineteenth century, the suburbs were more conducive to imaginative and ambitious urban design strategies than the city centre. Urban design in the city was constrained by the existing built fabric and the existing morphological form of established routes, whereas in the suburbs new streets could be laid out on previously undeveloped land. The ambitious design schemes prepared for the estate such as the Royal Paragon scheme from 1813 demonstrate this vision for suburban planning.[82] This scheme marked a key

---

82 Sherrard, Brassington and Greene, 'Survey of the town of Dunleary and Royal Paragon in the County of Dublin'.

shift in the perception of the area by its ground landlords, who no longer viewed it as semi-rural, with a seasonal function of providing a resort for city dwellers. They now understood the space as suitable for large-scale terraces of permanent residences. The development of Longford Terrace and Monkstown Crescent which evolved from the estate's plans show how domestic architecture of varying articulations and scales combined with road layout and landscape to create new spatial relationships in this nineteenth-century suburb. This was a landscape which sat between the rural and the urban, separate from but still linked to the urban core.

According to Stewart, there was not much investment by the ground landlords in developing or improving Kingstown before 1837.[83] In 1837, the estate bought back 'a considerable portion of the undeveloped part of the suburbs' from the original tenants, giving either a sum of money or an annual rent.[84] They paid about £25 an acre to buy back land they had leased at £3 to £4 an acre.[85] This investment in buying back land was a turning point in the development of the architectural and spatial character of the area. Subsequent investment by the estate would create a mid-nineteenth-century maritime suburb known for its elegant and orderly, formally arranged, seafront terraces. After 1837, the estate spent about £12,000 in developing Longford Terrace, Vesey Place, De Vesci Terrace, the Hill and Monkstown Crescent. Prior to 1837, the estate had only invested about £5,000 in the Monkstown area. This estate policy of regaining control over parts of the estate and setting them out had an impact on their design which can be recognised in the built form and character of these areas today. In the late nineteenth century, these areas were described as 'gentlemen's residences of an expensive character'.[86]

Wakeman's 1853 guidebook described taking the train from the city to Salthill and walking to Kingstown, and noted that the recently built suburban houses were 'generally handsome, displaying a variety of architecture and affording an idea of the taste and mode of life of the wealthier citizens of Dublin'.[87] D'Alton summarised the attractions of these new suburban spaces in his description of Salthill and Monkstown: 'A locality, so approximated to the sea, so accessible by railway communication, of such pure air, dry soil, bold scenery, and marine enjoyments ... crowded in every corner with villas and boarding-houses, bathing-lodges and cottages'.[88]

---

83 *Report from the select committee on town holdings*, May 1886, H.C. 1886 (213), 194.
84 In 1886, the estate was paying rents amounting to £400 a year.
85 Stewart, evidence to the select committee of the House of Commons, *Report from the select committee on town holdings*.
86 Ibid.
87 Wakeman, *Dublin: what's to be seen and how to see it*, p. 147.
88 D'Alton, *The history of the County of Dublin*, p. 870.

# 2

# Municipal Social Housing in Ireland, 1866–1914

## *Matthew Potter*

### Introduction

This chapter examines the impact of social housing in a number of Irish cities and towns from 1866 to 1914. It starts with a brief overview of housing conditions in urban Ireland, examines the legislative code governing Irish social housing, outlines the quantities built and discusses the impact on their respective towns.[1] An attempt will be made to examine the possible reasons for the differences in output between various comparable municipal authorities. The overall impact of the first half-century of Irish social housing will be assessed, in particular the manner in which it disproportionately benefited the more affluent sections of lower-income groups. Finally, this study uses a sample group of 11 municipal councils: Dublin, Cork, Limerick, Waterford, Galway, Drogheda, Kilkenny, Kingstown, Pembroke, Blackrock and Rathmines-Rathgar.

Social housing has been defined by Anne Power as:

> Housing that is not provided for profit and is often let at below market rents; it is allocated to lower-income groups, or to those whose income would not allow them to buy a home independently; the way it is produced – in quality and quantity – is laid down and regulated by the State. The social landlords themselves are also regulated in the way they provide housing. Social landlords can include local authorities, housing associations, co-operatives, limited dividend companies and private landlords.[2]

---

1 See Frank Cullen, 'The provision of working- and lower middle-class housing in late nineteenth-century urban Ireland' in *Proceedings of the Royal Irish Academy: archaeology, culture, history, literature*, cxi, sect. C, special issue: *domestic life in Ireland* (2011), pp 217–51.
2 Anne Power, *Hovels to high rises, social housing in Europe since 1850* (London, 1993), p. 3.

Chester McGuire has outlined four stages of housing development: intervention, provision, quality and withdrawal. In the first stage, severe housing shortage forces the state to intervene, generally by drawing up building regulations or facilitating private philanthropic bodies to provide housing. The second stage occurs when the state itself, at a national or local level, begins to provide social housing. In the third stage, the emphasis in state provision shifts from the quantity of units provided to their quality. The final stage arises when the majority of the population is well housed and the state scales back its involvement. This chapter examines Irish social housing during the first and part of the second of McGuire's stages.[3]

In 1996, the publication of *John Bull's other homes* by Murray Fraser established for the first time that the roots of Irish social housing lay firmly in the nineteenth century and, more significantly, that Ireland's system was one of the earliest and proportionately the largest such programme in the world.[4] Fraser himself states that 'within the context of Europe and America before 1914, it is clear that Ireland had by far the most socialised system of working-class housebuilding'.[5]

## Municipal government and urban space

Social housing in Ireland was but one aspect of the nineteenth-century state's expanding role. One of the most prescient accounts of this phenomenon was that of Foucault, who distinguished between 'sovereignty', exercised by medieval rulers over territory, and what he called 'governmentality', exercised by modern rulers over both territory and its population.[6] He wrote that 'in contrast to sovereignty, government has as its purpose not the act of government itself, but the welfare of the population, the improvement of its condition, the increase of its wealth, longevity, health, etc.'[7] While the functions of the medieval state were generally confined to foreign affairs and public order, the modern state became involved in a host of other areas, including health, education, social welfare, water supply, sanitation and culture. People were more closely and intensely governed and controlled than ever before. This phenomenon, sometimes called governmentalisation,

---

3 Chester C. McGuire, *International housing policies, a comparative analysis* (Lexington, Mass., 1981), p. 12.
4 Murray Fraser, *John Bull's other homes, state housing and British policy in Ireland 1883–1922* (Liverpool, 1996).
5 Ibid., p. 292.
6 Graham Burchell, Colin Gordon and Peter Miller (eds), *The Foucault effect: studies in governmentality with two lectures and an interview with Michel Foucault* (Chicago, 1991).
7 Michel Foucault, 'Governmentality', ibid., p. 100.

involved two processes pertinent to municipal government: first, the creation of a clear distinction between private and public space, and second, the establishment of sole jurisdiction over the latter by the state, national and local.[8]

In nineteenth-century Ireland, governmentalisation had a major impact on Irish cities and towns. Between 1828 and 1841, the old, corrupt, moribund borough corporations were replaced by reformed municipal authorities which paved, cleaned, lit and policed the streets; introduced systems of house numberings; established a state monopoly over naming streets, squares and other public spaces; and presided over the erection of increasing numbers of public monuments. From the 1880s onwards, nationalists took control of municipal councils all over Ireland outside north-east Ulster, which resulted in the 'nationalisation' of public space all over Ireland. This mainly consisted of changing street names for overtly political purposes and constructing public statues, particularly of the ubiquitous Maid of Erin and the 1798 pike man.[9]

In the same manner, social housing in urban Ireland was governmentalised. In nineteenth-century Europe, the prevalence of poor housing was highlighted because of its unprecedented concentration in the large cities created by industrialisation, which in turn led to the emergence of various social housing systems. Although Ireland did not experience widespread industrialisation outside Ulster, its housing conditions were as bad as any in Europe. Between 1700 and 1840, Irish improving landlords had frequently built what amounted to social housing for their poorer urban tenants, while borough corporations had sometimes administered privately funded almshouses. From the 1880s onwards, reformed municipal councils took over and greatly expanded the provision of social housing.

Internationally, the entry of the local state into social housing accelerated what has been described as the 'embourgeoisement' of the more affluent sections of the working classes. Beginning in the late nineteenth century, this phenomenon witnessed men becoming more domesticated, women becoming full-time housewives, the cultivation of privacy and respectability and increasing pride being taken in decorating and furnishing the home. Originally associated with the eponymous bourgeoisie, the process spread upwards and downwards to encompass both the elite and the proletariat, exemplified by the middle-class lifestyles adopted by Queen Victoria at one extreme and Karl Marx at the other.[10]

---

8   See S.E. Finer, *The history of government from the earliest times* (3 vols., New York, 1999), iii, 1609–35; Max Weber, *Economy and society: an outline of interpretive sociology*, 2 vols, ed. Guenther Roth and Claus Wittich (Berkeley, Calif., 1978), ii, 956–1005.

9   See M.J.D. Roberts, 'Public and private in early nineteenth-century London: the Vagrant Act of 1822 and its enforcement' in *Social History*, xiii, no. 3 (1988), pp 273–94.

10  John Scott, *A dictionary of sociology* (Oxford, 2014), pp 207–08.

In Ireland, the embourgeoisement process was to be significantly accelerated by the provision of social housing.[11]

## The problem

It is widely known that Irish cities and towns, particularly Dublin, had a major housing problem in the late nineteenth century. Indeed, such conditions were widespread, not only in the cities but also in the towns, large and small. The Third Report of the Royal Commission on the Housing of the Working Classes dealing with Ireland (1885) provided comprehensive information on the extent of the problem. Thus, it was stated that:

> The housing of the working classes at Cork appears to be in a very bad condition in many respects. There are in that city, 1,732 tenement houses, occupied by about 22,000 persons. The tenements are said to be in a disgraceful state, and the overcrowding has existed for fifty years with scarcely any improvement.[12]

Similar conditions existed in Limerick. In 1885, William Spillane, a former mayor and sheriff and proprietor of a large tobacco factory in the city, maintained that matters 'could not be much worse anywhere in the world'.[13] In Limerick city, employment was mainly concentrated in the areas of casual labouring on the docks, railways and related enterprises. In 1913, 20 per cent of the city's housing stock consisted of 1,050 tenement houses, and another 15 per cent were one-room flats.[14] In 1911, it was claimed that there was nowhere in Ireland 'with worse slum dwellings than Limerick or where proper houses for the poor are more necessary'.[15]

Waterford, which had a population of 23,000, contained 1,180 houses occupied by at least two families each, and in some instances 'there were as many as 10 families in one house'.[16] There were an estimated 360 tenement houses in the city. In Galway, with a population of between 15,000 and 16,000, 'There are from 1,000 to 1,200 houses in an unfit state for human

---

11 Maura Cronin, '"You'd be disgraced!": middle-class women and respectability in post-famine Ireland' in Fintan Lane (ed.), *Politics, society and the middle class in modern Ireland* (London, 2010), pp 107–29.
12 *Royal Commission for inquiring into the housing of the working classes. Third Report (Ireland), with minutes of evidence, appendices and indices*, H.C. 1884–85 [C 4547], xxxi (hereinafter, *Report on the housing of the working classes*), 194.
13 Ibid., p. 195.
14 Fraser, *John Bull's other homes*, p. 68.
15 *Irish Builder*, 18 Mar. 1911.
16 *Report on the housing of the working classes*, p. 196.

habitation. There is considerable overcrowding both in tenement houses, which are numerous and in cottages containing only one apartment'.[17]

Smaller towns also presented appalling housing conditions. New Ross, County Wexford was a case in point. In 1885, it had

> The melancholy distinction of having the highest average death-rate in the United Kingdom, the average for the last 10 years being 31 per thousand. Three-fourths of the houses of the labourers have no sanitary arrangements whatever, and some 'respectable houses' to quote the expression of the medical officer, have none either. ... The houses are generally overcrowded and badly ventilated and though the tenement houses are in a deplorable condition no attempt has been made to enforce regulations under section 100 of the Public Health Act.[18]

Navan, County Meath was almost as bad, with one witness to the 1885 Royal Commission on the Housing of the Working Classes stating that although he was familiar with conditions in Cork, Limerick and Waterford he had 'never seen houses there anything to equal those in Navan, as far as regards their miserable state'.[19]

## Attempts at a solution

In order for a social problem to be addressed, three factors need to be present: a pressing need, the financial resources and the political will. The catalogue of misery described in the 1885 Royal Commission on the Housing of the Working Classes and innumerable other contemporary accounts leaves no doubt that housing conditions prevailing in nineteenth-century Ireland were appalling. However, this does not explain why the state at both local and national levels assumed a much more active role in housing provision than almost anywhere else in the world at the time. If need was the sole catalyst for producing an activist state in the sphere of housing, the Russian Empire and British India, to name but two, would probably have emerged as pioneers in the field.

Similarly, financial resources were not a determining factor. On the one hand, municipal socialism was less important in Ireland due to the relative smallness of Irish cities and towns, the poverty of Irish municipalities compared with their British or Continental counterparts (as a result of economic stagnation), the consequent parsimony of the ratepayers who controlled them and the

17 Ibid.
18 Ibid., p. 197.
19 Ibid., p. 294.

predominance of political over social issues in the Irish political system. On the other hand, while the financial resources of the British Government were enormous (in 1914, Britain enjoyed the third largest national income in the world, and British per capita gross domestic product was only exceeded by those of the U.S.A., Australia and New Zealand), it did not necessarily mean that it was prepared to embark on a programme of social housing in Britain, let alone Ireland. If financial resources alone determined state involvement in social housing, the lead would have been taken by the U.S.A. and Australasia.[20]

What made the Irish case special was the additional factor: the presence of the political will. During the 1880s, the Irish Party attempted to overcome the traditional rivalry between farmers and labourers and unite them in support of a monolithic Home Rule movement. The Irish Party used the provision of labourers' cottages to win and retain the support of the labourers. In turn, the Party was able to wrest this concession from British governments anxious to ameliorate social discontent in Ireland, especially after the Conservative Party embraced the policy of 'killing Home Rule with kindness'.[21]

The Irish Party pursued a similar strategy with regard to municipal social housing, where it sought to ward off the potential threat to its hegemony posed by organised labour. Although this spectre never actually materialised, it seemed to assume dangerous proportions on a number of occasions. The first of these was the Parnellite split in the 1890s, which created a dangerous political vacuum and caused both sides to compete for labour support. Soon after, the Local Government (Ireland) Act 1898 caused a dramatic widening of the municipal franchise, which resulted in the emergence of a host of local labour parties that contested the municipal elections of 1899. Most of these made the provision of social housing one of their principal policy aims. After 1900, there was also the rise of the Irish Transport and General Workers' Union under James Larkin, the establishment of Sinn Féin in 1905 and the creation of a national Labour Party in 1912.[22]

Accordingly, the role of the Irish Party was crucial in creating the most significant state housing programme in the world by channelling the financial resources of the British state into the provision of Irish social housing. Two other factors were also significant. Outside north-east Ulster, the output of affordable private housing was very small, due to the weakness of the building industry, while the role of philanthropic private companies, dominant until around 1908, declined rapidly thereafter.[23]

---

20 Angus Maddison, *The world economy, historical statistics* (Paris, 2003), pp 184–85.
21 Fraser, *John Bull's other homes*, pp 20–45.
22 Ibid., pp 77–95.
23 Ibid., pp 91–92.

Table 2.1  Social housing legislation in Ireland, 1866–1914

| Act | Provisions | Results |
| --- | --- | --- |
| Labouring Classes Lodging Houses and Dwellings (Ireland) Act (1866)[a] | The Irish Board of Works gave loans to private companies and municipal councils, to finance up to half the cost of a housing scheme. | 3,416 dwellings completed |
| Artisans and Labourers Dwellings Act 1868 (Torrens Act)[b] | Municipal councils could repair or demolish individual insanitary dwellings. | Ineffective |
| Artisans and Labourers Dwellings Improvement Act 1875 (Cross Act)[c] | Loans were provided to municipal authorities to clear slums. On the cleared land, houses could be provided by themselves or private companies. | Until 1883, applicable only to towns of over 25,000 people, thus excluding all but the five largest Irish municipalities. In 1883, population limit reduced to 12,000. |
| Labourers (Ireland) Acts (1883, 1885 and 1886)[d] | Empowered boards of guardians to provide social housing in rural areas, including towns without municipal authorities. | 50,000 labourers' cottages completed by 1914, including large numbers in non-municipal towns. |
| Housing of the Working Classes Act (1885)[e] | Reduced interest rates and increased term of loans. | Smaller and poorer municipal authorities could build social houses for the first time. |
| Housing of the Working Classes Act 1890[f] | For the first time, local authorities were empowered to build new houses on greenfield sites. | 4,400 dwellings completed (1890–1908). Remained principal Irish housing act until 1966.[g] |
| Housing of the Working Classes (Ireland) Act 1908 (Clancy Act)[h] | First Irish housing subsidy towards interest repayments. Paid from a new Housing Fund.[i] | 2,600 dwellings completed (1908–14).[j] |

[a] 29 & 30 Vict. c. xliv (1866).   [b] 31 & 32 Vict. c. cxxx (1868).   [c] 38 & 39 Vict. c. xxxvi (1875).
[d] Murray Fraser, *John Bull's other homes, state housing and British policy in Ireland 1883–1922* (Liverpool, 1996), pp 28–29, 31–37.
[e] 48 & 49 Vict. c. lxxii (1885).   [f] 53 & 54 Vict. c. lxx (1890).
[g] Cathal O'Connell, *The state and housing policy in Ireland: ideology, policy and practice* (New York, 2007), p. 15.
[h] 8 Edw. 7 c. lxi (1908).
[i] After independence, the Housing Fund continued to pay subsidies relating to houses built before 1921. It was abolished under the provisions of the Housing Amendment Act 1958.
[j] Fraser, *John Bull's other homes*, pp 91–94.

## The legislative framework, 1851–1914

All municipal authorities, large and small, were empowered to provide social housing. Municipal authorities were created under the Lighting of Towns Act 1828, Municipal Corporations (Ireland) Act 1840 and the Towns Improvement Act 1854. The number of municipal authorities in Ireland expanded continuously in the period under review from 100 in 1861 to 126 in 1914 (they reached their greatest number at 129 in 1920). In towns without municipal self-government, the responsibility for social housing was given to boards of guardians under the Labourers (Ireland) Act 1883.[24]

The social housing legal code in Ireland consisted of both general British legislation and specific Irish acts (see Table 2.1). It commenced with the two Shaftesbury Acts (1851), which consisted of the Common Lodging Houses Act and the Labouring Classes Lodging Houses Act. The first of these was a routine measure, but the second, 'so much ahead of its time and far-sighted in its scope, must be said to mark the introduction of municipal socialism (construed, admittedly, in a narrow sense) in housing'. This was because 'it did, quite clearly, introduce the principle of local government construction and ownership of working-class dwellings'.[25] It permitted parish vestries to purchase land, build working-class dwellings on it, and borrow money against the rates for this purpose. Although largely unused due to its complex provisions and adoptive nature, the Labouring Classes Lodging Houses Act played a role in social housing legislation similar to Gladstone's Land Act 1870 in Irish agrarian reform, being of vital importance for the precedents it set rather than for its actual effectiveness. The local authority was permitted to become builder and landlord without restrictions as to house size or type and was not limited to rehousing alone.[26]

## The output

For over 40 years (1867–1908), Irish social housing was dominated by philanthropic private companies, though the vast majority of units were provided in Dublin, totalling around 4,500 by 1914. The Dublin Industrial Tenements Company was the pioneer and built 50 units in 1867. It was followed by the Dublin Artisans Dwellings Company, which built 3,600 units; the Guinness/

---

24 Matthew Potter, *The municipal revolution in Ireland: a handbook of urban government in Ireland since 1800* (Dublin and Portland, Oreg., 2010), pp 146–47, 209–10.
25 Anthony S. Wohl, *The eternal slum, housing and social policy in Victorian London* (2nd ed., New Brunswick, NJ, 2002), p. 76.
26 14 &15 Vict. c. xxxiv (1851).

Iveagh Trust, which provided 586 units; and the Dublin and Suburban Workmen's Dwelling Company, which constructed 288 units. The other major philanthropic bodies were the Cork Improved Dwellings Company (420 units); Limerick Labourer's Dwelling Company (50 units); Thomond Artisans Dwellings Company, Limerick (70 units) and the Waterford Improved Dwellings Company Ltd (24 units). In total, philanthropic private companies had provided around 5,000 units of social housing in Ireland between 1867 and 1914.[27]

Between 1879 and 1914, Irish municipal authorities built a total of 7,600 housing units, compared with 24,000 in British urban areas, which meant that the Irish output of municipal housing was nearly seven times that of Britain. Of these, Dublin Corporation built a total of 1,450; Cork Corporation, 546; Waterford Corporation, 250; Galway Town Commissioners, 194; Kilkenny Corporation, 140; Limerick Corporation, 133; and Drogheda Corporation, 128. Four Dublin townships were especially prolific: Kingstown Urban District Council provided 450 units, Pembroke Urban District Council, 354; Rathmines and Rathgar Urban District Council, 354; and Blackrock Urban District Council, 205. Belfast Corporation, the main exemplar of municipal socialism in the country, built a 222-bed hostel, but otherwise did not provide any social housing, as private developers built sufficient numbers of cheap, good-quality housing.[28]

However, a more useful measurement of output is to quantify social housing as a percentage of total housing units in a municipality. In Table 2.2, the total number of dwellings in the sample group of boroughs and municipal towns has been taken from the 1911 census and compared with the total number of social housing units provided in each of them by 1914. Of the major urban areas, Kingstown municipal social housing accounted for the largest percentage of the total dwellings in its operational area, at 12.6 per cent, followed by Blackrock at 11.6 per cent, Galway at 7.9 per cent, Kilkenny 6.5 per cent, Pembroke 6.4 per cent, Waterford 5.2 per cent, Rathmines 5.2 per cent, Drogheda 4.5 per cent, Cork 4.2 per cent, Dublin 4.1 per cent and Limerick 2.1 per cent. However, the picture is dramatically altered if the contribution of private philanthropic companies is included. In Dublin, philanthropic companies raised social housing units as a percentage of total housing units in 1914 to 16.8 per cent and in Cork and Limerick to 7.5 per cent and 4 per cent respectively.[29]

Perhaps the most interesting question to be addressed is why there were such notable differences between the outputs of various municipal authorities.

27  Fraser, *John Bull's other homes*, pp 69–74, 336 n. 70.
28  Ibid., p. 92.
29  1911 census of Ireland.

Table 2.2 Number of housing units in a sample group of eleven municipal authorities by 1914

| Municipality | Total number of houses | Number of municipal social housing units | Percentage of total | Number of philanthropic companies' social housing units | Percentage of total | All social housing units as percentage of total number of houses |
| --- | --- | --- | --- | --- | --- | --- |
| Dublin | 35,477 | 1,450 | 4.1% | 4,500 | 12.7% | 16.8% |
| Kingstown | 3,582 | 450 | 12.6% | | | 12.6% |
| Blackrock | 1,771 | 205 | 11.6% | | | 11.6% |
| Galway | 2,448 | 194 | 7.9% | | | 7.9% |
| Cork | 12,850 | 546 | 4.2% | 420 | 3.3% | 7.5% |
| Kilkenny | 2,135 | 140 | 6.5% | | | 6.5% |
| Pembroke | 5,497 | 354 | 6.4% | | | 6.4% |
| Waterford | 4,791 | 250 | 5.2% | 24 | 0.5% | 5.7% |
| Rathmines | 6,843 | 354 | 5.2% | | | 5.2% |
| Drogheda | 2,833 | 128 | 4.5% | | | 4.5% |
| Limerick | 6,305 | 133 | 2.1% | 120 | 1.9% | 4.0% |

This may be examined under a number of headings: the scale of housing need; the financial resources available to municipal councils; ideological/political factors; and the social composition of municipal councils.

## Housing need

The most significant factor influencing housing output should be perceived housing need. Accordingly, the 1881 census returns have been examined to create a model of housing in a selection of Irish urban areas before the advent of municipal social housing. These returns generally followed the format of earlier census returns, by classifying housing into four divisions. Fourth-class houses were built of mud or other perishable material and had only one room and one window. Third-class houses had from one to four rooms and one to four windows. Second-class houses had from five to nine rooms and an equal number of windows. First-class houses consisted of all those but of a higher standard than the preceding categories.

Accommodation within the various categories of house was also dealt with under four headings: first-class accommodation consisted of a first-class house occupied by one family; second-class accommodation consisted of a second-class house with one family or a first-class house occupied by two or three families; third-class accommodation consisted of third-class houses with one family each, second-class houses with two or three families or first-class houses occupied by four or five families; and fourth-class accommodation consisted of all fourth-class houses, third-class houses with more than one family, second-class houses with four or more families and first-class houses inhabited by six or more families (see Table 2.3).[30]

An examination of the sample group, including units provided by both municipal councils and private philanthropic companies, shows that there was some link between housing need and social housing output. Dublin, which had the worst housing in 1881, had the highest percentage output by 1914, 75 per cent of which was provided by private philanthropic companies. By contrast, Belfast had the best housing in 1881 and the lowest output by 1914. Similarly, Galway and Kilkenny had among the highest levels of need and the largest percentage housing outputs. On the other hand, the link was very weak in the case of Limerick, which had the fourth worst housing in 1881 but the second lowest build by 1914.

30 Ibid.

Table 2.3  *Percentages of families in Irish urban areas by class of accommodation, 1881*

| Municipality | Class 1 | Class 2 | Class 3 | Class 4 | Classes 3 and 4 |
|---|---|---|---|---|---|
| Dublin | 8% | 20% | 29% | 43% | 72% |
| Galway | 11% | 26% | 42% | 21% | 63% |
| Cork | 10% | 38% | 34% | 18% | 52% |
| Kilkenny | 10% | 39% | 39% | 12% | 51% |
| Limerick | 9% | 41% | 32% | 18% | 50% |
| Drogheda | 11% | 40% | 39% | 10% | 49% |
| Dublin Townships | 17% | 40% | 32% | 11% | 43% |
| Waterford | 11% | 47% | 22% | 20% | 42% |
| Belfast | 7% | 65% | 26% | 2% | 28% |

## Financial resources

The financial resources of the sample group have been tested against housing output. Between 1828 and 1860, a property tax (rates) became the main source of income for Irish municipal authorities.[31] The Poor Relief Act 1838 created the modern system by stipulating that the basis for the rateable valuation of a property was the letting or 'net annual' value (the amount of rent per year that could be obtained on premises when the costs of repairs, maintenance, improvements etc. are deducted). Between 1852 and 1865, the whole country was valued under the direction of Sir Richard Griffith, Commissioner of Valuation, using net annual letting value as a systematic basis for the assessment of the various rates.[32]

Although Griffith's valuations subsequently ceased to have any real connection with the rental value of a hereditament, they continued to be used as a yardstick against which new premises were rated and existing ones altered. Accordingly, estimates of the sample group's comparative wealth at the outset of social housing has been obtained by dividing the total rateable valuation in 1885 by the population in 1881 to obtain a per capita rateable valuation (see Table 2.4).[33]

---

31 Howard A. Street, *The law relating to local government in Ireland* (Dublin, 1955), pp 1313–24.
32 Roche, *Local government*, p. 165.
33 *Return as to each municipal borough and municipal town or township in Ireland showing how on 1st day of January 1885, each borough or town stood in respect of the following particulars. The rateable valuation, the population, etc.*, H.C. 1886 (53).

Table 2.4  *Rateable valuation in Irish urban areas per head of population, 1881–85*

| Municipality | Population | Total rateable valuation | Rateable valuation per head of population |
| --- | --- | --- | --- |
| Blackrock | 8,902 | £49,450 | £5 11s. 0d. |
| Rathmines | 24,370 | £11,3969 | £4 13s. 7d. |
| Kingstown | 18,586 | £78,053 | £4 4s. 0d. |
| Pembroke | 23,222 | £96,980 | £4 3s. 7d. |
| Belfast | 208,122 | £604,234 | £2 18s. 0d. |
| Dublin | 249,602 | £675,673 | £2 14s. 2½d. |
| Cork | 80,124 | £157,662 | £1 19s. 5d. |
| Waterford | 22,457 | £40,421 | £1 16s. 0d. |
| Limerick | 38,562 | £66,339 | £1 14s. 5d. |
| Galway | 15,471 | £26,212 | £1 13s. 9½d. |
| Drogheda | 12,297 | £19,199 | £1 11s. 2½d. |
| Kilkenny | 12,299 | £17,447 | £1 8s. 5d. |

When these results are cross-referenced with the housing output of both municipal councils and private philanthropic companies (Table 2.2), a number of extrapolations are obtained. Blackrock had the highest per capita rateable valuation and the third highest percentage housing output, while Kingstown had the third highest per capita rateable valuation and the second highest percentage housing output. Similarly, Rathmines, Pembroke and Dublin had both high per capita rateable valuations and large housing outputs. On the other hand, Limerick, Waterford and Galway had similar per capita rateable valuations, but while Galway had one of the highest percentage housing outputs, Limerick had one of the lowest. Kilkenny had one of the highest percentage housing outputs but the lowest per capita rateable valuations. In short, the link between financial resources and housing output is a weak one.

## Ideology

Ideological and political factors seem to have played a decisive role in at least one important instance. The Irish Parliamentary Party had brought social housing to the forefront of official policy for the reasons already outlined above. Conversely, unionists 'were generally opposed to legislation so clearly associated with the Nationalist cause'.[34] This resulted in a much smaller output of social housing in the Six Counties (the future Northern Ireland) than in the rest of Ireland. By 1919, a total of only 634 municipal social housing units had been built in the Six Counties. Derry/Londonderry Corporation built none at all by 1914.

Donegal Town provides an interesting example of how housing policy was influenced by the transition from unionist to nationalist control of a local authority. In the absence of a municipal council, the responsibility for social housing in the town rested with Donegal Board of Guardians. However, none was built during the period of unionist control (1840–99) despite considerable evidence of housing need. The situation changed as a result of the 1899 local elections which abruptly replaced the unionist hegemony with a nationalist one. Even then, Donegal Town did not acquire its first social houses for almost a decade. Finally, in August 1908, Donegal Rural District Council entered into a contract with local (nationalist!) builder Patrick Diver to erect ten 'labourers' cottages' in the townland of the Mullans at a cost of £116 10s. 0d. per cottage.[35]

Unionists justified the low input of social housing in the local authority areas under their control on the grounds that there was not the same pressing need in the future Six Counties as in the rest of the country. Whether this is actually true requires further research. However, a similar divide emerged in the South Dublin townships, where Nationalists actively promoted social housing in contrast to the Unionists' comparative lack of interest.

On the other hand, the emergence of Labour in the 1899 local elections produced no such clear-cut policy differences. Of the major municipal authorities, only Limerick Corporation came under Labour control, where the local party won 24 out of a total of 40 seats. This event attracted national and even international attention and resulted in the local authority being described as the 'Labour Corporation'. This contrasted with Labour's poor performance in other borough corporations: 2 out of 40 seats in Waterford, 3 out of 24 in Drogheda, 7 out of 60 in Dublin and none in Galway. Not only was there no positive correlation between the success of Labour and the output of social housing in this sample, but in fact the opposite would appear to have been the case. By 1914, social housing comprised 7.9 per cent of the total housing in Galway where Labour had won no seats in 1899 (and the uber-capitalist Máirtín Mór McDonogh (1860–1934) exercised a dominating influence over the municipal authority) compared with 2.1 per cent in Limerick, the home of the 'Labour Corporation'.[36]

---

34 Fraser, *John Bull's other homes*, p. 29.
35 *Derry People and Donegal News*, 29 Aug. 1908.
36 Potter, *The municipal revolution in Ireland*, pp 196–237. McDonogh served as chairman of

## Social composition of municipal councils

Finally, a similar disassociation emerges between the social composition of municipal councils elected in 1899 and subsequent social housing output. In Limerick, the working-class element on the new council was composed of ten 'journeymen', four master traders and one unskilled labourer, making a total of 15 on the 40-member council. Two other councillors (a fisherman and a river pilot) might also be classified as working-class. Yet, by 1914, social housing comprised only 2.1 per cent of the total in Limerick. On the other hand, the number of tradesmen on the 60-member Dublin City Council increased from 2 in 1890 to only 7 in 1900, while clerical/shop assistants went from none in 1890 to 2 in 1900. Here social housing comprised 4.1 per cent of the total in 1914.[37] Likewise, 7 'journeymen' were elected to Cork City Council in 1899, but even if the 4 master tradesmen are included, the working-class element was vastly outnumbered by the other 45 councillors. By 1914, social housing made up 4.2 per cent of the total in Cork.[38]

## Interpreting the data

Although it remains unclear what were the decisive factors in determining output in individual municipalities, a number of tentative conclusions may be drawn from the data presented in this chapter. The link between perceived housing need and output is strong in Dublin, Belfast, Galway and Kilkenny, but weak in Limerick. In the Dublin townships, there is both high per capita rateable valuation and large outputs of social housing, but in Kilkenny, this link is very weak. Limerick, Galway and Waterford had similar per capita rateable valuations, but sharply contrasting percentage housing outputs in the case of the first two. Ideology exercised a paradoxical influence, as there is a positive correlation between Nationalism and social housing, but hardly any between Labour and social housing output.

The lack of a link between Labour and social housing output is easily explained. In 1899, Labour gained an outright victory on only a few councils, and the old urban elites remained in power. Even where Labour parties took control, it generally disintegrated or became absorbed by the Irish

Galway Urban District Council on three occasions: 1899–1902, 1909–20 and 1925–34, but even when not in the chair was easily the most powerful man in Galway. See Jackie Uí Chionna, 'He was Galway': Máirtín Mór McDonogh, 1860–1934 (Dublin, 2016).

37 Mary E. Daly, Dublin: the deposed capital: a social and economic history, 1860–1914 (Cork, 1985), p. 205.
38 Maura Cronin, 'The economic and social structure of nineteenth century Cork' in David Harkness and Mary O'Dowd (eds), The Town in Ireland (Belfast, 1981), p. 126.

Parliamentary Party. In addition, the membership of the 'Labour parties' were generally not socialists, though some of them were more interested in social issues than their predecessors on the councils. Similarly, the administrative structures, functions, procedures and financial base of municipal authorities underwent no significant changes in 1898–99. The permanent officials remained in office and continued to direct affairs on a day-to-day basis, as before.[39]

### The embourgeoisement of Irish working-class housing

Social housing accelerated the embourgeoisement of the higher working classes in three principal ways. First, the penury of Irish municipal councils obliged them to charge comparatively high rents in order to defray the cost of providing the houses. Consequently, they could only be afforded by the more prosperous elements in the working classes. In turn, the municipal councils could not reduce rents to a level that would make them affordable by the poorest applicants. In this manner, social housing benefited only the aristocracy of labour (craftsmen, clerks and shop assistants) and excluded most of those in need of it. Thus, in 1898, it was reported in County Tipperary that the Thurles Town Commissioners were completing a scheme of nine social houses on the Mall in the town centre which it was claimed 'were so nicely situated and are of such a substantial kind that we have no doubt but that the Commissioners would easily find tenants willing to give twice the rent they intend to charge'.[40] Not until the 1930s did a solution to this dilemma emerge, when central government increased the level of subsidy.

Secondly, the spatial arrangements of the social housing facilitated embourgeoisement. In contrast with the overcrowding of the tenements, social housing units usually made provision for bedrooms separate from the spaces used for food preparation and dining. This was evident from the very beginning of the Irish social housing programme. Thus, in the Dublin Artisan Dwelling Company's large housing schemes in Stoneybatter, houses were either one storey and had three rooms, or two-storey with four rooms. Likewise, the country's first municipal social housing scheme, which was built in 1879 by Waterford Corporation, consisted of seventeen two-storey, four-room terraced houses. Cork Corporation constructed two-storey terraced houses with water closets that had either three rooms (living room with

---

39 Arthur Mitchell, *Labour in Irish politics 1890–1930: The Irish labour movement in an age of revolution* (Dublin, 1974), p. 20.
40 *Nenagh Guardian*, 8 Sept. 1898.

attached scullery downstairs and two bedrooms upstairs) or four rooms (living room and bedroom downstairs and two bedrooms upstairs).[41]

In many instances, social housing contained that most 'respectable' of domestic spaces, the parlour, which became the focus of family sociability and display (however modest) and the interface with the outer world, a semi-public space where visitors were received in a formal setting.[42] Indeed, the parlour symbolised an entire lifestyle of temperance, order and cleanliness of which 'the universally recognised signifiers were spotlessly clean windows and doorsteps whitened by scrubbing; lace window curtains which could be draped to reveal an aspidistra in a parlour window'.[43]

Few first-hand accounts of this process exist, but Limerick author Críostóir Ó Floinn has described his family's experience of social housing, albeit a quarter of a century after this chapter's terminal date.[44] In 1919, his parents Richard and Elizabeth O'Flynn, moved into a privately rented three-room flat at 2 Old Church Street, King's Island in the centre of Limerick city. Accommodation consisted of two bedrooms and a 'combined kitchen, sitting room and living room'. The flat was one of two in a terraced house, so the O'Flynns shared the front door, hallway and stairs with the family renting the other apartment. The two families also had 'to share the small yard with its single toilet and one tap on the wall'.[45] However, the O'Flynns were 'decent, respectable people. His [Críostóir's] father works away steadily delivering coal and supplements the family income playing the sax in a dance band'.[46] Even in the tiny kitchen/living room, Mrs O'Flynn created a bourgeois interior where 'the essential furniture consisted of a table, a dresser, a corner press, some chairs and the big black range' plus a gas ring and gas lamp.[47] In 1938, the O'Flynns moved to 36 O'Dwyer Villas, Thomondgate, part of a new Limerick Corporation housing scheme of 94 two-storey houses. It was an end house in a terrace, with only two bedrooms, but Ó Floinn refers to 'the splendour of the new house, all to ourselves, with electricity, hot and cold water in the kitchen, a bathroom and gardens', a veritable 'paradise regained'.[48]

Thirdly, social housing reinforced the reconfiguration of urban space along socio-economic lines. The flight of the upper and middle classes to the

---

41 Fraser, *John Bull's other homes*, pp 74–100.
42 Alison Ravetz, *Council housing and culture: the history of a social experiment* (London, 2003), pp 8–20.
43 Ibid., p. 27. See also Thad Logan, *The Victorian parlour: a cultural study* (Cambridge, 2001).
44 Críostóir Ó Floinn, *There is an isle: a Limerick boyhood* (Cork, 1998).
45 Ibid., pp 25–30.
46 *Irish Times*, 25 Apr. 1998.
47 Ó Floinn, *There is an isle*, p. 29.
48 Ibid., p. 332.

suburbs was one of the most characteristic features of the Anglophone world in the nineteenth century. It was paralleled on a lesser scale by the creation of social housing enclaves for the higher working classes in the city and town centres. The spatial distancing may not have been as stark, but the tendency was similar.

The comparison must not be overdrawn, however. The suburbs of Irish cities and larger towns were often large enough to create self-contained streetscapes into which no inferior housing could intrude. In Dublin, this process culminated with the creation of separate municipal councils to administer what had become a garland of sufficiently large 'townships' to warrant the creation of these bodies. Thus, in 1901, the population of Rathmines and Rathgar was 32,602, of Pembroke 25,799 and of Kingstown 17,377.[49] Although there was as wide a variety of housing classes in these local authority areas as in any other in the country, they contained a disproportionately large number of first- and second-class houses, thus facilitating the creation of 'upper-class ghettoes' like Ballsbridge and Sandymount.

By contrast, no social housing scheme had a population on that scale, although, predictably, Dublin provides examples of some that came close. The most radical reconfiguration of pre-1914 urban Ireland by social housing providers was the construction of 1,000 houses in Stoneybatter by the Dublin Artisans Dwellings Company between 1879 and 1908.[50] Also of significance were the 336-unit Kevin Street scheme and the 250-unit Iveagh Buildings provided in Dublin by the Iveagh Trust between 1894 and 1900.[51]

## Conclusion

Social housing had a significant ameliorative impact on Irish cities and towns before 1914. A total of 12,600 units were constructed, of which 60 per cent were municipal and 40 per cent provided by the private sector. Greater Dublin was the principal beneficiary, followed by Galway, Cork and Waterford in all of which it exceeded 5 per cent of total housing units. Clearly, output was not on the same scale as it was to be after independence, when the provision of social housing was one of the most important functions of local government, particularly between 1932 and 1987. However, such a comparison is both anachronistic and invalid. It is more instructive to situate pre-1914 Irish

---

49 Joseph V. O'Brien, *Dear, dirty Dublin: a city in distress, 1899–1916* (Berkeley, Calif., 1982), p. 284 taken from the 1901 census of Ireland.
50 Christine Casey, *Dublin: the city within the Grand and Royal Canals and the circular road with the Phoenix Park* (New Haven, Conn., 2005), pp 270–71.
51 O'Brien, *Dear, dirty Dublin*, pp 128–29.

output in the context of contemporary urban social housing, an exercise which suggests that it was one of the most advanced systems in the world. Fraser has established that this was due to the espousal of social housing by the Irish Parliamentary Party rather than because Irish housing need was particularly acute or that there were more abundant resources available than in other jurisdictions.

Irish social housing between 1867 and 1914 had a significant impact on the embourgeoisement of the country's working classes. If each housing unit was inhabited by an average of four to six people, an estimated 50,000–75,000 people benefited from moving into a better standard of housing. The link is not absolute, of course, and the provision of mass social housing from the 1930s to the 1980s did not prevent the survival to the present of a residualised underclass.[52] Nevertheless, a benchmark for acceptable housing standards was established before 1914 to which the vast bulk of lower income groups could aspire.

Finally, the significant involvement of both the public and private sectors in social housing before 1914 represented a significant acceleration of the governmentalisation process. On the one hand, the division between public and private space was decisively breached insofar as the state entered the dwellings of a large minority of the population by directly providing them with housing. On the other hand, the new social housing units promoted the cult of domestic privacy and thus accelerated the division between public and private space. In this and in so much else, Irish social housing in the half century before 1914 established trends that continued until the late twentieth century.[53]

---

52 Tony Fahey (ed.), *Social housing in Ireland: a study of success, failure and lessons learned* (Dublin, 1999), pp 3–13.
53 Fintan Lane, *Politics, society and the middle class in Modern Ireland* (Basingstoke, 2010).

# 3

## 'The Donegalls' Backside': Donegall Place, the White Linen Hall and the Development of Space and Place in Nineteenth-Century Belfast

*Jonathan Jeffrey Wright*

During the late eighteenth and early nineteenth centuries, as is well known, the town of Belfast experienced growth and development. One obvious indication of this growth was the expansion of its population. Following a visit to the town in 1812, the writer John Gamble estimated that Belfast's population stood at 30,000, which number included some 4,000 Catholics. 'A few years ago', he remarked, emphasising the significance of this latter figure, 'there was scarcely a Catholic in the place'.[1] If Gamble's estimate of 30,000 was correct, then Belfast had grown by over 11,000 since 1791, when its population had stood at just 18,320, and in the decades that followed it continued to grow, rising to 37,277 in 1821 and 75,308 in 1841.[2] But it was not just in terms of the expansion and diversification of its population that the changing nature of Belfast could be measured. Transformation could also be seen in the shape and appearance of the town. Between c.1760 and 1790, as Sean Connolly has recently noted, 'an extensive programme of urban improvement pushed the town well beyond its historic boundaries and gave it both a new appearance and a much-extended range of urban amenities'. During this period Belfast acquired 'some of its most significant older buildings', including the Exchange and Assembly

---

I wish to thank Professor Sean Connolly and Professor Raymond Gillespie for their comments on earlier drafts of this chapter and for their generosity in sharing references.
  1 John Gamble, *Society and manners in early-nineteenth-century Ireland*, ed. Breandán Mac Suibhne (Dublin, 2011), p. 268.
  2 S.J. Connolly and Gillian McIntosh, 'Imagining Belfast' in S.J. Connolly (ed.), *Belfast 400: people, place and history* (Liverpool, 2012), p. 17.

Rooms, First Belfast Presbyterian Church, the Poor House and the White Linen Hall, and in the years that followed more were to come.[3] The Belfast Academical Institution, an impressive building based on a plan by Sir John Soane, opened in 1814, and a General Hospital was erected the following year in Frederick Street.[4] In 1816, St George's Church appeared on High Street and the Commercial Buildings, combining 'an excellent commercial hotel, a spacious and handsome news-room, and behind these an area with a piazza for the use of merchants', were constructed on Waring Street in 1822.[5]

These interrelated processes of demographic growth and urban development were to have significant impacts on the lives of Belfast's inhabitants. Population growth, for instance, altered the nature of sociability and personal relations in the town. Prior to 1750, as Raymond Gillespie has noted, 'Belfast remained an intimate town ... a place still based on face-to-face encounters in which people knew the genealogical matrix within which they operated'.[6] If it did not disappear entirely by the early nineteenth century, such intimacy became more difficult as the town grew in size and underwent what one long-established resident described as 'almost an entire change of inhabitants'.[7] Likewise, the physical development of the town reflected, and contributed to, a shift in the nature of urban life. Drawing on the work of Peter Borsay, Connolly has placed the development of Belfast in the late eighteenth century within the wider context of the 'urban renaissance', suggesting that 'Belfast, in common with other provincial towns, was becoming not just a larger urban centre, but a different kind of urban society'.[8]

The aim in what follows – which might be read as an experiment in spatial microhistory – is to explore the development of one of the new spaces that Belfast acquired as it experienced the 'urban renaissance' and transformed into a new type of society. 'A central feature of the Urban Renaissance', as Borsay has observed, 'was the renewal and transformation of the landscape'.[9]

---

3 S.J. Connolly, 'Improving town, 1750–1820', ibid., pp 161–97 at 161–78 (161 and 162 for quotes).
4 C.E.B. Brett, *Buildings of Belfast, 1700–1814* (rev. ed., Belfast, 1985), pp 14–15. For more on the Belfast Academical Institution, see [Royal Belfast Academical Institution], *Centenary volume, 1810–1910* (Belfast, 1913) and John Jamieson, *The history of the Royal Belfast Academical Institution, 1810–1960* (Belfast, 1959).
5 Brett, *Buildings of Belfast*, pp 15–17 (17 for quote). See also Raymond Gillespie, *Early Belfast: the origins and growth of an Ulster town to 1750* (Belfast, 2007), pp 167–73.
6 Gillespie, *Early Belfast*, p. 167.
7 Martha McTier, quoted in Jonathan Jeffrey Wright, *The 'natural leaders' and their world: politics, culture and society in Belfast, c.1801–1832* (Liverpool, 2012), p. 39.
8 Connolly, 'Improving town', pp 164 and 169.
9 Peter Borsay, *The English urban renaissance: culture and society in the provincial town, 1660–1770* (Oxford, 1989), p. 41.

What this meant, in everyday terms, was that the 'urban renaissance' brought about the construction of new spaces or, to be more precise, new physical spaces and symbolic places. Following the recent work of Katrina Navickas and Leif Jerram, 'space' and 'place' are understood, in what follows, as distinct: whereas 'space shapes physical action by its materiality', 'place ... is invested with meaning, association, performances and codes'.[10] In his earliest articulation of the concept, Borsay argued that the 'urban renaissance' was characterised by 'four areas of development in town life': 'leisure facilities, the economy, public amenities and architecture'.[11] Developments in each of these areas were manifest spatially. While the appearance of ballrooms, walks and theatres reflected growing leisure opportunities, the shops of skilled tradesmen reflected economic growth. Likewise, architectural developments and public amenities were manifest in wider streets, water pipes and increasingly planned and regulated streetscapes.[12] These spatial manifestations of the 'urban renaissance' functioned, on an obvious level, as 'spaces' which shaped and influenced behaviour: ballrooms and assemblies, for instance, were for dancing and self-projection; they were 'arenas of display' with their own rules and behavioural standards.[13] Shops, likewise, were for shopping in, though in an era of increasing middle-class consumption there was, no doubt, an element of display here too.[14] However, these new spaces could also function symbolically as places: as Borsay has put it, 'a town's physical form ... expressed the social and cultural aspirations of those who resided there'.[15] Thus, to take just one example, a ballroom was not only a space in which people danced, but a place which might be said to have symbolised the fact that people wanted to dance and, indeed, that they had the leisure time, politeness and refinement to do so.

In Belfast, the functional and symbolic aspects of the 'urban renaissance' may be traced in the White Linen Hall and its immediate environs, Donegall Square and Donegall Place. First laid out and developed in the early 1780s, this area came to constitute a distinctive quarter within the town by the early

---

10 Katrina Navickas, *Protest and the politics of space and place, 1789–1848* (Manchester, 2016), pp 15–16 (for quotes). See also Leif Jerram, 'Space: a useless category for historical analysis?' in *History and Theory*, lii, no. 3 (2013), pp 400–19.
11 Peter Borsay, 'The English urban renaissance: the development of provincial urban culture, c.1680–c.1760' in *Social History*, ii, no. 5 (1977), pp 581–603 at 590.
12 Borsay, 'English urban renaissance', pp 582–90, *passim*.
13 Borsay, *Urban renaissance*, pp 150–72.
14 See, for shops and shopping, John Stobart, 'Leisure and shopping in the small towns of Georgian England' in *Journal of Urban History*, xxxi, no. 4 (2005), pp 479–503.
15 Borsay, *Urban renaissance*, p. 41. See also Katrina Navickas, '"Why I am tired of turning": a theoretical interlude', seminar paper delivered at the Institute of Historical Research in December 2011, available at www.historyworkingpapers.org/?page_id=225 (accessed 7 July 2016).

nineteenth century, and the ensuing discussion seeks to explore the ways in which this quarter worked as both place and space. To begin, the quarter will be discussed as a place. Here, attention will focus first on the White Linen Hall itself, before broadening out to take into account the wider street-scape that surrounded it. Following this, the discussion will turn from place to space and will focus on the multiple ways in which the White Linen Hall, a building ostensibly erected for commercial purposes, was utilised.

Although it was dismantled in 1896 and replaced with the Belfast City Hall, finished a decade later in 1906, the White Linen Hall stands, in historiographical terms, as one of Belfast's best-known buildings, and its 'biography' is well known.[16] Described by the Belfast historian George Benn, in 1823, as 'a large quadrangular building, enclosing an extensive area', the White Linen Hall was erected on what was, at the time of construction, an undeveloped site, 'lying and being on the south side of the Town and Castle of Belfast in the County of Antrim and near the ancient ramparts of the said Castle'.[17] This site was granted to a committee of prominent citizens by Belfast's landlord, Arthur Chichester, the fifth earl of Donegall, in 1783; work commenced that same year with the laying of a foundation stone, and the building was opened in 1784.[18] Just two years later, however, further work was taking place. In the journal he wrote during his tour of Ireland in the Autumn of 1787, the Reverend Daniel Beaufort made reference to the 'new linen hall', but noted that 'the foundations here are so bad, that the gateway, & many houses in a very handsome street building in front of it, have sunk or given way considerably & [the] gate is now rebuilding'.[19] Further work appears to have occurred in the mid-1810s, when a decorative cupola was added and thus, by 1823, Benn could write approvingly of its appearance.[20] 'The front, or rather the

---

16 See, for instance, Peter McIvor, 'The rise and fall of Belfast's White Linen Hall, 1783–1896' in *Long Room*, xxvi–xxvii (1983), pp 7–11; Brett, *Buildings of Belfast*, pp 7 and 65; Connolly, 'Improving town', pp 169–74; Brenda Collins, Trevor Parkhill and Peter Roebuck, 'A White Linen Hall for Newry or Belfast?' in *Irish Economic and Social History*, xliii (2016), pp 1–12.
17 George Benn, *A history of the town of Belfast: from the earliest times to the close of the eighteenth century* (London, 1877; repr. Belfast, 2008), p. 102; 'Copy counterpart re lease and conveyance of ground for building a linen hall', Public Record Office of Northern Ireland (hereinafter P.R.O.N.I.), Papers of White Linen Hall, Belfast, FIN/1/29/1/1.
18 'Copy counterpart re lease and conveyance of ground for building a linen hall'; McIvor, 'Rise and fall', p. 7; Brett, *Buildings of Belfast*, p. 7; Collins, Parkhill and Roebuck, 'A White Linen Hall for Newry or Belfast?', p. 10. For the Donegall family's connection with Belfast, see Peter Roebuck, 'The Donegall family and the development of Belfast, 1600–1850' in P. Butel and L.M. Cullen (eds), *Cities and merchants: French and Irish perspectives on urban development, 1500–1900* (Dublin, 1986), pp 125–36.
19 'Journal of a tour through part of Ireland', P.R.O.N.I., Beaufort journal, MIC250/1.
20 Brett, *Buildings of Belfast*, p. 7.

centre, of this edifice has a very pleasing effect', he remarked, 'being handsome and light with an extremely neat spire'.[21]

In all likelihood, this pleasing edifice was designed by Roger Mulholland, an architect patronised by Donegall.[22] Although an absentee, Donegall was, in the words of one historian, 'a paragon of proprietorial virtue', and his willingness to spend money, issue leases and grant land was in no small degree responsible for the development, already referred to, which Belfast experienced during the second half of the eighteenth century.[23] That being said, it would be a mistake to view the construction of the White Linen Hall as a straightforward manifestation of landlord-led improvement. To be sure, the construction of the building could not have taken place without Donegall's involvement. However, it was only following the establishment of a public subscription 'for raising money for the purpose of erecting and building a large commodious Hall or Market House in or near the said Town of Belfast for the public sale therein of white linen' that Donegall granted the land on which the White Linen Hall was built.[24] Thus the White Linen Hall's construction owed as much to the initiative of Belfast's citizens as it did to Donegall's improving inclinations, and it is here that we can begin to trace its significance as a symbolic place.

Having been funded by public subscription, which raised some £17,550, the White Linen Hall served, in a very obvious sense, to symbolise the willingness of Belfast's citizens to invest in the fabric of their town, and, no less significantly, their ability to do so.[25] As Marianne Elliott has suggested, the Linen Hall stood, alongside the Poorhouse, another building funded by public subscription, as 'something of a monument to the Presbyterian mercantile community which dominated the town's civic life'.[26] Here, of course, Belfast was far from unique: throughout Britain, such spaces served, in Navickas's words, 'to project the commercial wealth and sobriety of the merchant and manufacturing middle classes who formed the "principal inhabitants" of towns'.[27] But there were more particular ways in which the White Linen

---

21 Benn, *History of the town of Belfast*, p. 102.
22 C.E.B. Brett, *Roger Mulholland: architect of Belfast, 1740–1818* (Belfast, 1976), pp 13–16. See also McIvor, 'Rise and fall', p. 7.
23 Roebuck, 'The Donegall family', p. 133; Connolly, 'Improving town', pp 161–64; C.E.B. Brett, 'The Georgian Town: Belfast about 1800' in J.C. Beckett and R.E. Glassock, *Belfast: the origin and growth of an industrial city* (London, 1967), pp 67–77 at 70–71.
24 'Copy counterpart re lease and conveyance of ground for building a linen hall'.
25 John Suffern to Commissioners of Charitable Donations and Bequests for Ireland, 5 Dec. 1884, P.R.O.N.I., Papers of White Linen Hall, Belfast, FIN/1/29/1/1.
26 Marianne Elliott, *Wolfe Tone: prophet of Irish independence* (New Haven, Conn., 1989), p. 135. For the Belfast Poorhouse, see R.W.M. Strain, *Belfast and its charitable society* (London, 1961).
27 Navickas, '"Why I am tired of turning"'.

Hall functioned as a symbolic place: it was a place that was also symbolic in commercial terms.

As the work of W.H. Crawford has demonstrated, the process whereby Belfast's White Linen Hall was constructed was linked directly to the growing autonomy of Ulster's linen merchants, and to conflict between the merchants of Belfast and Newry concerning whose town should control the province's linen market.[28] Prior to the 1780s, Ireland's linen trade had been controlled by the Dublin Linen Board and bleached ('white') linen was sent to the White Linen Hall in Dublin for sale. By the 1780s, however, the Linen Board's increasing interference and attempts to regulate the linen trade had caused frustration. Thus, in August 1782, the linen drapers of Ulster met in Armagh to signal their opposition. At this meeting the possibility of opening a white linen hall in Ulster was discussed, and this prompted a dispute as to where such a building might be located. While the merchants of Newry, at that point a significant hub of trade and commerce, proposed that the new linen hall be established in their town, Belfast's increasingly assertive merchants argued that *their* town offered the best location. At a meeting of Ulster's linen merchants held in Armagh on 2 December 1782, Newry's claim won out, but by this point Belfast's merchants had already opened a public subscription to fund their linen hall and, notwithstanding the decision of the Armagh meeting, work began on Belfast's White Linen Hall in the months that followed. In the end, two new linen halls were constructed – one in Newry and one in Belfast – but it was Belfast that became the centre of the linen trade in Ulster.[29] The opening of Belfast's White Linen Hall was, as Crawford has observed, 'cardinal in the development of Belfast', and the story of its establishment serves neatly to bear out Jon Stobart's observation that 'the character of towns is influenced by their interaction with other places'.[30] Competition with Newry prompted Belfast's merchants to erect a White Linen Hall, and this move was central to the emergence of Belfast as the capital of Ulster. Thus, as a symbolic 'place', the White Linen Hall was doubly significant: in addition to symbolising the drive and ambition of the citizens whose subscriptions facilitated its construction, it also symbolised Belfast's victory over Newry and its emergence as the leading centre of trade

---

28 The account that follows draws on W.H. Crawford, 'The Belfast middle classes in the late eighteenth century' in David Dickson, Daire Keogh and Kevin Whelan (eds), *The united Irishmen: republicanism, radicalism and rebellion* (Dublin, 1993), pp 62–73 at 66–68; and Collins, Parkhill and Roebuck, 'A White Linen Hall for Newry or Belfast?', pp 1–12.

29 Conrad Gill, *The rise of the Irish Linen Industry* (Oxford, 1925), pp 190–91.

30 Crawford, 'Belfast middle classes', p. 66; Jon Stobart, 'County, town and country: three histories of urban development in eighteenth century Chester' in Peter Borsay and Lindsay Proudfoot (eds), *Provincial towns in early modern England and Ireland* (Oxford, 2002), pp 171–94 at 193.

and commerce in Ulster. 'Its White Linen Hall became', as Crawford has put it, 'a symbol of its success'.[31]

A third layer of symbolic significance can be identified if we turn from commerce to politics. In the late eighteenth century the two were, of course, closely related, and it is by no means insignificant that Belfast's White Linen Hall was constructed at a time when the Volunteering movement, which sought free trade and legislative independence for Ireland, was at its height.[32] Indeed, as Peter McIvor has noted, the laying of the building's foundation stone in April 1783 occurred in the days immediately following the passage of the Renunciation Act (whereby Westminster relinquished its legislative authority over Ireland), and a copy of the said act was secreted within the foundation stone, alongside a document that explained that 'by the Firmness and Unanimity of the Irish Volunteers this Kingdom (long oppressed) was fully and completely emancipated'.[33] It is difficult to escape the conclusion that the laying of the White Linen Hall's foundation stone was a decidedly political occasion, and it was not to be the only occasion on which the White Linen Hall would provide a stage for the performance of Volunteering politics. Some seven years later, in July 1791, it was at the heart of another political display when Belfast's Volunteers celebrated the second anniversary of the storming of the Bastille. On this occasion the town's Volunteers marched 'through every street of any consequence in the town' before halting outside the White Linen Hall, where '*feu de joyes*' were discharged. Following this, the gathered masses – 'two very full companies, a Troop of Light Dragoons, and two Artillery Corps, with four brass six-pounders, together with such a multitude of our unarmed inhabitants as no former event ever was the means of assembling' – entered into the Linen Hall's central square and 'unanimously agreed to, and afterwards announced with cheers, a Declaration of their sentiments on the French Revolution'. Later that same day the Volunteer Corps, having earlier dispersed, 'returned to the Hall with side arms, and sat down to dinner at a single table in the south wing of the Hall, with a number of the citizens, which remained, amounting to *three hundred and fifty-four*'.[34]

The events of July 1791 were, without doubt, unusual. Granted, a subsequent attempt to utilise the White Linen Hall for political purposes was made early

---

31 W.H. Crawford, 'The creation and evolution of small towns in Ulster in the seventeenth and eighteenth centuries' in Borsay and Proudfoot, *Provincial towns in early modern England and Ireland*, pp 97–120 at 111.
32 The significance of this political context has been highlighted in Crawford, 'Belfast middle classes', pp 66–67 and McIvor, 'Rise and fall', p. 7.
33 McIvor, 'Rise and fall', pp 7 and 10 (for quote). See also A.T.Q. Stewart, *A deeper silence: the hidden roots of the United Irish movement* (London, 1993), pp 164–65.
34 Henry Joy, *Historical collections relative to the town of Belfast from the earliest period to the Union with Great Britain* (Belfast, 1817), pp 348–50.

in January 1797 when a sizeable gathering of Belfast citizens met, in the aftermath of the failed French landing at Bantry Bay, 'to discuss the propriety of arming themselves in defence of the country against the common enemy'. In this instance, however, attempt is the operative word. The 1797 meeting was convened, initially, in the ballroom of the Belfast Exchange. This venue was soon full to overflowing, whereupon '[i]t was ... proposed to adjourn to the White Linen Hall; but no preparation having been made for their reception, they at length collected on the pavement in front of it'.[35] Yet if the gathering of July 1791 was, then, an uncommon occurrence, it nevertheless remains significant. It serves, on a very obvious level, to illustrate the impressive scale of the building: here, after all, was a space where 354 could gather at a 'single table'. But, more particularly, it highlights the extent to which the White Linen Hall was, in its early years, associated symbolically with Volunteering. Some memory of this association was to survive throughout the nineteenth century, albeit confused. As late as 1895, the *Belfast News-Letter* could remark that the building was 'erected in 1785, a time of stirring deeds and historic events'. That imprecise 1785 (the building was opened in 1784) highlights the confusion, as also does the paper's subsequent claim that the presence of 'members of the Orange Institution' when the buildings foundation stone was laid 'shows that then they were a recognised power in the city'.[36] To be blunt, they were not. The Orange Order was not established until 1795, and the Orangemen present at the laying of the White Linen Hall's foundation stone were, as A.T.Q. Stewart has explained, freemasons.[37]

The *News-Letter*'s comments on the White Linen Hall were included in a lengthy report on the opening of an Art and Industrial Exhibition held in the building in 1895, and it is tempting to read some political significance into the paper's factual confusion. In his intriguing discussion of the White Linen Hall's 'rise and fall', McIvor has noted that the debate over the 1890 Belfast Corporation Bill, which empowered the town's corporation to demolish the White Linen Hall in 1896, was divided along Unionist/Nationalist lines: whereas Unionists supported the measure, believing that the building should be demolished and replaced with a City Hall befitting Belfast's status as an industrial powerhouse, Nationalists, for whom the White Linen Hall constituted a 'symbolic link' with the 1780s and '90s, the era of 'Protestant Nationalist politics and culture', opposed it.[38] Could it be that the *News-Letter*'s

35   Ibid., pp 450–51.
36   *Belfast News-Letter*, 12 Apr. 1895.
37   Stewart, *Deeper silence*, pp 164–65. On Orangeism, see, most recently, David Fitzpatrick, *Descendancy: Irish Protestant histories since 1795* (Cambridge, 2014), part 1. For freemasonry, see Petri Mirala, *Freemasonry in Ulster, 1773–1813: a social and political history of the masonic brotherhood in Ulster* (Dublin, 2007).
38   McIvor, 'Rise and fall', pp 9–10; *Belfast News-Letter*, 12 Apr. 1895.

association of the White Linen Hall with Orangeism at the time of the 1895 Art and Industrial Exhibition reflected an attempt (whether consciously or unconsciously) to provide a palatable past for the building at a time when the Unionist-dominated city was placing itself on display? Perhaps. But it is equally plausible that the writer in question had simply made an unwarranted assumption, or that, over the years, the precise details of the laying of the building's foundation stone had become confused.[39] Nevertheless, the mere fact that such questions might be raised demonstrates the density of the White Linen Hall as a symbolic place, rich in overlapping and intersecting commercial, political and civic associations.

We can discern a similar symbolic density if we broaden our focus to look beyond the White Linen Hall at the streets which immediately surrounded it. In granting the land on which the White Linen Hall was constructed between 1783 and 1784, the fifth earl of Donegall – who became the first marquis of Donegall in 1791 – was not simply obliging the ambitious linen merchants of the town but encouraging development in unused space.[40] Although formerly encompassed within the grounds of Belfast Castle, the land lay outside the limits of the town in the early 1780s and a new, planned streetscape developed in the vicinity of the White Linen Hall. In addition to Donegall Place, which connected the building to Belfast itself, streets would, over time, develop on the four sides of the building and become known as Donegall Square.[41] Here, Belfast was conforming to wider trends, both within Ulster, where squares were common enough in urban settlements, and, more broadly, within Britain, where the 'urban renaissance' brought 'a new consciousness of the relationship between buildings', and planned streets and squares became de rigueur.[42] Admittedly, Donegall's more ambitious plans for the area did not come to fruition. A 1785 newspaper article, for instance, refers to an 'intended Canal which is to pass in front of the Linen Hall'. This idea was dropped, as also were plans to adorn the entrance to Donegall

---

39 Subsequent writers have, certainly, fallen into similar confusion. See, for instance, McIvor, 'Rise and fall', p. 7.
40 W.A. Maguire, *Living like a lord: the second marquis of Donegall, 1769–1844* (Belfast, 2002), p. 1.
41 These comments draw on 'Copy counterpart re lease and conveyance of ground for building a linen hall'; Gilbert Camblin, *The town in Ulster: an account of the origin and building of the towns of the province and the development of their rural setting, with 62 plates and maps from contemporary sources* (Belfast, 1951), pp 801–81; Stephen Royle, 'The growth and decline of an industrial city: Belfast from 1750' in Howard B. Clark (ed.), *Irish cities* (Dublin, 1995), pp 28–40 at 30; Raymond Gillespie and Stephen A. Royle, *Irish historic towns atlas: Belfast: part 1, to 1840* (Dublin, 2003), p. 6; Gillespie, *Early Belfast*, pp 171–72; Connolly, 'Improving town', pp 169–70.
42 Camblin, *The town in Ulster*, p. 79; Borsay, *Urban renaissance*, pp 60–79 and 85–101 (60 for quote).

Place with 'elegant iron Pallisading and adequate Globe Stands raised from clean brick walls'.[43] Nevertheless, the uniformity Donegall imposed on those erecting buildings in the new streets ensured that a striking urban space emerged. Arriving in Belfast in June 1802, Anna Walker, the wife of a military officer posted to the town, judged Donegall Place 'a very Handsome Street' and at least one visitor in the 1790s drew favourable comparisons with London.[44]

The aim in establishing this new sector was to create a 'high status residential area', and in this it was successful.[45] The memoirs produced by historically minded residents later in the nineteenth century invariably recalled that the area around the White Linen Hall had, earlier in the century, been notably well-heeled. Writing in 1857, Benn thought it 'unnecessary to say that Donegall Place was until lately the residence of that extinct body, the aristocracy of Belfast', and the neighbourhood's social cachet has been confirmed by the research of the historical geographers Emrys Jones and Stephen A. Royle.[46] Occupied by merchants, bankers and 'country gentlemen who came to Belfast for society in winter', the houses in Donegal Place reflected the social standing of their occupants.[47] 'One of the main agents through which a person established social position was', Borsay has suggested of eighteenth-century England, 'the home'.[48] This was no less true in Belfast, and Donegall Place functioned, until well into the nineteenth century, as a symbolic 'place' that signified its inhabitants' taste and affluence.

Wealth aside, however, the new quarter of the town was also symbolically significant insofar as it became associated closely with the Donegall family. Given that the first marquis of Donegall had granted the land on which the White Linen Hall was constructed, and had encouraged development in the surrounding area, this would seem to be an obvious connection. But it was, in fact, as a result of the actions of the second marquis of Donegall, George Augustus Chichester, that the quarter became associated with the

---

43 Benn, *History of the town of Belfast*, pp 550–51; Camblin, *The town in Ulster*, p. 80.
44 Anna Walker diary, p. 31, P.R.O.N.I., Anna Walker document, T/1565/1; Gillespie and Royle, *Belfast: part 1*, p. 6; Connolly, 'Improving town', p. 170.
45 Gillespie and Royle, *Belfast: part 1*, p. 6.
46 George Benn, 'Reminiscences of Belfast – No. 2' in *Ulster Journal of Archaeology*, 1st series, v (1857), pp 144–50 at 148; Emrys Jones, *A social geography of Belfast* (Oxford, 1960), pp 36 and 230; Stephen A. Royle, 'The socio-spatial structure of Belfast in 1837: evidence from the first valuation' in *Irish Geography*, xxiv (1991), pp 1–9 at 6–7. See also Thomas McTear, 'Personal recollections of the beginning of the century' in *Ulster Journal of Archaeology*, 2nd series, v, no. 3 (1899), pp 162–74 at 173 and, for the account of a former resident of Donegal Place, Narcissus G. Batt, 'Belfast sixty years ago: recollections of a septuagenarian' in *Ulster Journal of Archaeology*, 2nd series, ii, no. 2 (1896), pp 92–95.
47 Batt, 'Belfast sixty years ago', p. 92.
48 Borsay, *Urban renaissance*, p. 232.

family. A seemingly inveterate gambler, George Augustus was in considerable financial difficulty when he succeeded his father as marquis of Donegall and, in a bid 'to escape the more rigorous laws in regard to debt which prevailed in Britain', he settled in Belfast in 1802.[49] This plan was not wholly successful: creditors, predictably, followed, as also did gossip and scandal.[50] Nevertheless, Donegall's connection with Belfast endured; indeed, as Maguire has noted, he spent the remainder of his life in the town.[51]

In Belfast, Donegall lived between 1802 and 1807 in an impressive house – known, inevitably, as Donegall House – which was located on Donegall Place's south-western corner; and following this he moved to Ormeau House, a country residence located in Belfast's immediate, south-eastern hinterland.[52] To illustrate the extent to which the area immediately surrounding the first of these residences became associated with Donegall, we need only consider its street names. Donegall Place, for instance, did not become known as such until around 1805; in the 1790s it was known as Linen Hall Street (not to be confused with today's Linen Hall Street, laid out at the rear of the White Linen Hall in the mid-1810s) or the Flags. Likewise, prior to 1806, Donegall Square North was known as South Parade, and the earliest references to Donegall Square East, Donegall Square South and Donegall Square West date to 1813, 1808 and 1813 respectively.[53]

Beyond street names, the second marquis also influenced the appearance of the quarter. Writing in November 1802, the Belfast woman Martha McTier informed her brother, the well-known reformer, William Drennan, that changes were afoot in the neighbourhood, explaining that 'the centre ground is to be railed in, and ornamented on both sides fronting the L[inen] Hall, and a walk round it, 80 feet wide'.[54] This development was made possible by a grant of additional land made by the second marquis, who also enclosed a row of houses located on South Parade, in the immediate rear of his own

---

49  Roebuck, 'The Donegall family', pp 133–34 (134 for quote); Maguire, *Living like a lord*, pp 1–15; Connolly, 'Improving town', p. 186.
50  Maguire, *Living like a lord*, pp 16–25.
51  Ibid., p. 15.
52  Isaac Ward, 'Belfast Castle, Donegal House, and Ormeau House, the residences of the Donegall Family' in *Ulster Journal of Archaeology*, 2nd series, xi, no. 3 (1905), pp 126–30 at 127–28, 129; Maguire, *Living like a lord*, pp 25–32. See also W.A. Maguire, 'A resident landlord in his local setting: the second marquis of Donegall at Ormeau 1807–1844' in *Proceedings of the Royal Irish Academy*, lxxxiii, sect. C (1983), pp 377–99.
53  Gillespie and Royle, *Belfast: part 1*, pp 13–16; George Benn, 'Reminiscences of Belfast' in *Ulster Journal of Archaeology*, 1st series, iii (1855), pp 260–64 at 261; Thomas Gaffikin, *Belfast fifty years ago: a lecture delivered by Thomas Gaffikin, in the Working Men's Institute, Belfast on Thursday evg, April 8th, 1875* (3rd ed., Belfast, 1894), p. 14.
54  Martha McTier to William Drennan, 21 Nov. 1802, *The Drennan–McTier Letters*, ed. Jean Agnew (3 vols, Dublin, 1998–99), iii, 84.

house, which sat on the corner of South Parade and Donegall Place.[55] As McTier lived, with her mother, in one of the houses in question, she took a particular interest in the latter scheme and detailed its progress in her letters to her brother. In a letter dated 18 March 1804, she announced excitedly that 'Lord Donegall is going to enclose the ground before my mother's and the other three houses, as they all belong to ladies, in the same way he has done his own, and the whole will be as pretty a place as is to be seen in any town'. Equally important, it promised to 'make the houses much more valuable'.[56] In response, Drennan agreed that the houses would 'be increased in value', before turning to tease his sister: 'I suppose', he wrote, 'the name of the South Parade will then be changed to the Donegalls' B–ks–de – for the row will then have the appearance of little houses in his lordship's garden'.[57] He was, of course, closer to the mark than he realised. South Parade did not become known as the Donegalls' Backside but, as we have seen, it did become known, at around the same time, as Donegall Square North.

Work on the enclosure of South Parade proceeded slowly. McTier complained, in a letter dated 12 January 1805, that it was 'still in an unfinished state' and returned to the theme, several weeks later, reporting that 'Lord Donegall's finances do not allow him to perform his promise of railing in our ground'.[58] By the end of the year, however, the railings had been erected, landscaping had been completed and South Parade was judged 'pretty and genteel'.[59] This description – 'pretty and genteel' – might be applied with some justice to the Donegall Square/Donegall Place quarter as a whole, but some early-nineteenth-century inhabitants would have added one further descriptor: 'conservative'.

As is well known, Belfast was, in the late eighteenth century, a stronghold of political radicalism.[60] In the aftermath of the 1798 rebellion, the political enthusiasms of its inhabitants abated somewhat, but by the 1810s political disputation re-emerged and a group of reformers challenged the authority of the Belfast corporation, an unrepresentative body which comprised a sovereign and twelve burgesses and was dominated by Donegall and his relatives. This dispute came to a head in November 1820, when the sovereign of Belfast, Thomas Verner, unsuccessfully attempted to prevent an illumination being

55 H.C. (10 June 1890), vol. 345, c. 488, available at http://hansard.millbanksystems.com/commons/1890/jun/10/second-reading#S3V0345P0_18900610_HOC_3 (accessed 12 May 2018); Ward, 'Belfast Castle', p. 128; McIvor, 'Rise and fall', p. 7.
56 Martha McTier to William Drennan, 18 Mar. 1804, *Drennan–McTier Letters*, iii, 207.
57 William Drennan to Martha McTier, 4 Apr. 1804, ibid., iii, 213.
58 Martha McTier to William Drennan, 12 Jan. 1805 and undated, ibid., iii, 305 and 330.
59 Martha McTier to William Drennan, 3 Dec. 1805, ibid., iii, 396.
60 The following paragraph draws principally on Wright, *The 'natural leaders'*, chap. 2 (esp. pp 50–57, 80–85 and 91–104).

held in support of Queen Caroline, the estranged wife of George IV. Related to Donegall through marriage, Verner lived in his former Belfast residence, Donegall House, and on 17 November, when the illumination was held, his unlit windows were smashed by a mob of exuberant youths.[61] So, too, were the windows of numerous other properties located in Donegall Place, including those of the conservative Nelson Club, which had been established in 1806 to commemorate Nelson's victory at Trafalgar.[62] Indeed, even those properties that were illuminated in Donegall Place were attacked. 'Several houses that were lighted up, suffered as severely as those that were dark', one observer wrote, 'in short every house in Donegall Place received some damage'.[63] Not merely a socially symbolic place, Donegall Place was, within the context of the conflict between Belfast's reformers and its corporation, a politically symbolic one, and on the evening of 17 November 1820 its residents paid for this in broken glass.

The White Linen Hall and its surrounding streets can, then, be viewed as symbolically significant places, but how did they function as spaces? In what ways were they used? And how, if at all, did their uses change over time? Over the course of the nineteenth century a clear shift occurred in the use of Donegall Place and Donegall Square. 'This locality was formerly the St James' of Belfast', James Adair Pilson noted, in the mid-1840s, 'but it has recently been encroached upon by enterprizing merchants and traders, who have so closely pressed upon the *elite* as to compel them to retire to the new and more appropriate *locale* of Wellwood-place, Glengall-street, College-square, Wellington-place, &c.'[64] This process continued as the century progressed, and the former residential district was transformed into a commercial district, albeit a prestigious one.[65] As early as the 1840s, the shops appearing in Donegall Place were said to 'rival, in every respect, the first establishments of their kind in London, Dublin, or Edinburgh' and similar claims were being made at the end of the century.[66] Indeed, by the 1890s, Donegall Place was

---

61 Ward, 'Belfast Castle', p. 129; Maguire, *Living like a lord*, p. 21; Connolly, 'Improving town', pp 188–89.
62 William Mitchell to Robert James Tennent, 24 Nov. 1820, P.R.O.N.I., Tennent papers, D/1748/G/457/8; Batt, 'Belfast sixty years ago', pp 92–93; Connolly, 'Improving town', p. 195.
63 James Montgomery to Robert James Tennent, 28 Nov. 1820, P.R.O.N.I., Tennent papers D/1748/G/465/4.
64 James Adair Pilson, *History of the rise and progress of Belfast, and annals of the county Antrim, from the earliest period till the present time* (Belfast, 1846), p. 25.
65 Jones, *Social geography of Belfast*, p. 230; Royle, 'The socio-spatial structure of Belfast', p. 8; Stephen A. Royle, 'Workshop of the empire, 1820–1914' in Connolly, *Belfast 400*, pp 199–235 at 222–25.
66 Pilson, *History of the rise and progress*, p. 25.

being described as 'the Bond Street of Belfast' and 'the *locale* of many of the city's most superb temples to trade'.[67] But what of the White Linen Hall? The remainder of the discussion will seek to unpack the multiple ways in which this more distinctive space was used.

Most obviously, the White Linen Hall was used as a marketplace for the sale of linen. Under the terms of the original indenture whereby the marquis of Donegal granted the land on which the White Linen Hall was erected, the building's trustees were required to 'permit and suffer a Hall or Market House to be erected and to stand and be continued thereon for the public sale of white Linens and to be used as such at all times thereafter'.[68] However, despite this seemingly prescriptive stipulation, the building was not used for commerce alone. It was also used as a cultural, civic and recreational space.

Evidence of the White Linen Hall's use for non-commercial purposes may be found in the fact that Gaetano Fabbrini, an Italian art teacher, formerly employed in the Belfast Academical Institution, opened a drawing school 'in one of the central rooms' in February 1821. This school appears to have remained in the building for some fifteen years, before moving to new premises in 1836, and it is by no means the only example we have of the building being used for wider civic and cultural purposes.[69] Samuel Lewis's 1837 *Topographical dictionary of Ireland*, for instance, notes the existence of a 'large news-room in one of the wings of the White Linen Hall', and it is known that the building was used, from time to time, by the Belfast Law Society and the Botanic Gardens' managing committee.[70] But, more significant than Fabbrini's school, the news-room or the occasional use of the building by organisations representing civic society and associational culture, was the presence, within the White Linen Hall, of the library of the Belfast Society for Promoting Knowledge. In 1801, the White Linen Hall's management committee suggested that the society, which had been established in 1788 and was then searching for new premises, might have accommodation 'over the central part of the Linen Hall for the library free of all expense'.[71] The Society for Promoting Knowledge agreed and so began a process whereby its library would take over a series of rooms within the White Linen Hall, and become closely associated with the building. The library moved, in 1892, to its current

67 [Historical Publishing Company], *The industries of Ireland, part 1: Belfast and towns of the North* (1891), pp 41–42.
68 'Copy Counterpart re Lease and Conveyance of Ground for Building a Linen Hall'.
69 Eileen Black, *Art in Belfast, 1760–1888* (Dublin, 2006), pp 16–18.
70 Samuel Lewis, *A topographical dictionary of Ireland comprising the several counties, cities, boroughs, corporate, market and post towns, parishes and villages, with historical and statistical descriptions* (London, 1837), p. 193; John Killen, *A history of the Linen Hall Library, 1788–1988* (Belfast, 1990), p. 57.
71 Killen, *Linen Hall Library*, pp 7 and 24.

home on Donegal Square North, but remains known, to this day, as the Linen Hall Library.[72]

The best-known description of the library as it existed in the White Linen Hall relates to its late-nineteenth-century heyday. In his autobiography, *Apostate*, the Belfast novelist Forrest Reid wrote of the library as 'a charming place ... very like a club'. 'Its membership', he continued, 'was comparatively small; its tone was old fashioned; it belonged to the era of the two- and three-volume novel; it had about it an atmosphere of quiet and leisure'.[73] Perhaps what is most striking about this description is the extent to which it corroborates descriptions of the library at earlier points. George A. Birmingham, born ten years earlier than Reid, in 1865, made similar remarks in his memoir, *Pleasant Places*. No fan of the White Linen Hall, which he judged 'would not have been out of place in a fifth-rate provincial town, though even there not a source of pride', Birmingham recalled the library as 'rather a poor affair' but conceded that 'it was a great help to me'. There, he recalled, he 'could get the most recent English poets', access being facilitated by the fact that '[n]o one else ever seemed to want them'.[74] Earlier still, following an 1812 visit to Belfast, Gamble wrote of spending 'solitary hours' in the library and mused that 'the bustling inhabitants of this great commercial town have little leisure – I do not know that they have little inclination – for reading'.[75] Overall, one is left with the impression that Reid's description, with its references to the library's limited membership and 'atmosphere of quiet and leisure', holds true for much of the nineteenth century and that the Linen Hall Library was never a popular or oversubscribed institution.[76] Indeed, it was arguably the case that the grounds of the White Linen Hall were used more widely than the rooms occupied by the Belfast Society for Promoting Knowledge.

In the late eighteenth century, Belfast's leisured classes – joined, in 1791, by Theobald Wolfe Tone and Thomas Russell – had taken constitutionals on the 'Mall', a walk proceeding south from the White Linen Hall and linking it with Joy's Paper Mill.[77] However, as has been discussed, additional land

---

72 Ibid., pp 57, 75–77; Hardy, *Twenty-one views*, p. 18.
73 Forrest Reid, *Apostate* (London, 1928), pp 52–53.
74 George A. Birmingham, *Pleasant places* (London, 1934), p. 9. For biographical details on Reid and Birmingham, see James Maguire and James Quinn (eds), *Dictionary of Irish biography from the earlies times to the year 2002* (9 vols, Cambridge, 2009), iv, 444–47; viii, 429.
75 Gamble, *Society and manners*, p. 268.
76 For further discussion of the Linen Hall Library in the early nineteenth century, see Wright, *The 'natural leaders'*, pp 141–60 *passim*.
77 Elliott, *Wolfe Tone*, p. 142; Robert Scott, *A breath of fresh air: the story of Belfast's parks* (Belfast, 2000), p. 3; Gillespie and Royle, *Belfast: part 1*, map 9.

surrounding the White Linen Hall was granted by the second marquis of Donegal in 1802. This land was duly planted and enclosed with railings and thus, when he visited Belfast in 1812, Gamble found 'a public walk, prettily laid out with flowers and shrubs'.[78] Here, albeit in the context of the nineteenth century, was a classic space of the 'urban renaissance' – 'an arena for overt personal display', whose users 'were propelled into contact with each other to gossip and flirt, to see and be seen'.[79] Granted, this was not Gamble's experience. As noted, he had described his hours in the Society for Promoting Knowledge's library as 'solitary', so few users had he encountered, and he continued to riff on this theme as he discussed the public walk: 'I meet with as few people here as in the library', he quipped. 'Young women appear to walk as little as the men read'.[80] Here, Gamble's experience was unrepresentative. The walk was a popular recreational space until at least the 1860s, and one former user, writing from the vantage point of the early twentieth century, remarked that 'the new generation ... can have little idea of the part that the enclosure played in the life of the inhabitants long ago'.[81] Indeed, there is clear evidence that the walk was being used in the early 1810s. When she visited Belfast at this time, Mary Craig judged 'a walk round the Linen Hall' sufficiently interesting to report it in a letter to her sister Margaret, and in July 1812 the *Belfast News-Letter* reported on 'judicious improvements' being made to what it described as 'the pleasure grounds', and publicised a proposal to install benches for the use of 'infirm persons, or nurses with children'.[82] By 1823, Benn could confidently assert that the walk was 'the principle promenade in the town', and in 1837 P.D. Hardy seemed to concur, noting that it 'affords a most agreeable promenade for the inhabitants at all seasons'.[83]

At the height of its popularity, the White Linen Hall was, in the words of the Belfast journalist Frederick Frankfort Moore, 'decorously lively ... with the crinolines and flounces and "Dolly Vardens" of the 'sixties'.[84] This suggests a space which, if popular, was also polite, middle class and respectable. As such, it raises questions as to how the walk was regulated and respectability maintained. One means of regulation, employed elsewhere in the city, was financial. Those who wished to stroll in Belfast's Botanic Gardens, opened in 1829, were required to pay, and this had the effect of limiting visitors from

78 Gamble, *Society and manners*, p. 268; Hardy, *Twenty-one views*, p. 18.
79 Borsay, *Urban renaissance*, pp 150 and 162–72 (150 and 162 for quotes).
80 Gamble, *Society and manners*, pp 268–69.
81 Frank Frankfort Moore, *In Belfast by the sea*, ed. Patrick Maume (Dublin, 2007), p. 53.
82 Mary Craig to Margaret Craig, undated (catalogue suggests c.1810), P.R.O.N.I., Bound volume of c. 20 letters from Mary Cuming [née Craig], T1475/2; *Belfast News-Letter*, 10 July 1812.
83 Benn, *History of the town of Belfast*, p. 102; Hardy, *Twenty-one views*, p. 18.
84 Moore, *In Belfast by the sea*, p. 53.

the working classes.[85] There is, however, no evidence that a similar system was employed in the grounds of the White Linen Hall. By contrast, it is known that the building had a staff: porters and a 'paid Chamberlain' were employed, and it is possible that these figures helped to regulate the walk.[86] But, perhaps above all, respectability was regulated by unspoken rules and codes of conduct – codes which relied, ultimately, on users acquiescing with them. Recalling his childhood in Belfast in the 1820s, Thomas Gaffikin noted the popularity of performances, 'on the space in front of the present archway or entrance to the hall', of a 'military band' and described the convoluted perambulations that took place during these performances. 'The main walk round the Hall', he noted,

> was enclosed from this space by an iron railing on each side, with small gates for ingress and egress. The most respectable of the persons listening to the music were distributed on both sides, and it was the practice to turn and walk round between each piece, which rendered it necessary at times for the great crowds at the rear of the hall, to change sides in succession. During this ceremony the democrats stood their ground, with the bandsmen in the centre.[87]

Here, it seems, was a space in which people knew how to behave, a space with a code of unwritten rules – rules that could be pointedly violated, as by the 'democrats', in order to snub one's nose at the 'respectable' elite of the town.

Clearly, then, the White Linen Hall was not used for the sale of linen alone. Nevertheless, despite these additional uses, commerce was its principal function. It was designed as a marketplace for the linen trade and was used for this purpose until at least the mid-nineteenth century. In some respects, however, it was an architecturally unconventional linen hall. Indeed, while one nineteenth-century writer viewed the White Linen Hall as 'particularly well calculated for the purpose for which it was designed', being 'fitted up with different offices and rooms for the factors', the architectural historian C.E.B. Brett judged it 'unusual in eighteenth-century Irish linen markets in not having open arcades where purchasers could inspect the bolts of linen in full daylight'.[88] Yet, if it lacked arcades, it is nevertheless clear that the White

---

85 William Whitaker Barry, *A walking tour round Ireland in 1865 by an Englishman* (London, 1867), p. 5; Eileen McCracken, *The Palm House and Botanic Garden, Belfast* (Belfast, 1971), pp 8, 13–14.
86 John Suffern to Commissioners of Charitable Donations and Bequests for Ireland, 5 Dec. 1884.
87 Gaffikin, *Belfast fifty years ago*, p. 39.
88 P.D. Hardy, *Twenty-one views in Belfast and its neighbourhood*, repr. with notes and introduction by C.E.B. Brett (Belfast, 2005), p. 18.

Linen Hall did serve as a venue for the sale of linen. As noted, the building was divided internally, with 'different offices and rooms'. One account lists '223 large rooms, and 19 offices besides other large accommodation', and Benn, writing in the early 1820s, noted that '[t]he numerous apartments which the building contains are chiefly occupied as the rooms and offices of the linen drapers', before proceeding to explain the way in which the trade operated. 'The cloth is here received from the bleachers', he explained, 'and prepared for sale or exportation, being chiefly carried either to England, America, or the West Indies'.[89] Echoing Benn, Conrad Gill has remarked that the White Linen Hall's 'chief function was always the collection and sorting of packs for transatlantic cargoes', and a sense of the scale of this trade is indicated by the fact that, during the period 1810–19, Belfast's merchants acquired 4,537 packages of linen for export, at an average cost of £65 per package.[90]

By the early 1840s, the White Linen Hall remained an important centre of commerce and trade. In the narrative he penned following his visit to Ireland in 1842, the German traveller John George Kohl recalled a visit to the bustling, industrious commercial space. Linen, he informed his readers, was 'the life and soul of Belfast' and the White Linen Hall was 'the great centre of attraction'. 'Here', he explained, 'almost all the linen of northern Ireland destined for exportation, is brought together and sorted … Each firm of importance has its counting-house and warehouse in this place, and a walk through the hall is therefore full of interest and instruction for the curious stranger'. By this point, parcels of linen were being despatched from Belfast 'to London, to Spain, to Brazil, to the United States, to British America, and lately also to China', and Kohl was advised – presumably by the 'opulent linen-merchant … who had the goodness to show me his store and counting-house' – that '[e]very market is partial not only to some particular kinds of linen, but also to particular ways of packing, and particular external decorations to the packages'.[91] Had Kohl visited forty years later, however, he would have encountered a very different space, for during the second half of the nineteenth century the character of the once-bustling White Linen Hall was dramatically altered.

As previous scholars have noted, over the course of the nineteenth century the White Linen Hall was increasingly used as a space for storage, rather than

89 John Suffern to Commissioners of Charitable Donations and Bequests for Ireland, 5 Dec. 1884; Benn, *History of the town of Belfast*, pp 102–03.
90 Gill, *Irish linen industry*, p. 190; Thomas Bradshaw, *Belfast general & commercial directory for 1819 … with a directory and history of Lisburn* (Belfast, 1819), p. xvii.
91 J.G. Kohl, *Ireland, Scotland and England* (London, 1844), 'Ireland', p. 198 (each section of this edition (Ireland, Scotland and England) is paginated separately. For Kohl, see Glenn Hooper (ed.), *The tourist's gaze: travellers to Ireland, 1800–2000* (Cork, 2001), p. 69.

trade, and 'came more and more to consist of private warehouses and offices rather than a centre of exchange'.[92] This development has been attributed to the growth of communications infrastructure: 'at the time of its demolition', McIvor has argued of the White Linen Hall, 'modern commercial practices – in particular, the use of the telegraph, which allowed for the facilitation of trade from the premises of the manufacturers' themselves – had rendered its use as a public auction-place redundant, and it had passed into the hands of private merchants for warehousing purposes'.[93] Some further light can, however, be shed on this alteration in the building's use by the consideration of a detailed letter John Suffern, 'the Representative of a deceased Subscriber', addressed to the Commissioners of Charitable Donations and Bequests for Ireland in December 1884. Working on the principle that the White Linen Hall was, in fact, 'a Charitable institution founded in the year 1782 for the Encouragement, Extension and improvement of the linen trade of the north of Ireland', Suffern sought to highlight the way these ends had been subverted through the mismanagement of the building. While the White Linen Hall had previously been open to 'any linen Draper from the remotest part of the kingdom', and had been used for public linen sales, this was no longer the case. As Suffern explained, 'the manner of conducting linen business entirely changed … the Hall ceased to be used as a public market for the sale of linens' and this had a knock-on effect on the way in which the building was managed: 'Less interest consequently came to be taken in the Hall by the public; no person hardly attended the annual meetings save the members of the Committee of Management and these Gentlemen yearly elected at the annual meetings such of their own number as retired by rotation from the Committee'. What concerned Suffern, however, was not the fact that the management committee perpetuated itself in this way, but the fact that it abused the power it had acquired: 'this committee of management', he wrote, 'in Contravention of the terms of the Trust for the public let to some of their own members at rents fixed by themselves the entire of the premises'. What was worse, those granted access to the building 'exclude the public from the use of or access to the Hall treating it as their own private property'; the rents collected – 'quite under the letting value' – were inadequate to the costs of the building; and some, profiting from this arrangement, had 'sublet portions of their lots'. While the changing nature of the linen trade clearly played a part in bringing about this state of affairs, Suffern's account suggests that

---

92   Gill, *Irish linen industry*, p. 190.
93   McIvor, 'Rise and fall', p. 8. For the importance of the postal service and the telephone, see Edwin James Aiken and Stephen A. Royle, 'Markets and messages: linenopolis meets the world' in Olwen Purdue (ed.), *Belfast: the emerging city, 1850–1914* (Dublin, 2013), pp 1–23.

the management committee's cronyism, corruption and, as he put it, 'illegal practices' were equally significant.[94]

By the mid-1880s, then, the White Linen Hall had ceased to fulfil what Suffern viewed as its function – 'the Encouragement, Extension and improvement of the linen trade'. Quite the reverse: it had come to have 'a very injurious effect on the linen trade of Belfast', insofar as it conferred a commercial advantage on those who rented its rooms cheaply and avoided the '[e]xceedingly high rents' their competitors were required to pay elsewhere in the city. Consequently, Suffern suggested that the building be repurposed, in accordance with the aims of its founders, to provide accommodation for a technical school, or that it be let 'at fair rents' to raise money for an institution of this nature, reasoning that '[t]he want of technical schools now is being much felt in the linen trade'.[95] In the end, this proposal would not come to fruition, and within little more than a decade the building was demolished. Nevertheless, Suffern's suggestion highlights the fact that some believed that the White Linen Hall could be used to promote the linen industry in its broader sense.

Such thinking was by no means unique. Throughout its life the White Linen Hall appears to have been used, by those connected with the linen trade, as rather more than a marketplace. On 5 and 6 January 1816, for example, 'a number of the most respectable bleachers, dealers, and manufacturers' gathered in the building to view a demonstration of James Lee's patented system of flax preparation, and the following October it was used by 'the principal merchants' as a venue to meet with the secretary of the Dublin Linen Board, who was informed that the system of customs inspection then in operation was considered 'very inconvenient to shippers'.[96] In these instances we see the White Linen Hall being pressed into service as a space for deliberation and discussion, but it was also used, on at least one occasion, to display and promote the linen trade. When Queen Victoria visited Belfast during her Irish tour of 1849 she was taken to the White Linen Hall, where an exhibition, demonstrating the way in which linen was produced, was laid out in a 'range of rooms' that ran 'the entire length of the East side' of the building. 'These', the *Belfast News-Letter* reported proudly, 'which have been justly considered the finest suite of rooms any where occupied for the purposes of the linen trade, presented a very handsome appearance'. 'The floor was carpeted with crimson cloth, covered with yard-wide bleached damask; and each room was fitted up with two tables, on which the articles were placed,

---

94 John Suffern to Commissioners of Charitable Donations and Bequests for Ireland, 5 Dec. 1884.
95 Ibid.
96 F.W. Smith, *The Irish linen trade hand-book and directory* (Belfast, 1876), p. 61; William Charley, *Flax and its products in Ireland* (London, 1862), pp 12–15 (15 for quote).

and the floor carpeted with unbleached damask'.[97] Whether or not the Queen was impressed by these rooms is unclear, but she does appear to have been struck by the exhibition. 'It is really very interesting to see', she noted in her diary, 'and it is wonderful to what a perfection it [the production of linen] has been brought'.[98]

The White Linen Hall's role as an exhibition space was reprised in 1895 when, as has already been noted, it played host to an Art and Industrial Exhibition. There were, however, striking differences between the 1849 and 1895 exhibitions. In the intervening period, a well-developed culture of 'industrial exhibition' had developed. Belfast's manufacturers had displayed their wares at exhibitions held in Dublin, Glasgow, London, Manchester, Paris and Philadelphia, and such events had come to be 'seen as an opportunity both to celebrate economic achievement and to boost it still further by self-advertisement and the dissemination of ideas and expertise'.[99] Thus, in contrast to the 1849 exhibition, which focused solely on linen and provided an opportunity for the industry to display itself to the Queen, the 1895 exhibition, which was organised in order to raise money for the Belfast Working Men's Institute and Temperance Hall, encompassed far more than linen. Indeed, while 'the various departments of the linen trade' were displayed in a section of the exhibition given over to 'textile fabrics', competition was provided by five additional sections, displaying 'art', 'scientific and mechanical appliances', 'economic products', 'natural history and antiquities' and 'domestic industries and sanitation'.[100] In short, the 1895 exhibition was an exhibition on a much grander scale than that of 1849, and this was reflected in the way in which the White Linen Hall was used. While the 1849 exhibition made use of the east side of the building, the 1895 exhibition made use of the entire building, and led to a dramatic alteration in its appearance. Early in February 1895, the *Belfast News-Letter* reported that 'the traditional landmarks of our good old Linen Hall are rapidly disappearing', before proceeding to explain that '[a]n army of busy workmen are transforming the enclosure into a spacious building, which will

---

97 *Belfast News-Letter*, 14 Aug. 1849. For a full account of Victoria's visit to Belfast, see S.J. Connolly, 'Like an old cathedral city: Belfast welcomes Queen Victoria, August 1849' in *Urban History*, xxxix, no. 4 (2012), pp 571–89.
98 *The industries of Ireland*, p. 49. It was later claimed, in Belfast, that the White Linen Hall's 1849 exhibition provided Prince Albert with the inspiration that led, ultimately, to the famous London exhibition of 1851. See John Vinycomb, *Historical and descriptive guide to the city of Belfast* (Belfast, 1895), p. 32 and Aiken and Royle, 'Markets and messages', pp 18–19.
99 Connolly and McIntosh, 'Imagining Belfast', pp 33–35 (33 for quote).
100 Philip Shrapnel, *Art & industrial exhibition, Belfast, 1895: official catalogue* (Belfast, 1895), p. 18; *Belfast News-Letter*, 12 Apr. 1895.

occupy the largest space ever yet enclosed under one roof in Belfast'.[101] By 11 April 1895, when the exhibition was formally opened by the Marchioness of Londonderry, it was reported that 'little now remains but the outside walls of the premises', though even these were altered by the addition of 'flags and bunting' and 'battle-mented towers'.[102] That the building could be altered so radically for the 1895 exhibition is telling. Such alterations would, of course, have been highly disruptive to everyday business and were possible precisely because the White Linen Hall was no longer being used for business.

While the 1849 exhibition represented the apotheosis of the White Linen Hall as a space associated with the linen industry, the 1895 exhibition appears as its nadir, and the shift is represented neatly in the columns of the *Belfast News-Letter*. In 1849, the paper heaped praise on the 'great and much-admired establishment'. 'A department of our commerce', it claimed, 'and one so immense and important to the inhabitants of this province as the linen trade, should have an establishment in its capital worthy of its importance, and such a one we find in the universally-admired Belfast White Linen-Hall'.[103] By 1895, the tone was commemorative, rather than celebratory. The White Linen Hall was 'once the centre of active business life and closely identified with the staple trade of the province', but 'once' was the operative word. Times had changed. Belfast had grown, experiencing 'wonderful progress and development, scarcely surpassed by that of any modern town', and the White Linen Hall, although connecting the 'city of the present to the town of the past', had been judged surplus to requirements. Indeed, it was, by this point, slated for demolition: 'before many months have passed away', the *News-Letter* explained, 'scarcely a vestige will remain of buildings which for years formed one of the permanent features of the city, and from which was directed a large percentage of those operations which have had as their result the establishment of the linen trade of Ulster upon a sound and substantial basis'.[104] Here, fittingly, the White Linen Hall was associated with the rise of the linen trade, but, equally fitting, its association was couched in the past tense: the White Linen Hall's centrality to the Ulster's linen trade was, by August 1895, a matter of historical record, rather than contemporary reality.

The history of Belfast's White Linen Hall is, on one level, a story of decline. Surviving for just 112 years, the building was erected during a phase of

101 *Belfast News-Letter*, 4 Feb. 1895.
102 *Belfast News-Letter*, 12 Apr. 1895. Surviving photographs confirm that the White Linen Hall was 'transformed, by a mock castellated entrance and a huge temporary structure covering its inner courtyard'. W.A. Maguire, *A century in focus: photography and photographers in the North of Ireland, 1839–1939* (Belfast, 2000), p. 76.
103 *Belfast News-Letter*, 14 Aug. 1849.
104 *Belfast News-Letter*, 12 Apr. 1895.

improvement and economic expansion in the late eighteenth century but came to appear increasingly obsolete in the face of Belfast's continued growth and development. Thus, in January 1896, the *Belfast News-Letter* could remark that its destruction was 'rendered necessary by modern requirements'.[105] Nevertheless, as the preceding discussion has demonstrated, it was at the centre of a new and for many years vibrant quarter of the town that developed in the late eighteenth century. It functioned as a commercial space, a recreational space and a cultural space, and it was symbolically significant, with important commercial, civic and political associations. So, too, was the streetscape that surrounded it: Donegall Place and Donegall Square were not merely residential streets, they constituted a fashionable, elite neighbourhood which had distinctive social and political associations. Approaching the White Linen Hall and its surrounding streetscape from the perspective of place and space thus reveals a complex multifaceted urban area, an area with a history that intersects at multiple points with the wider social, political and economic developments which shaped Belfast, and which was, for nearly a century, at the heart of life in the town.

105 *Belfast News-Letter*, 21 Jan. 1896.

# 4

# The School and the Home: Constructing Childhood and Space in Dublin Boarding Schools

*Mary Hatfield*

In 1825, an unhappy female student at the Loreto Abbey Boarding School in Rathfarnham, Dublin wrote a letter to her parents complaining about ill treatment and severe discipline while in residence at the school. Mother Frances Mary Teresa Ball (1794–1861), mother superior of the Loreto order in Ireland, after reading the student's complaints, included her own letter along with the student's, explaining the cause of the disciplinary action. The incident had occurred because the young girl had stamped her foot violently, refused to hold her head up and constantly interrupted her classmates during their lessons. Ball stated that consequently,

> Your daughter was removed from her place at table and in the school room, until she merited return. She has resumed her usual station in the refectory, but she remains one seat lower in the school room till she becomes more satisfactory. On one occasion when she refused to comply with a very easy request, she was not allowed to sit down until she had accomplished what had been asked.[1]

In what seems to be a mundane episode of student discipline, controlling student space appears to be a typical form of classroom management. Mother Superior Ball believed that the removal of students from the classroom was

---

1 Reading students' private correspondence was the policy of all Irish Loreto boarding schools because *belles lettres* was considered part of the educational curriculum. Unfortunately, the student's original letter is not extant. Papers of M. Frances Teresa Ball, 1794–1861, copybook, M. Teresa Ball letters, TB/COR/8, June 1825, Loreto Central and Irish Province Archives, Dublin (hereinafter L.C.I.P.A.).

an appropriate disciplinary method for her genteel female students.[2] Of course for this tactic to be effective teachers and pupils had to understand the significance of embedded spatial hierarchies and their corresponding social consequences. This chapter examines the spatial policies, urban morphology and educational missions of the Loreto Abbey Boarding School, Rathfarnham, and the Royal Hibernian Military Academy, Phoenix Park, to consider ways in which adults literally and figuratively constructed spaces for urban childhood in the first half of the nineteenth century. The production of space, as Henri Lefebvre famously insisted, happens in the physical world, the social world and the imagined world. There is a dynamic relationship between a physical place, its social construction, and the idealised category of childhood.[3] When Irish educators built schools within Dublin's bourgeoning urban environment, they envisioned a space to facilitate a range of social functions and educational goals. Concerns about the unhealthy physical and moral environment of Dublin city resulted in gates, walls and enclosures which would protect children from the dangers of city life, while simultaneously serving as public symbols of the school's exclusivity. However, as the two schools selected for analysis demonstrate, spatial policies varied widely depending on the gender and class composition of the school.

Irish boarding schools were versatile spaces, serving simultaneously as public institutions, charitable organisations and private residences for pupils and teachers. In Dublin, as in other colonial metropoles, educational institutions were a mechanism for providing a stable form of association among the bourgeoisie.[4] Though the most elite Irish families probably opted to send their child abroad for an education, Dublin was a more feasible option for middle-class and petty bourgeois families, hosting an array of private academies, boarding schools and day schools.[5] At a basic level, the middle classes were differentiated from the aristocracy and gentry by participation in the productive economy, and from the working classes by property ownership and lack of engagement in manual labour. As the middle classes expanded during the nineteenth century, urban schools became important regulatory institutions for the professional classes, serving as gatekeepers for university attendance and professional credentials. Margaret Hunt's study of the 'middling sort' in Britain identified the rise of the bourgeoisie as an urban phenomenon, but tied less to professional or economic status, and more as

2 Ibid.
3 Henri Lefebvre, *The production of space* (Oxford, 1991).
4 Robert Rotenberg, 'Metropolitanism and the transformation of urban space in nineteenth-century colonial metropoles' in *American Anthropologist*, ciii, no. 1 (2001), p. 9.
5 Ciaran O'Neill, *Catholics of consequence: transnational education, social mobility, and the Irish Catholic elite 1850–1900* (Oxford, 2014).

a cultural group espousing prudential virtue.[6] Boarding schools operated to impose values of order, discipline and industry on children, but these values were expressed differently depending on the class and gender of the pupils. Social capital, conferred through education and family genealogy, was a form of advantage that operated on a symbolic level, but was tied to real economic circumstance.[7] The institutional space created within these schools was intended to shape pupil and teacher behaviours in a common habitus.[8] The two schools considered in this chapter had diverse aspirations for their pupils and this is evident in their respective pedagogy, curriculum and ethos. The Loreto order's boarding school for girls in Rathfarnham, Dublin, founded in 1822, was a Catholic secondary school for bourgeois girls providing a liberal education in languages and female accomplishments. Attendance at this convent school signified familial wealth, social capital and confessional identity. In contrast, the ethos of the Royal Hibernian Military School in Phoenix Park, established in 1769, reflected its close, though not official, relationship with the British Army. The school began as a charitable home for orphaned sons and daughters of military men and became a semi-elite military school by the end of the nineteenth century. After 1808 the school had more direct ties to the British military establishment and was purposefully designed to encourage enlistment among its male pupils.

The experience of children in these schools diverges from the historiographical emphasis on urban childhood as inevitably impoverished and 'at risk'.[9] Dublin could indeed be a hostile environment for children. In 1851, at

---

6 Margaret R. Hunt, *The middling sort: commerce, gender, and the family in England, 1680–1780* (San Diego, Calif., 1996).
7 Pierre Bourdieu, *The Logic of Practice* (Cambridge, 1990), pp 119–38.
8 Pierre Bourdieu's concept of the habitus as a 'structuring structure' is utilised in this context to highlight the social dimensions of space in the school milieu maintained through individual and collective social practices and experiences. The boarding school habitus privileged particular social and cultural capital relationships that fit within the institution's pedagogical vision. The term is useful in shifting attention from the formalised functions of the school, delineated in prospectuses or curricular choices, to the more informal practices of social reproduction that shaped students' values, expectations and behaviours. See Pierre Bourdieu, *The logic of practice* (Cambridge, 1990); Pierre Bourdieu, *Distinction: a social critique of the judgement of taste* (London, 1984); Pierre Bourdieu, *The state nobility: elite schools in the field of power* (Oxford, 1996).
9 The dominant historiography of urban children depicts the anxiety of the 'child-saver' movement to remove working-class children from the streets and place them in institutions. Timothy J. Gilfoyle, 'Street-rats and gutter-snipes: child pickpockets and street culture in New York City, 1850–1900' in *Journal of Social History*, xxxvii, no. 4 (2004), pp 853–62; Jane Read, 'Gutter to garden: historical discourses of risk in interventions in working-class children's street play' in *Children & Society*, xxv, no. 6 (2011), pp 421–34; Donald M. MacRaild and Frank Neal, 'Child-stripping in the Victorian city' in *Urban History*, xxxix, no. 3 (2012), pp 431–52.

the end of the famine, William Wilde reported that 62 per cent of children living in the impoverished south inner city died before they were ten years old.[10] The impact of poor sanitation, a more limited diet and general poverty affected urban children disproportionately. Cormac Ó Gráda suggested that children born at the Dublin Rotunda Hospital had a one-in-two chance of reaching the age of five, though these figures admittedly represent the health of the poorest in a poor city.[11] However, the city could also enable children, and their families, to access an array of educational, cultural and economic opportunities which simply did not exist in isolated rural areas. The longevity of these two schools must be at least partially due to their location in the capital city, their access to financial support from private and state benefactors located therein and their ability to leverage the cultural capital of their school in the educational marketplace.[12] These two schools were bourgeois constructions, one created by Dublin's Catholic elite to provide education for upper-class Catholics and the second established by a Protestant elite to ameliorate the social plight of orphaned military children. The spatial policies and morphologies of these two schools offer an example of how bourgeois constructions of childhood were consolidated during the first half of the nineteenth century to emphasise children's innocence and vulnerability, and conterminously expressed anxiety about the menace children posed to wider society if corrupted. Bourgeois constructions of ideal childhood gained official sanction by the end of the century with legislation on children's labour, compulsory education and child welfare.[13] The nascent formation of these discourses was already manifest in the abstract and representational depictions of spaces for children in the Irish boarding school by the mid-nineteenth century.

By the middle of the nineteenth century, constructions of bourgeois childhood throughout the Western world were increasingly centred on the removal of children from public spaces and their enshrinement within the

---

10 As quoted in Jacinta Prunty, *Dublin slums, 1800–1925: a study in urban geography* (Dublin, 1999), p. 46.
11 Cormac Ó Gráda, 'Dublin's demography in the early nineteenth century: evidence from the Rotunda' in *Population Studies*, xlv, no. 1 (1991), p. 51.
12 The boarding school at Loreto Abbey, Rathfarnham remained in operation until 1996; the Royal Hibernian Military Academy was relocated to Shorncliffe Camp, Folkestone, Kent in 1922. See Howard Robert Clarke, 'The attempt to re-locate the Royal Hibernian Military School in Northern Ireland, 1922–1924' in *Irish Sword: The Journal of the Military History Society of Ireland*, xxviii, no. 114 (2012), pp 399–410.
13 Sarah-Anne Buckley, *The cruelty man: child welfare, the NSPCC and the state in Ireland, 1889–1956* (Manchester, 2013); Gillian McIntosh, 'Children, street trading and the representation of public space in Edwardian Ireland' in Maria Luddy and James M. Smith (eds), *Children, childhood and Irish society, 1500 to the present* (Dublin, 2014), pp 46–64.

home.[14] Especially for children, the space of home became identified as an idyllic refuge, a place of moral goodness, spiritual succour and familial bonds.[15] While 'separate spheres' has become a convenient catch-all term for gender ideologies during the nineteenth century, the chronology of the public/private divide and the effects of rhetoric on practice have become points of contention.[16] Leonore Davidoff, 20 years after publication of the classic *Family Fortunes*, defended the dichotomy of the public–private divide, arguing that the spatial practices of bourgeois families underwent significant material change by the mid-nineteenth century.[17] She argued that changing gender relations can be mapped through examination of the built environment and the practices of the gendered body in social space. The sacralisation of home life during the nineteenth century accompanied a growing concern for those children whose childhoods did not match a bourgeois conception of innocence, dependence and vulnerability. The construction of childhood as a period of impressionability and purity became significant in the spatial organisation of home and school life for many children, with greater division drawn between adult/child, male/female spaces by the last quarter of the nineteenth century in an effort to keep children's spaces protected from contamination by the adult world.[18]

Twinned with the removal of children from public spaces was an emphasis on childhood education. Optimism about the reformative role of education

---

14 Hugh Cunningham, *Children and childhood in western society since 1500* (Harlow, 2005), 137–71.
15 Susan Galavan, *Dublin's bourgeois homes: building the Victorian suburbs, 1850–1901* (London, 2017).
16 Amanda Vickery argued that, rather than an invention of the eighteenth century, the separation of home life from public duty has been a trope in Western writing since ancient times. See Amanda Vickery, *The gentleman's daughter: women's lives in Georgian England* (London, 2006). See also Linda K. Kerber, 'Separate spheres, female worlds, woman's place: the rhetoric of women's history' in *Journal of American History*, lxxv, no. 1 (June 1988), pp 9–39.
17 Leonore Davidoff, 'Gender and the "great divide": public and private in British gender history' in *Journal of Women's History*, xv, no. 1 (2003), pp 11–27. See also Kathryn Gleadle, 'Revisiting family fortunes: reflections on the twentieth anniversary of the publication of L. Davidoff and C. Hall (1987) *Family Fortunes: men and women of the English middle class, 1780–1850*' in *Women's History Review*, xvi, no. 5 (2007), pp 773–82.
18 The designation of particular spaces for particular uses was well established by the Victorian era: see Marta Gutman and Ning de Coninck-Smith (eds), *Designing modern childhoods: history, space, and the material culture of children* (New Brunswick, NJ, 2008); Jane Hamlett, '"The dining room should be the man's paradise, as the drawing room is the woman's": gender and middle-class domestic space in England, 1850–1910', *Gender & History*, iii, no. 21 (2009), pp 576–91; Rachel Remmel, 'The spaces of the schoolhouse and the city: gender and class in Boston education, 1830–1832' in *Journal of the History of Childhood and Youth*, ii, no. 7 (2014), pp 199–218; Susie Steinbach, *Understanding the Victorians: politics, culture, and society in nineteenth-century Britain* (London, 2012).

had been circulating since the early eighteenth century, but these ideas began to impact on a broader section of society with an expanding print culture, private philanthropic initiatives and the establishment of the Commissioners for National Education in Ireland (C.N.E.I.) in 1831.[19] The adults who designed, constructed and monitored school spaces based their decisions on an understanding of childhood as a period particularly susceptible to corruption and immoral influence. As historians have noted, the category of 'children in danger' emerged from an urban context, where industrialisation, the breakdown of traditional family life and pressures of overpopulation provoked episodic moral panics about juvenile delinquency, criminality and moral decline.[20] Legislation limiting children's street-trading, proposed in 1902, centred on anxieties about children's exposure to immorality in urban streets and the moral and physical degeneration of the Irish working class. Gillian McIntosh argued that child street traders in Irish urban centres were a visible reminder that middle-class formulations of childhood did not match the realities of life for Ireland's poorest families.[21]

Didactic tracts intended to encourage religious habits among the working classes often provided cautionary tales about the dangers of the city streets, particularly for children. Abigail Roberts (1748–1823) from County Laois, wrote tracts for the Kildare Place Society which characterised education as the best method of inculcating moral values in working-class children. Her stories promoting early education implied that schools would effectually serve *in loco parentis* to compensate for the lack of supervision provided at home. In her tract *The Schoolmistress* (1824), an Irish mother, Mrs Moloney, tells Mrs Wilman, the schoolteacher, 'many a time I am obliged to send them out to play on the road, and then afterwards find they have been fighting amongst themselves or with others, so that I see how much it is our duty, at all events, to put them in better hands'.[22] Roberts portrayed city streets as places where children fought and

---

19  Mary E. Daly and David Dickson (eds), *The origins of popular literacy in Ireland: language change and educational development 1700–1920* (Dublin, 1990); David Dickson, Justyna Pyz and Christopher C. Shepard (eds), *Irish classrooms and British Empire: imperial contexts in the origins of modern education* (Dublin, 2012); Niall Ó Ciosáin, *Print and popular culture in Ireland, 1750–1850* (Basingstoke, 1997).

20  For the concept of moral panic, see Eileen Janes Yeo, '"The boy is the father of the man": moral panic over working-class youth, 1850 to the present' in *Labour History Review*, lxix, no. 2 (2004), pp 185–99. See also Peter King, 'The rise of juvenile delinquency in England 1780–1840: changing patterns of perception and prosecution' in *Past & Present*, clx, no. 1 (1998), pp 116–66; Conor Reidy, *Ireland's 'moral hospital': the Irish borstal system, 1906–1956* (Dublin, 2009).

21  McIntosh, 'Children, street trading and the representation of public space in Edwardian Ireland', pp 51, 64.

22  Abigail Roberts, *The schoolmistress; or, instructive and entertaining conversations between a teacher and her scholars* (Dublin, 1824), p. 77.

misbehaved, while the school brought them under the watchful eye of a schoolmistress. In New Englander John Abbott's didactic tract, appropriately entitled *The child at home* (1833), city streets were rife with opportunities for children to learn bad habits, pick up profanities from their peers and become generally idle.[23] His tract, published originally in New York, reprinted in London and distributed in Dublin, depicted common fears about the moral environment of the city caused by industrialisation and urban expansion. Especially for boys, the sorts of entertainment found in the streets were thought to lead to an adult life of dissipation and criminality. Abbott warned that boys who spent their evenings looking for amusement outside of the home were likely to lose their appreciation for domestic life and would forever be seeking out excitement and pleasure, a sure sign of moral decline.[24] Principal among Abbott's concerns was the nature of play on city streets which took place beyond parents' purview. The unsupervised space of the streets and the flow of people in and out of neighbourhoods meant children could easily form friendships with unscrupulous characters. Abbott suggested that girls walking alone at night could be harassed and chased by drunken men or gangs of boys.[25]

For girls, the perils of city life were presented as a threatening encounter with implicit sexual danger, whereas for boys the threat of moral corruption was read as an embedded feature of urban space and its ability to amuse and entertain through superficial spectacle. Didactic literature throughout the period delineated a feminine responsibility for making home life an attractive alternative to the potentially depraved leisure pursuits available in the urban sphere. The *Catholic offering* (1859), a book intended for Irish girls returning home after a convent school education, suggested that it was young girls' role to ensure that their brothers were welcomed into the domestic circle. 'Elder brothers would be often induced to spend their evenings blamelessly at home, if that home were rendered attractive, and those evenings cheerful and agreeable; ... to what higher or holier object can the varied resources of a well educated and highly accomplished woman be directed, than that of shielding from evil those she is bound to love!'[26] This theme was well rehearsed in literary works, with children, and girls in particular, singled out as paragons of morality and innocence in a corrupted world.[27]

---

23 J.S.C. Abbott, *The child at home: or the principles of filial duty familiarly illustrated* (London, 1833), pp 77–78.
24 Ibid., pp 78–80.
25 Ibid.
26 Anon., *The Catholic offering: counsels to the young on their leaving school and entering into the world* (Dublin, 1859), p. 200.
27 Claudia Nelson, *Boys will be girls: the feminine ethic and British children's fiction, 1857–1917* (New Brunswick, NJ, 1991); Catherine Robson, *Men in wonderland: the lost girlhood of the Victorian gentleman* (Princeton, NJ, 2003).

During the first three-quarters of the nineteenth century, the language of domesticity and motherhood permeated the language and logic of female schooling. *The Catholic offering* reminded Irish pupils:

> Home is to you as it should be to every woman – your world, your empire, your sun, your centre of attraction; a worthy sphere for your energies; a legitimate field for the exercise of your accomplishments, acquirements, and varied mental resources. It seems but a little while to look back to the day when you left that home, a happy, thoughtless, petted child; how different are your feelings on your return to it.[28]

This transformation from petted child to thoughtful woman was the aim of convent boarding schools, and, rhetorically at least, schools for girls framed their argument for female education within the bounds of familial duty, maternal care and religious devotion. However, the spatial hierarchies and daily practices in schools catering for girls did not always reflect feminine ideals. The experiences of girls attending the Loreto boarding school certainly suggest that the discourse of domestic femininity was not necessarily reflective of actual practice.

The establishment of the Loreto Abbey Boarding School by the Loreto sisters was part of a boarder reorganisation of Irish Catholic educational provision during the early nineteenth century. Archbishop of Dublin Daniel Murray (1768–1852) recognised the need to provide more educational establishments for Catholics in Ireland. Frances Ball (1794–1861), founder of the Loreto Order in Ireland, was educated at the Institute of the Blessed Virgin Mary (I.B.V.M.) boarding school in York, England. After her noviciate with the I.B.V.M. community, she returned to Dublin in 1821, accompanied by two other sisters. With Archbishop Murray's help, they moved to Loreto Abbey, Rathfarnham, on 5 November 1822.[29] The site of the congregation's first institution in Ireland was an imposing campus replete with all the decorations and ornamentations of a respectable, public institution. Significantly, the convent's architectural distinctions accrued over time, in stages which reflect changing ideals of female education and the growing status of the Catholic Church in Irish society.[30] Formerly the home of the Protestant Archbishop of Cashel, the house was built in 1725 and probably designed by Sir Edward Lovett Pearce (1699–1733), also the designer of

---

28  *The Catholic offering*, p. 188.
29  Papers of Loreto Abbey, Rathfarnham, Dublin, Rathfarnham annals, 1821–60, Rath/LAC/1/1, L.C.I.P.A.
30  For a similar study of the architecture of a Loreto school in Canada, see Christine Lei, 'The material culture of the Loretto School for Girls in Hamilton, Ontario 1865–1971' in *Canadian Catholic Historical Association Historical Studies*, no. 66 (2000), pp 92–113.

4.1 Building and grounds of Loreto House, Rathfarnham, Dublin (c.1900)
(Institute of the Blessed Virgin Mary (Loreto),
Institute and Irish Province Archives)

Parliament House in College Green (Figure 4.1).[31] Its tall castellated spires were a landmark in the south of Dublin. Mother Superior Ball took personal interest in redesigning the interior to fit the requirements of a convent and school, coordinating building renovations and additions during her lifetime. Ball's initial impressions of the estate left much to be desired. She stated 'the demesne was a complete desert, there had been a walk around the back lawn but no trace then remained of it. The weeds in the garden had grown six feet high and no sign of a walk could be discovered in them. The orchard was a bog …'[32] This commentary on the 'wildness' of the landscape fit within the community's narrative of playing a civilising role in Irish society. Among the first modifications made to the Abbey was the enclosure of the property, and 'the walls of the gardens were raised several feet' to maintain the privacy of the community.[33] The enclosure was advertised to parents in school prospectuses as a benefit to their daughters' safety. It had the added benefit of keeping visitors and curious neighbour at a distance. The appearance of women

31 The house was purchased from the Archbishop of Cashel by George Grierson, the king's printer in Ireland during the 1790s. During the economic depression following the Act of Union the house was uninhabited and fell into disarray. Anne Dempsey, 'The Abbey': an appreciation of Loreto Abbey, Rathfarnham (Rathfarnham, 1999), p. 5.
32 Rathfarnham annals, 1821–60, Rath/LAC/1/1, L.C.I.P.A.
33 Ibid.

in religious habits created a sensation in the surrounding neighbourhood according to the community's annals. The problem of uninvited guests was sometimes so great a neighbouring farmer had to come and warn the visitors to leave.[34] The constant intrusion of the public disrupted children's education and more worryingly presented the convent 'like a hotel, where everyone was at liberty to come and go as she fancied'.[35] This reference to a hotel-like atmosphere had worrying implications for the virtue of the females residing there; a few decades earlier the Ursulines in Cork had been accused of being 'seminaries of prostitution' by disgruntled neighbours.[36] One way to counter these accusations was to restrict the movement of nuns and pupils and limit physical access to the convent grounds. Ball also tried to keep a tight rein on the grounds surrounding the abbey. She told her solicitor to raise a sum of money to offer to a neighbour to take over their property, stating, 'Archbishop thinks we ought to take the house, to prevent inconvenience from unsuitable neighbours'.[37]

Other early modifications to the property included enlarging the student dormitory to provide more light and better air circulation. The ceilings were raised 12 feet and windows installed on the south of the dormitory room.[38] During the first decade of operation, the boarding school had approximately 40 boarders; by the 1840s, student numbers had increased to 80. As a socially elite school, it catered for Catholic girls typically between the ages of 11 and 16. The relatively large student numbers affected the day-to-day management of the school, necessitating transactional arrangements, regulatory discipline and high student-to-teacher ratios. Three years after the Abbey's establishment, the annals noted, 'some trouble was occasioned in the Schools by the insubordination of the children which was found to proceed from over indulgence and neglect of vigilance, which obliged the introduction of "School Regulations" found to be most beneficial in reproducing order and regularity'.[39] One of the regulations introduced, which continued in Loreto schools during the twentieth century, was the constant presence of an adult with the pupils. A nun slept in the student dormitories, accompanied girls on their way to class and chapel and presided over meals. Anxieties about moral corruption, bad language and disobedience prompted this highly regulated environment. One

---

34  Ibid., p. 7.
35  Ibid.
36  William Coppinger, *The life of Miss Nano Nagle as sketched by the right Rev. Dr Coppinger in a funeral sermon preached by him in Cork, on the anniversary of her death* (Cork, 1794), p. 23.
37  Papers of M. Frances Teresa Ball, letter from Frances Ball to J. Connolly, Esq, 8 Lower Sackville St., 20 Apr. 1837, TB/RAT/1/2, L.C.I.P.A.
38  Rathfarnham annals, 1821–60, Rath/LAC/1/1, L.C.I.P.A.
39  Ibid.

of the few forms of privacy reserved for students was a small locked desk in which a girl could keep her school books and painting supplies, but even this was somewhat tempered, since the mistress of schools retained a master key.[40] Privacy for students may also have been available in the extensive grounds surrounding the convent, where trees and walking paths could give students cover from the watchful eye of their teacher.

The congregation very quickly cemented its reputation as a purveyor of elite female education by advertising their students' successful transformations into genteel ladies at student exhibitions and prize ceremonies. Their curricular offerings privileged foreign language tuition, dance, music and other feminine accomplishments. The visits of such prestigious figures as Daniel and Maurice O'Connell, the Earl Carlisle, Lord Lieutenant of Ireland and Lady Bellew helped to augment the reputation of the Loreto order.[41] In 1831, Ball wished to expand to the north side of Dublin to a more central urban location. According to the annals, 'numerous were the invitations given by parents and many more complaints of children being obliged to walk across the city to partake of the advantages derived in a convent day school'.[42] For middle-class girls, a daily journey through Dublin's city centre, and the attendant dangers of their exposure to the streets, was not easily amenable to the genteel respectability the convent cultivated. After searching for a suitable house for two years, three Loreto sisters established St Patrick's day school in July 1831. The school was a short-lived project. It lasted less than a year, a failure which the community attributed to bad timing, since many wealthy citizens retired to their country homes for the summer, only returning to Dublin for the winter season. The lack of respectable families from which to draw pupils contributed to its closure, as the pupils who did attend were considered unruly and unrespectable.[43] Though St Patrick's failed, Ball established several other schools in Dublin city including a day school at Harcourt Street in 1833, an establishment on North Denmark Street in 1836 and St Stephen's Green boarding school in 1841. It became established policy to carefully interview and select day pupils to ensure that they would not corrupt boarders by bringing in outside influences. The foundation in Rathfarnham remained the central motherhouse of the Irish Loreto order, serving as residence for the administrative branch of the community as well as a spiritual homeplace for nuns who perceived the Abbey as the centre of the imagined topography of the expanding community.

40 Papers of M. Frances Teresa Ball, letter, TB/CAN/3/17, 3 Nov. 1854, L.C.I.P.A.
41 Papers of M. Frances Teresa Ball, letter, TB/CAN/3/24, 7 Apr. 1857, and letter, TB/COR/9/131, 20 Nov. 1849, L.C.I.P.A.
42 Rathfarnham annals, 1821–60, Rath/LAC/1/1, L.C.I.P.A.
43 See 1831, ibid., p. 14.

The Loreto sisters also ran free schools for less advantaged pupils alongside their paid boarding schools, further emphasising how categorised and channelled they saw their own social mission. Within the Rathfarnham area, flour, cloth and pin manufacturers were in operation.[44] The free school at the Abbey held classes on Sundays to accommodate the mill children working during the week. When the free school was opened in 1823, 90 students attended on the first day. The community's annals noted that within a short time of their establishing the free school, a Protestant school was opened in neighbouring White Church, offering the enticement of blankets in exchange for enrolment. Consequently, the number of students at the Abbey dropped to 60. However, the sisters began to offer dinner to some of the most destitute children and some of their students then returned.[45]

The free school and the boarding school were separated through physical and social demarcation of separate spaces. Established to the southern end of the Abbey on the Grange road, the free school maintained its own buildings and recreation grounds for pupils, outside the walls of the Abbey. At the Loreto House in St Stephen's Green, established in 1841, the free school and the boarding school operated more closely to one another, but free school pupils were instructed to enter through the field at the rear of the building rather than the main entrance.[46] The uniform of boarding school pupils, as well as the ribbons or sodality badges the girls wore, also served as demarcations of belonging to the boarding school, not the free school. The students' class identities were inscribed not only through their movement and location in the school space, but also displayed on their bodies.

Despite rhetoric which placed familial bonds at the centre of female education, upon attendance at Rathfarnham school, students were effectively cut off from regular contact with their families. Until the 1840s, boarders generally remained at school for 12 months a year, with leave granted at the discretion of the headmistress. The intrusion of any visitors, including parents, was discouraged. Ball advertised in one of the early prospectuses that, 'Parents are most earnestly besought not to break in upon the habits of application so requisite for the improvement of their children, by numerous and unnecessary visits. Visits on Sundays can at no time be allowed'.[47] When visits were permitted, they took place in the parlour and were overseen by the Mistress of the House; only a pupil's parents were allowed to be alone with her.[48] In general, the parlour and the chapel were the only spaces for public access to the

---

44  See the Ordnance Survey map for Rathfarnham (1837–42).
45  Rathfarnham annals, 1821–60, Rath/LAC/1/1, pp 11–12, L.C.I.P.A.
46  Papers of M. Frances Teresa Ball, letter, TB/CAN/3/15, 18 Mar. 1854, L.C.I.P.A.
47  Papers of M. Frances Teresa Ball, School prospectus, TB/RAT/4/2, undated, L.C.I.P.A.
48  Papers of M. Frances Teresa Ball, letter, TB/CAN/3/6, 29 Nov. 1851, L.C.I.P.A.

convent.[49] Students were only allowed access to certain areas of the Abbey and the nuns retained an entirely separate refectory and living quarters. When one student from Spain received the privilege of eating dinner in the nuns' dining hall after seven years at the school it was considered unusual enough to be included in the community annals.[50]

Among the nuns there were further demarcations of class, with divisions between lay sisters, choir sisters and novices.[51] While making recommendations on proper housing structures to Teresa Dease, a founder of the Loreto community in Canada, Ball described how, 'Our community sisters have separate lecture [and] ... apartment for recreation. Novices have an adjoining house; Lay sisters separate apartment for lecture, recreation and needlework'.[52] Services in the chapel were similarly required to maintain assigned hierarchical order. A notice in Rathfarnham insisted that if it became necessary for the sisters to convene for prayer outside the chapel, 'the changing of place will not require the sisters to go out of their ranks for kneeling'.[53] Students would have been aware of these subtle markers of hierarchy, since lay and choir sisters wore different uniforms and had different tasks. Lay sisters were not supposed to have extended interaction with boarders, so their access to the main staircase and student dormitories was restricted. One of the rules of the religious order insisted that sisters must not have favourites or cultivate exclusive friendships. In order to maintain this detachment teachers were prohibited from 'visiting the Infirmary, the cells, speaking alone with pupils in the dormitory, music room, passage, walking out or elsewhere'.[54] When one student transgressed these spatial boundaries, Ball personally issued a school-wide notice. 'A new boarder at 10 O'c walked up to stare at the company ... The nun in the class should prevent so forward and rude acts'.[55]

The boarding school was a highly supervised, hierarchical space for children. While residing at the Abbey each individual was assigned a place within the community's structure. This designation held physical implications for managing student bodies and inculcating respectable, feminine behaviour.

---

49 Maria Luddy, 'Convent archives as sources for Irish history' in Rosemary Raughter (ed.), *Religious women and their history: breaking the silence* (Dublin, 2005), p. 106.
50 Rathfarnham annals, 1821–60, Rath/LAC/1/1, 31 May 1855, L.C.I.P.A.
51 Choir sisters traditionally paid a dowry upon entering the convent and held higher positions within the community such as teaching or administration. Lay sisters generally performed manual labour and domestic tasks.
52 Papers of M. Frances Teresa Ball, letter, TB/CAN/3/18, 15 Mar. 1856, L.C.I.P.A.
53 Papers of M. Frances Teresa Ball, Regulations, assembling in the choir, TB/REG/7, undated, L.C.I.P.A.
54 Papers of M. Frances Teresa Ball, Regulations, rule on ordinary and recreation days, TB/REG/10, undated, L.C.I.P.A.
55 Papers of M. Frances Teresa Ball, Regulations, new boarders, TB/REG/23, Apr. 1847, L.C.I.P.A.

The interior hierarchy was more nuanced than a simple separation between adults and children. Boarding school students were kept separate from free school pupils, their classes were further divided according to age, and rankings within classes were based on merit. Access to privileged spaces within the school was negotiated and renegotiated daily. When students refused to comply with the school's procedures, their place among their peers fell accordingly. For example, the student described in the introduction was removed from her place at table and in the school room until she 'merited return'. Central to the organising logic of the Abbey was the separation between public and private spaces. The convent's enclosure and careful cordoning of public spaces for visiting, such as the parlour or the chapel, signalled the necessity of privacy to notions of feminine respectability. However, within the privatised school space, teacher–student relationships were characterised by transactional, business-like interactions. The day-to-day schedule of a convent school responded to the order's primary mission; to inspire Catholic devotion and a sense of moral duty within their pupils. However, despite the rhetoric of familial domesticity which permeated pedagogical texts, students lived in an environment far removed from a typical family home. The large student numbers, expansive school grounds and competitive nature of exams and exhibitions created an experience of education which was less focused on practical housekeeping skills and more on the social capital which would enhance a girl's status and prepare her to enter bourgeois society. The topography of students' lives was institutionally structured to ensure that relationships were cultivated horizontally among classmates, maintaining and enhancing class distinctions.

In contrast to the cultivated privacy of the Rathfarnham Boarding School, the Royal Hibernian Military School (R.H.M.) stood on an elevated bluff of land in the southern corner of Phoenix Park.[56] The physical presence of the school, measuring 300 feet across and three storeys high, reflected the iconography of eighteenth-century military and civic institutions.[57] The central building was set between two outward projecting wings, with a courtyard extending from the rear (Figure 4.2). The original architect is unknown; however, the two front-facing wings were the work of Francis Johnston (1760–1829) approximately 30 years after the school's initial construction in 1769.[58] The school was one of several building projects initiated by the British state in Phoenix Park between 1734 and 1788. During this period,

---

56 The school is currently the site of St Mary's Hospital, Phoenix Park.
57 *Hibernian school in the Phoenix Park, seventh report from the Commissioners of the Board of Education, in Ireland*, H.C. 1810 (177) (Ireland), 2.
58 Howard Robert Clarke, *A new history of the Royal Hibernian Military School, Phoenix Park, Dublin, 1765–1924* (Yarm, 2011), p. 22.

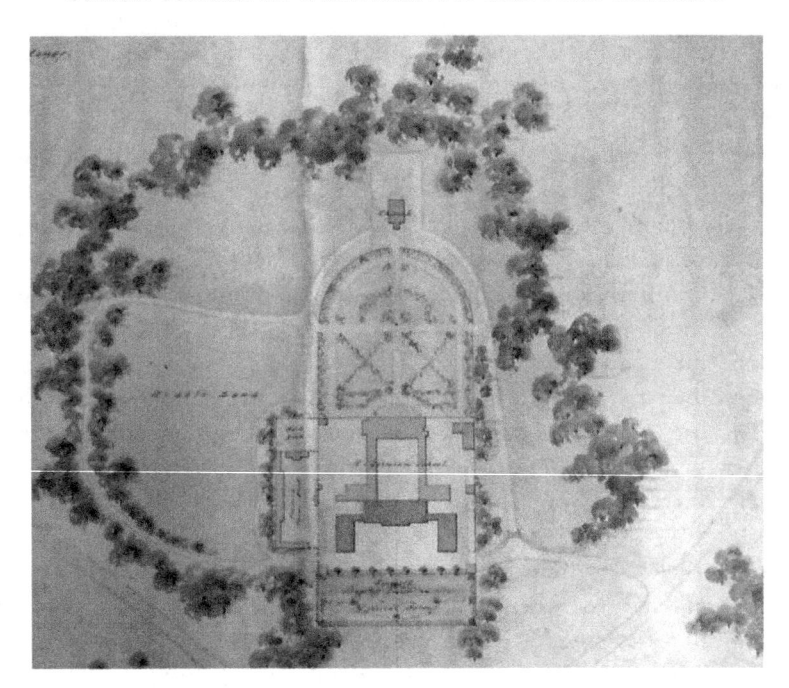

4.2 Decimus Burton's ground plan of proposed farm buildings for the Royal
Hibernian Military School, January 1836
(Office of Public Works, National Archive of Ireland, OPW/5HC/2/65–68.
Thanks to the Director of the National Archives
for permission to reproduce the image)

the Magazine Fort, Chapelizod barracks and the Royal Military Infirmary designated the Phoenix Park as an institutional, militarised and imperial space.[59] The R.H.M.'s classical symmetry and imposing design fit the model of other institutions for orphaned children, including the Green Coat Hospital in Cork, constructed in 1715 for destitute Protestant children, and the 1773 rebuilt Blue Coat Hospital in Blackhall Place, Dublin.[60] From the outside there was little to suggest the domestic function of the school as a home for children and staff.

The school in Phoenix Park originated as a philanthropic endeavour of the Hibernian Society. Founded in the parish of St Paul near the Royal Barracks (now Collins Barracks), the Society formed to ameliorate the plight of orphaned children of military men in the aftermath of the Seven Years

---

59 Robin Usher, *Protestant Dublin, 1660–1760: architecture and iconography* (Basingstoke, 2012), pp 134–35.
60 Christine Casey, *Dublin: the city within the Grand and Royal Canals and the Circular Road with the Phoenix Park* (New Haven, Conn., 2005), p. 238.

War (1756–63). The initiative can be characterised as part of a wider scheme to provide for impoverished children in institutions designed specifically for them. By the end of the eighteenth century, there was a growing belief that children who shared spaces with adults in municipal workhouses were likely to emulate immoral habits or become corrupted by adult criminality.[61] The Hibernian Society was founded to prevent 'popery, beggary and idleness' and its proselytising mission remained a feature of the curriculum until at least the 1840s.[62] From 1808 to 1846, the Society was granted a charter which allowed it to place boys directly into military service, though the function of the school still aimed towards providing both boys and girls with education and training in the trades. In 1846, the philanthropic involvement of the Hibernian Society effectively ended, and the school came under direct control of the War Office with the explicit mission of producing boys who would serve in the British Army. For the sake of comparison, this chapter will focus primarily on the workings of the school before 1846, when both boys and girls were in residence.

In 1769, the Hibernian Society was granted a royal charter and three acres of land in Phoenix Park by the Lord Lieutenant. The location of the land parcel in the park became an issue of contention during the planning phase with the originally allocated plot declared unsuitable for children. During the eighteenth century, aetiological models linked humoral imbalance with atmospheric miasmas: bad air meant bad health.[63] Dr John Nicholls, former surgeon general of the army in Ireland, told the ranger of Phoenix Park, Nathanial Clements, that the proposed location would be detrimental to children's health because it was low-lying and susceptible to damp, poor-quality air. He suggested relocation of the site 184 yards away to a higher position. Although Nicholls's suggested site lay outside the boundaries of the official land grant, Clements consented to the change and moved the plans to their present location, believing it indefensible to erect a building injurious to children's health. The move caused some consternation among the Board of Governors. When the issue was referred to a panel of medical doctors for review they sided with Nicholls's observations about the health benefits of an elevated location.[64] Once constructed, the school was declared to have an 'extensive and cheerful view over a rich and variegated tract of country'

---

61 Joseph Robins, *The lost children: a study of charity children in Ireland 1700–1900* (Dublin, 1980); Audrey Woods, *Dublin outsiders: a history of the Mendicity Institution, 1818–1998* (Dublin, 1998).
62 *Hibernian school in the Phoenix Park, seventh report from the Commissioners of the Board of Education.*
63 Tony Farmar, *Patients, potions and physicians: a social history of medicine in Ireland 1654–2004* (Dublin, 2004).
64 Clarke, *A new history of the Royal Hibernian Military School*, pp 24–25.

situated two miles from the nearest part of the city, and three miles from Dublin Castle.[65]

Typically, children were between the ages of 7 and 12 when admitted to the school, with preference given to orphans of military officers, followed by children who had lost either parent or had a father in foreign military service. In 1799, the school had 202 children. Within ten years, the attendance grew to 450, 150 of whom were female, evidence of the social impact of the Napoleonic Wars.[66] Although the charter of the school stated that one of its aims was providing homes for orphaned children, roughly a quarter of the student body had at least one living parent and returned to them at the end of their schooling. From 1800 to 1809, 3,269 children were admitted to the school. Of these, 25 per cent of boys and 15 per cent of girls returned to a parent. Surprisingly, only 23 boys entered the army. Working in trades was the more popular choice of career, with 44 per cent of the boys placed in apprenticeships. In 1810, the Commissioners of the Board of Education believed that boys from the R.H.M. were competently trained to get positions as petty officers in the army when reaching the proper age. However, they noted, 'the parents of these children, where such exist, almost universally prefer their being apprenticed to some trade, that may enable them to acquire a future maintenance, to the life of a solider'.[67] The Commissioners saw this as a flaw in the former charter which did not give the school explicit authority to place boys in the army. Although they thought that as many as three-fourths of the students of the R.H.M. went on to serve the army of the line as tailors and shoemakers, from 1808, a new charter was drafted to allow the school authority to place children in their care directly into the regular army, with the student's consent.[68]

The daily schedule of the school emphasised the creation of strong, fit, masculine bodies able to fulfil the duties of military service. The Board of Education reported the school's physical arrangements 'are obviously calculated to impress martial ideas, and inspire an early taste for a military life ... the classes are called companies, are regularly drilled, perform all their evolutions by beat of drum, and are judiciously encouraged by the commandant in running, leaping, and such other exercises as produce agility of body and firmness of nerves'.[69] The centre building, and focal point of the institution's architecture, contained the boys' schoolrooms, dining hall and dormitories. The school's initial layout placed the chaplain, steward and

65 *Hibernian school in the Phoenix Park, seventh report from the Commissioners of the Board of Education*, p. 12.
66 Ibid., p. 12
67 Ibid., p. 7.
68 Ibid., p. 1.
69 Ibid., p. 6.

masters in apartments within this centre building. By 1810, construction of a separate eastern wing was completed to house them, effectively separating adults from the pupils, reinforcing the military hierarchy and delineating the privilege of privacy conferred upon adults. The students' bedrooms were designed like a barracks, with 81 student beds housed in each dormitory measuring 133 feet long by 20 feet wide.[70] This was reported as detrimental to physical (and perhaps moral) health, as there was no space between the boys' beds. One serjeant-assistant [sic] slept in each of the five male dormitories to ensure order. This sergeant accompanied the students to their meals, to chapel and supervised them during recreation to 'prevent them from doing mischief, or acting improperly'.[71] The students woke to the sound of a beating drum at 5:30 in summer, 6:30 in winter, with the first order of the day being a parade exercise on the outer lawn, inspected by the Adjutant and Secretary for cleanliness and neatness.[72] If found to be improperly washed the boys were sent to the sergeant who headed their company. Multiple infractions resulted in a report to the Commandant.[73] Children's access to the city was limited and their daily routines subject to constant supervision by adults. However, children were allowed to leave the school if granted a pass from the Commandant. There is no record of how frequently these passes were given or on what grounds, but since they were issued directly by the Commandant it seems probable that passes were an exception, not a rule.

According to the school's regulations, the students' day involved approximately five hours of recreation and drills. This time included parades, marching drills and gymnastics classes, though some of the time was given to free play. To facilitate the physical demands of drilling, covered corridors connecting the dining hall with the school rooms were constructed in the first decade of the nineteenth century. The purpose of these porticos was to allow boys to exercise outside in rainy weather. By 1810, the school had acquired 19 acres of farmland and plans were made to move offices and outbuildings from the front of the school to the farmyard at the rear. A report by the Commissioners stated that in order to provide suitable spaces for the boys' exercise, the grounds at the front of the school needed to be elevated to 'form a noble area, in which the boys may play, and perform their military evolutions'.[74] This selection of ground at the front of the school signalled the publicised nature of students' exercises and the wish to advertise pupils'

---

70  Ibid., p. 2.
71  *Regulations for the establishment and government of the Royal Hibernian Military School for the orphans and children of soldiers* (Dublin, 1819), p. 62.
72  Ibid., p. 50.
73  Ibid., p. 58.
74  *Hibernian school in the Phoenix Park, seventh report from the Commissioners of the Board of Education*, p. 6.

discipline and health in a masculine, militarised fashion. In 1856, when Revd George R. Gleig inspected the school, he examined the boys in English and military education in front of an audience. *The Times* reported that, 'The examination having concluded, the pupils were paraded on the plateau in front of the building, and put through a variety of military evolutions, all of which they performed with the ease and dexterity of trained soldiers'.[75] These military parades were a memorable feature of life at the school. W.R. Fanu, who lived at the school until the age of ten while his father served as school chaplain, described the school 'as happy a home as a boy could have. Never can I forget our rambles through that lovely park, the delight we took in the military reviews, sham fights, and races held near the school'.[76] However, the park was not always such an idyllic space for children's play. In 1819, a ten-year-old boy from Chapelizod was playing in the park near the school when a musket ball fired by the 42nd Highland regiment hit him in the arm. He underwent surgery at the R.H.M. and the *Freeman's Journal* praised him for undergoing the ordeal with 'astonishing fortitude'.[77]

Military parades were public rituals that advertised a variety of imperial, national and local narratives of childhood health and masculinity. The urban setting, and the surety of an audience for student parades, accommodated and raised the importance of these daily exercises into public performances. The R.H.M.'s proximity to military barracks and state offices within the Phoenix Park lent symbolic capital to its place within a broader imperial imagination. Male pupils were touted as the future army of Britain with emphasis on their moral character, industry and discipline. In 1848, when pupils were taken on an outing to Kingston (now Dún Laoghaire) for a tour of the frigate *H.M.S. Amphion*, they paraded onto the pier with fife and drum. Nearly 300 students participated in the day's events, given free passage on the railway, allowed to roam the ship, and provided with a treat of cakes and oranges. Reporting on the event, the *Belfast News-Letter* wrote that commandant Colonel Columb 'had every reason to be proud of the healthful and creditable appearance of his tiny troops'.[78] The public presentation of the school operated on the staunchly masculine overtones of creating a corps of 'tiny troops'. The newspaper made small mention of the group of 40 or 50 female pupils who also enjoyed the day out with their mistresses. The presence of young girls on the outing was merely an aside to the spectacle of the boys' fife and drum performance.

75 *The Times*, 11 June 1856.
76 W.R. Fanu, *Seventy years of Irish life being anecdotes and reminiscences* (London, 1894), p. 1.
77 *Freeman's Journal*, 17 July 1819.
78 *Belfast News-Letter*, 16 May 1848.

The manner in which female students and their mistresses were an anomaly within the institutional ethos of the school is evident in the physical segregation demarcating female and male spaces. Located in the peripheral western wing, the 150 female pupils in the establishment were spatially segregated from the rest of the school.[79] Judiciously detached from other parts of the building, they had their own dormitories, school rooms, dining-hall and playground, essentially a school within a school, physically removed from the main institution. The kitchen, bread-room and storage facilities, functional sites intended to be hidden from public view, were placed between the male and female parts of the institution as a spatial buffer. Girls followed a similar daily schedule to the boys but were taught feminine skills such as making their own clothes, knitting, mending and making linen. Females were usually apprenticed out as milliners, seamstresses or servants at the end of their education, typically around the age of 14.

While the public gaze reified the masculine legitimacy of boys' exercise, girls' recreation remained hidden from public view in a back garden or indoor gymnasium.[80] During the 1830s, female exercise was believed to help equalise imbalances of the feminine mind caused by gender-specific ills and encourage development of an idealised feminine physique.[81] Professor J.A. Beaujeu was hired by the R.H.M. to conduct classes in calisthenics and gymnastics for girls. His exercises, 'designed for female anatomy', included use of bars, pull-ups on hanging rings and pulling on ropes. Beaujeu noted, 'exercise produces unclouded serenity of mind: hence moral, as well as intellectual health, is deeply indebted for its existence to the exercise of physical powers'.[82] These exercises were designed to inculcate feminine self-regulation, developing control of the body and encouraging development of feminine posture. Beujeu argued that exercise for females was essential for 'strengthening the body, and giving activity and grace to the motions; and, at the same time, by affording a pleasing amusement to youth, who have need of recreation after their hours of more serious employment'.[83] Commentary on female recreation thus emphasised attributes of grace, personal development and amusement,

---

79  *Hibernian school in the Phoenix Park, seventh report from the Commissioners of the Board of Education*, p. 6.
80  Decimus Burton's ground plan of proposed farm buildings for the school, Royal Hibernian Military School plans, Office of Public Works, National Archive of Ireland, OPW/5HC/2/65–68.
81  Ann Chisholm, 'Nineteenth-century gymnastics for U.S. women and incorporations of buoyancy: contouring femininity, shaping sex, and regulating middle-class consumption' in *Journal of Women's History*, xx, no. 3 (2008), pp 84–112.
82  J.A. Beaujeu, *A treatise on gymnastic exercises, or calisthenics, for the use of young ladies* (2nd ed., Dublin, 1828).
83  Ibid., p. 5.

whereas boys' activities were seen as demonstrations of discipline and strength indicating their preparedness for future adult roles.

The two urban boarding schools selected as case studies in this chapter demonstrate ways in which the public–private divide structured the everyday lives of children within these spaces. Enclosed areas, gates or separate buildings often delineated female spaces and established privacy as a dominant feature of feminine respectability. In contrast, boys were paraded and drilled in public spaces to illustrate institutional success in creating healthy, disciplined children. Within the boarding school, children were taught what spaces were appropriate for certain activities. Their movements from dormitory, to chapel, and on excursions to the city required negotiation of a complex habitus. Teaching and discipline practices reinforced the social meanings attributed to certain spaces, and removal from the schoolroom, or displacement from one's place in the class hierarchy, had real social implications. The other theme which emerges is the growing insistence on the conceptual and spatial segregation of children from adult spaces. The creation of pupil and teacher divisions hinged on an understanding of private–public spaces within the buildings. The convent parlour, or the R.H.M.'s elevated front garden, served as places for public display and pageantry, while dormitories remained private spaces with a domestic function. While these two schools served a minority of Irish children, their method of disciplining student bodies, maintaining gendered distinctions and delineating adult–child spaces was a feature of many schools in the Western world. The spatial practices in these boarding schools, adapted from continental and British boarding school traditions, informed children of their place within Irish gender and class hierarchies.[84] This aspect of socialisation was just as integral to the schooling process as students' lessons in religion, reading and writing. Dublin's bourgeoning urban topography was more than a passive backdrop to these schools' construction. The institutions relied upon the cultural, social and financial capital provided by Dublin society to stake their claim in the educational landscape. The pageantry and ethos of the R.H.M. developed because of its proximity to the Protestant Ascendancy in the eighteenth century and its publicised role as a home to military orphans and future members of the British Army. Loreto Abbey's status as an elite school for Catholic girls benefited from the perceived cosmopolitanism of the capital city and its close relationship to the Catholic hierarchy in Dublin. Their elevated urban spaces enabled the boarding schools to position themselves as positive counterpoints to the cramped, overcrowded, dirty urban spaces considered inhospitable to children. Their impressive public facades and extensive grounds reassured parents that children within their

---

84 The transnational features of Irish boarding school education are examined in O'Neill, *Catholics of Consequence*.

schools were appropriately insulated from urban life. Underlying the spatial polices and cultural discourses of both schools was an optimistic belief in the ability of the environment to shape children's physical and moral health. While construction of children's needs varied by class and gender, there was a similarity in how adults responded to the urban threats of degeneration, immorality and social breakdown by sequestering children away from sites of possible moral contamination and demarcating social hierarchies within the schools in greater detail. Imagining childhood as a period in which easily impressionable children were shaped by their educational environment augmented the importance of the boarding school as an intermediary between children and the city.

# 5

# 'High Walls and Locked Doors': Contested Spaces in the Belfast Workhouse, 1880–1905

## Olwen Purdue

In November 1880, Irish Poor Law inspectors Mr Brodie and Dr Bourke travelled from Dublin to Belfast in order to conduct an official inquiry into the management of the city's workhouse. The inquiry, held in the workhouse boardroom over a five-day period, saw the inspectors interviewing a wide range of witnesses, from David Wilson, Chairman of the Board of Guardians, and Robert Hamilton, one of the city's magistrates, to James Kinnear, assistant clerk in the master's office, and 17-year-old Sarah Slevin, mill worker and occasional inmate of the workhouse. The inquiry focused on recent 'scandals' which had reached the pages of the press concerning the conduct of the workhouse master, Captain Whitla, the manner with which he carried out his duties, and the extent to which Poor Law regulations were adhered to particularly with regard to the strict segregation and separation of workhouse inmates.[1]

This inquiry came about as a result of a series of allegations which had been made regarding the administration of Belfast workhouse in the pages of the local press, in a Belfast court and on the floor of the House of Commons. This particular episode was, however, just one of a series of public controversies surrounding the city's workhouse, all of which serve to highlight the tensions that existed in the late nineteenth century over the perceived role of the workhouse and its function as the principal provider of welfare for the city's poor. Much of this tension centred around the issue of space: pressure on welfare spaces in a city that was experiencing phenomenal growth; controversy

---

1 Copies of minutes of evidence taken at the recent inquiry held at the Belfast Workhouse by Inspectors Bourke and Brodie, together with their report thereon, H.C. 1881 (123), available at www.dippam.ac.uk/eppi/documents/12602/download (accessed 12 May 2018).

between central and local authority over the appropriate use of workhouse space; and dispute between those who administered the workhouse and those who used it in relation to access to and movement within those spaces.

These tensions had existed in some form or another since the conception of the Poor Law and were not unique to Ireland. Felix Driver, in his study of the new English Poor Law on which the Irish system was based, highlights the extent to which various pressures shaped and modified the system over time, arguing that 'despite the hopes of the architects of the new Poor Law in 1834, the subsequent history of workhouse administration bears the imprint of all kinds of conflicts, struggles and compromises'.[2] Driver sees these struggles as having taken place between central and local Poor Law authorities, while the paupers, those who made up the vast bulk of the people within the workhouse system, stood helplessly by, victims of an oppressive system and devoid of any influence or agency. While Driver's assessment of the relative position of the various players has considerable validity, it tends to overlook the important role played by the paupers themselves in these conflicts. As this chapter will show, an examination of contemporary concerns surrounding the use and control of space in Belfast workhouse as expressed in the pages of the press, Board of Guardians minute books and official reports, reveals the extent to which the principles and regulations that underpinned the Poor Law were being challenged and subverted by the poor of Belfast as they exercised agency in how they used the workhouse as a means of survival.

Space – its use, regulation and control – was fundamental to the very idea of the workhouse, part of the ideological underpinning of the Irish Poor Law.[3] The minimum amount of cubic space available per inmate was calculated to ensure the maximum number of people could be safely accommodated. Spaces for physical labour were specifically provided alongside the usual 'work' spaces within the workhouse – the kitchen, laundries, garden etc. – so that inmates engaged in the hard labour necessary to ensure their moral well-being and to implement the workhouse 'test'. And space was used to control and reform – the physical layout of the workhouse was constructed so as to maximise supervision as well as segregation; space was to be created for education and for punishment to ensure that workhouse inmates were suitably trained and controlled; and space was strictly regulated to prevent any form of interaction between 'normal' inmates and those deemed to be morally contagious. Even the location of the workhouse on what would have been the outskirts of a

---

2   Felix Driver, *Power and pauperism: the workhouse system 1834–1884* (Cambridge, 1993), p. 2.
3   Peter Gray, 'Conceiving and constructing the Irish workhouse, 1836–45' in *Irish Historical Studies*, xxxviii, no. 149 (May 2012), pp 22–35. For a discussion of the changing patterns of workhouse use over time and according to region, see Virginia Crossman, *Poverty and the poor law in Ireland 1850–1914* (Liverpool, 2013), pp 101–38.

town represented the very deliberate policy of separation and containment. Of London workhouses, David Green has written: 'Their location on the edge of towns or along main roads, no less than the high walls that enclosed them or their internal spatial arrangement, emphasised the principle and practice of strict separation of paupers from the rest of society'.[4]

The *Act for the Effectual Relief of the Destitute Poor in Ireland* (1838) introduced statutory welfare to Ireland along the lines of the new Poor Law passed in England four years earlier. Fundamental to this was the spatial segregation of the poor into workhouses built across the country. The system of outdoor relief which then dominated provision in England was not introduced in Ireland; Irish paupers had no right to receive relief in their own homes regardless of their circumstances until new legislation was passed in 1847 in response to Famine conditions and overcrowding in the workhouses.[5] The establishment of this 'workhouse test', which sought to differentiate the 'deserving' and the 'undeserving' poor by making admission to the workhouse the only form of relief available, ensured that none but the most desperate for relief would seek shelter within its walls. This idea was expressed most clearly by George Nicholls, architect of the Irish Poor Law, who claimed that the success of the 'workhouse test' lay in

> the improvident or idle being cast upon the parish, and forced to shelter into a workhouse, where, although screened from the extreme penalties for his neglect, the pauper is yet subjected to so many disagreeable circumstances that the desire to escape from these constantly urges him on to renewed exertion and to an observance of those virtues a neglect of which had entailed upon him privations so hard to be borne.[6]

Apart from the obvious deterrent of long hours of hard work, minimal provisions and harsh disciplinary regimes, the fact that family members were to be classified and separated on admission and would remain strictly segregated throughout their stay was a further means of ensuring that people would only seek relief as a very last resort. The workhouse building was designed to enforce this segregation. Green highlights the central importance of workhouse structure: interior segregation of space was to be absolute, ensuring the strict separation of different classes of pauper and, in particular,

---

4 David R. Green, *Pauper capital: London and the Poor Law, 1790–1870* (Farnham, 2010), p. 115.
5 Keith Snell, *Parish and belonging: community, identity and welfare in England and Wales, 1700–1950* (Cambridge, 2006), p. 220; Irish Poor Relief Act 1838 (1 & 2 Vict. c. lvi).
6 H. Willink, 'Life of George Nicholls' in George Nicholls, *A history of the English Poor Law* (2 vols, London, 1989), quoted in Peter Gray, *The making of the Irish Poor Law 1815–43* (Manchester, 2009), p. 132.

'the entire and absolute separation between the sexes, who are to live, sleep and take their meals in totally distinct and separate parts of the building, with separate yards for each'.[7] As this chapter will demonstrate, however, in the case of Belfast workhouse this was largely aspirational.[8]

The structure of Irish workhouses reflected this preoccupation with the use of space. On approaching the workhouse from the front entrance, a visitor would be met by a small, normally quite ornate, building which housed the Board of Guardians' boardrooms and offices as well as receiving rooms or probationary wards where applicants for admission would wait to have their admission approved and registered. Behind this was a much larger building – the main body of the workhouse, where inmates worked, slept and ate meals. At the centre of this, in a position to allow observation and control of the inmates' movements, were the master's and matron's quarters. To either side were boys' and girls' schoolrooms and beyond that men's and women's sleeping quarters. Boys and girls generally slept on the first floor, again strictly segregated from each other and from adults. Behind this again was the infirmary. On admission, inmates were separated and recorded as one of the following eight categories: able-bodied men, able-bodied women, aged and infirm men, aged and infirm women, boys aged 6–15, girls aged 6–15, children aged 2–5 and infants under 2.[9] Once admitted, men, women and children were to remain strictly separate from each other, with distinct exercise yards as well as accommodation for each of these three categories of inmate. The sick were housed in the infirmary and had their own exercise area. The importance of this controlled use of space was emphasised by Chief Commissioner Power in 1859 when he declared that effective management of a workhouse depended on the 'strict enforcement of classification and the continued appropriation of the several parts of the building to the uses for which they were originally designed'.[10]

It was not just the separation of sick from healthy inmates that concerned the Poor Law authorities; if anything, the separation of inmates on grounds of perceived morality was an even greater priority. The fear of 'moral contagion' that pervaded the thinking of the Victorian middle classes throughout much of the century was particularly acute in the context of institutions that housed those considered to be the lowest orders in society. As Maria Luddy has shown, Irish workhouses were frequently scrutinised to ensure that women of good character, and children in particular, were kept well away from

---

7 Green, *Pauper capital*, p. 117.
8 Elaine Farrell also explores these ideas in her essay, '"A very immoral establishment": the crime of infanticide and class status in Ireland, 1850–1900' in E. Farrell (ed.), *'She said she was in the family way': pregnancy and infancy in modern Ireland*, Institute of Historical Research (London, 2012), pp 205–22.
9 Belfast Board of Guardians minutes, 1842, P.R.O.N.I., BG/7/A/1.
10 Quoted in Crossman, *Poverty and the poor law*, p. 101.

the influence of women of dubious morality.[11] Workhouse separation wards represented designated spaces within which those deemed morally contagious should be confined. Belfast Union's Board of Guardians appears to have embraced the concept of segregated space with enthusiasm as their efforts to ensure the separation of the 'morally contagious' went well beyond the levels of classification as set down in the Poor Law. The 1862 annual report of the Poor Law Commissioners noted of Belfast workhouse that:

> the young are separated from the old and detached school buildings have been erected on the Workhouse grounds. A separation-ward has also been established, in which are placed all females labouring under venereal disease, and all women who have given birth to two or more illegitimate children. The Guardians are of opinion that the system of classification might, with advantage be carried still further by the separation of the younger of the adult class of both sexes from those of more mature age.[12]

If the use of space *within* workhouses was intended to be closely prescribed and strictly enforced, so was access *to* the workhouse, with guardians and workhouse officials alike tasked with the responsibility of monitoring and controlling entry to and discharge from the institution. Under the Irish Poor Law, all destitute people who applied for relief were eligible for admission to a workhouse and while some were refused relief on the basis that they were perfectly capable of supporting themselves or could be supported by other family members, the vast majority of applicants were admitted.[13] Anyone wishing to be admitted to the workhouse had first to get a ticket from the Relieving Officer who would ascertain their eligibility for relief. This ticket was then presented to the workhouse master who would admit them to a probationary ward where they would be examined before being admitted to the main body of the workhouse. The name, address and details of the applicant were recorded in the indoor register and their clothes were replaced by a workhouse uniform. In the case of urgent need the master himself could admit an applicant subject to approval by the guardians at their next meeting. Once admitted, able-bodied inmates were expected to engage in long hours of manual labour in return for their upkeep at the expense of the ratepayer, the preferred tasks being breaking stones, working the land attached to the

---

11 Maria Luddy, *Prostitution and Irish society 1800–1940* (Cambridge, 2007), pp 59–60.
12 *Annual report of the Commissioners for Administering the Laws for Relief of the Poor in Ireland, including the fifteenth report under the 10 & 11 Vic., c. 90, and the tenth report under the 14 & 15 Vic., c. 68: with appendices.* 1862 [2966] p. 81.
13 Crossman, *Poverty and the poor law*, p. 112.

workhouse or cleaning and doing laundry. Children were expected to attend the workhouse school and sometimes engaged in industrial training. Inmates could discharge themselves at any time, although they were expected to give three hours' notice before leaving. While registered as inmates they were strictly forbidden from coming or going as they pleased, although day passes could be issued which would allow them to leave the workhouse for specific purposes during the day. If they arrived back after the gates were locked at 9 p.m. they would have to seek permission from the master to be readmitted.[14]

While Poor Law regulations may have demanded strict control of the ways in which paupers used and negotiated workhouse spaces, the reality of managing a workhouse in the context of a rapidly growing industrial city made that control almost impossible to maintain. In the case of late-nineteenth-century Belfast, these regulations were regularly subverted both by the sheer numbers of those seeking admission and by those within the workhouse walls as they sought to exercise some degree of agency over their experience of welfare and relief. Belfast workhouse had been built on the Lisburn Road – originally well beyond the limits of the town – to the standard design and with capacity to house 1,000 paupers. When it opened in 1841 it was believed that this size of workhouse was appropriate for a town with a population of 70,000. What could not be foreseen at that stage was the population explosion Belfast experienced over the next 60 years as its rapid industrialisation sucked in people from all over rural Ulster. By the end of the century, Belfast had become one of Britain's major industrial centres and, with a population of almost 350,000, Ireland's largest city.[15] The rapid physical growth of the city over this period brought significant societal challenges, with overcrowding, inadequate water supplies and poor sanitation contributing to the spread of disease and increased mortality rates, while the large numbers working in heavy industry and factories resulted in high levels of work-related injuries. Inability to work, whether through injury, ill health, pregnancy or through lack of opportunity, meant that destitution was a very real possibility for those who had left the support networks of families and communities when moving to the city. Although an extensive network of charitable organisations existed, these were hindered by limited funding and minimal resources; for the vast majority of those who found themselves unable to fend for themselves the city's workhouse was the only option.[16] The growing numbers seeking relief in the workhouse are reflected in official statistics for the period. Annual reports

---

14 Belfast Board of Guardians minutes, 1 Jan. 1878, P.R.O.N.I., BG/7/A/42.
15 Ian Budge and Cornelius O'Leary, *Belfast: approach to crisis; a study of Belfast politics, 1613–1970* (London, 1973), p. 28.
16 For a survey of the network of voluntary welfare provision in nineteenth-century Belfast, see Alison Jordan, *Who cared? Charity in Victorian and Edwardian Belfast* (Belfast, 1994).

of the Poor Law commissioners show that during the period between 1850 and the mid-1870s the numbers admitted to Belfast workhouse in any given year had always remained in and around 10,000. By 1880, the annual intake had risen to around 20,000, while in 1913, over 29,000 people were registered as having been admitted.[17]

The absence of a night asylum where the temporary homeless or migrants from the country could find food and shelter led many recent arrivals to the city to seek temporary refuge in the workhouse. In January 1901, for example, 13 of those admitted to Belfast workhouse gave their place of residence as Antrim, 20 were from Killyleagh, 28 from Downpatrick, 93 from Lisburn and 132 from Newtownards, all in the neighbouring counties of Antrim and Down, while a further 8 came from Armagh and 14 from Lurgan, both in County Armagh.[18] For Belfast's Poor Law guardians, answerable to the city's ratepayers and anxious to keep the cost of poor relief to a minimum, this was a totally inappropriate use of workhouse space and of ratepayers' money. With no law of settlement in place, however, they had no option but to admit people from outside Belfast into the workhouse if they were destitute, regardless of where they had come from.

This increase in the number of admissions over the period was not just a result of a rapid population increase but also reflected changing attitudes towards and uses of the city's workhouse in the final decades of the nineteenth century. As Crossman's recent work on the operation of the Poor Law in Ireland has revealed, by the end of the century the population of workhouses across Ireland had become swollen by a transient body of causals who used them as places of short-term accommodation rather than long-term poor relief.[19] This was very evident in many rural unions, such as Ballymoney in County Antrim, where, by 1900, the vast majority of those admitted were single young men who stayed for one or two nights, generally on their way to another destination.[20] It was also seen in Belfast, where the workhouse was now serving a variety of purposes for many groups of people who were never included in the Poor Law's idea of the 'deserving poor' – those who turned up seeking admission during the day, spent one or two nights there and then moved on again. A picture emerges from the indoor registers of the city's poor coming and going from the workhouse on a regular basis, many of them shifting about constantly from one lodging house to another

---

17 *Annual report of the Local Government Board for Ireland 1880*, H.C. 1880 [C 2603] [C 2603-I], xxviii, 1, 39; *Annual report of the Local Government Board for Ireland 1913–14*, H.C. 1914 [Cd 7561], xxxix, 595.
18 Belfast workhouse indoor register, Jan. 1901, P.R.O.N.I., BG/7/G/52.
19 Crossman, *Poverty and the poor law*, p. 119.
20 Olwen Purdue, 'Poverty and power: the workhouse in a north Antrim town 1861–1921' in *Irish Historical Studies*, xxxvii, no 148 (Nov. 2011).

and using the workhouse as somewhere to stay in between times. A random selection of individuals identified in the workhouse registers during the four months of October 1900 and January, April and July 1901, for example, serves to highlight this. During these four months, John L. was admitted six times, each time from a different address; Joseph S. was admitted eight times during the same period, each time staying for a few days before moving on; and John B. was admitted nine times, each time with his wife and three children. Sixteen per cent of the 4,371 people admitted to Belfast workhouse during these four separate months appeared more than once; 212 people were admitted four or more times.[21] One can assume that many of these people appeared at the workhouse gate just as regularly for the rest of that year and in other years as well.

The workhouse seems to have been an important part of a network of shelter, particularly for many younger men who seemed to be permanently on the move around the city, shifting from one address to another, in some cases having none. Again, the workhouse registers for the four months listed above confirms this. To take one out of numerous examples, James K. was a young single Presbyterian labourer, aged 26. On 17 October 1900, he was admitted to the workhouse from 64 Great Patrick Street with sore eyes but discharged himself on the same day. He reappeared on 6 January 1901 from an address on the Newtownards Road to the east of the city, his condition simply registered as 'destitute'. He left the following day but reappeared on 17 January, this time staying for a full month. He reappeared twice in April, the first time his address given as Brown Square in Millfield while the second time he was back at Great Patrick Street. He appeared again on 15 July, his address given as 'none'. Many single men came to the workhouse from one of the city's numerous lodging houses. Some were admitted with an injury or illness; others whose condition was described as 'destitute' had presumably been forced to quit their lodgings when they could no longer afford to pay the rent. During the four sample months examined for 1900–01, 56 of the men admitted to the workhouse gave their address as 12 Great George's Street, one of the city's large lodging houses. Their ages ranged from 20 to 70 years of age and while some were widowers the majority of them were single. Of the men admitted from this address during the period examined, several returned at least once. John C., a 40-year old single labourer, for example, was admitted from 12 Great George's Street on 25 October 1900, remaining until 15 April 1901, when he was discharged. Four days later he was admitted again from the same lodging house, this time remaining in the workhouse until 17 September 1901. William C., a single, 32-year-old labourer, was admitted from that address on 23 October 1900 and remained until 2 January 1901. He was

---

21  Belfast workhouse indoor registers, 1900–01, P.R.O.N.I., BG/7/G/51–54.

readmitted from the same lodging house on 7 January 1901 and remained in the workhouse for another month.[22] As this is just a snapshot of the men admitted from this one lodging house in four separate months, it suggests a much wider picture of a highly mobile poorer class, dependent on a network of shelters, who moved to lodging houses when money allowed and to the workhouse when it did not.

This use of the workhouse did not escape the attention of the city's ratepayers, who repeatedly called on the Poor Law authorities to exercise more control over admission to the workhouse thus preventing what they saw as an abuse of the system and a form of behaviour that completely undermined the fundamental principles of the Poor Law. The *Belfast News-Letter*, a conservative and unionist paper whose readership would have largely represented the ratepaying classes, was particularly incensed by the apparent inability of the authorities to prevent people from using the workhouse as a means of free lodging. In November 1885, the newspaper declared, rather melodramatically, that the workhouse had been converted into a

> huge lodging house by a large number of lusty, happy-go-lucky tramps and vagrants who deemed it an honour and a privilege to be able to withdraw from the bustle and noise of the busy town to the shades of calm seclusion and philosophic retirement which the splendidly built edifice on the Lisburn Road known as the 'house' affords.[23]

Highly exaggerated as this assessment of workhouse use might have been, there is no doubt that it contained an element of truth. The records clearly demonstrate the extent to which the workhouse was used as casual accommodation, a situation which was very far from what had been intended by the architects of the Poor Law when it was passed in 1838 and which was a constant source of friction between those who administered welfare and those who used it.

## The workhouse wall

If the use of the workhouse as a place of shelter was becoming increasingly contested, the workhouse gates and walls often became the sites at which this contest played out: the space around which both those within and those seeking admission to the workhouse challenged some of the fundamental principles of the Poor Law as they sought to exercise some agency over

---

22 Ibid.
23 *Belfast News-Letter*, 18 Mar. 1885.

their experience of welfare. At a basic level, the workhouse walls were used, normally by younger inmates, as a means of escape; this had been an issue since the early days of the workhouse and was common to workhouses across Britain and Ireland.[24] While adult inmates were free to leave the workhouse if they pleased, some chose to abscond wearing the workhouse clothes which were, it may be presumed, in better condition than their own (even if they did bear the distinctive marking of the workhouse and therefore carried the risk of arrest for theft). In 1912, Charles T. was charged with absconding from Belfast workhouse and taking workhouse clothing with him, for which he received a prison sentence of two months.[25] Boys were particularly prone to escaping. On 13 May 1857, three boys absconded from the workhouse school 'during the time of Divine Service'. Two returned, but the third had disappeared complete with 'a suit of clothes, the property of the guardians'. A pencilled note in the margins of the minute book records the fact that the relieving officer was to be on the search for the missing boy – and the suit.[26] The following month saw 14-year-old James O'N. abscond while the rest of the boys were at Sunday dinner, returning the next day. The report stated that he had twice appealed to the Board of Guardians to allow him leave for a day and twice had been refused.[27] Just weeks later, the minutes recorded that 'Richard P\_\_\_, aged 11, and George D\_\_\_ 9 years, absconded over the boundary wall on the 10th inst. and returned in the evening'.[28] This seems to have been a perennial problem: a letter from the Local Government Board in May 1905 reprimanded Belfast's guardians and demanded a full explanation when four boys escaped from the school yard during the absence of the schoolteacher.[29]

The walls also represented an opportunity for appropriating workhouse property, with all manner of goods being thrown over the boundary wall, presumably to a waiting accomplice. In December 1879, the workhouse master reported the prosecution of Bridget D. and Maggie S. 'for larceny of Clothing, the property of the Union' for which they each received a sentence of six months' imprisonment. The women, who were housed in the separation ward, had prepared for this carefully by picking out the distinctive red threads from the workhouse sheets to render them less noticeable. They had then bundled up a collection of workhouse clothes in the sheets and thrown them over the workhouse wall where they were collected by an accomplice on the

---

24 Green has shown that this was one of the most common causes for committal among inmates of London workhouses in 1873: *Pauper capital*, p. 179.
25 Belfast Board of Guardians minutes, 2 Jan. 1912, P.R.O.N.I., BG/7/A/89.
26 Belfast Board of Guardians minutes, 13 May 1857, P.R.O.N.I., BG/7/A/20.
27 Belfast Board of Guardians minutes, 3 June 1857, P.R.O.N.I., BG/7/A/20.
28 Belfast Board of Guardians minutes, 15 July 1857, P.R.O.N.I., BG/7/A/20.
29 Local Government Board for Ireland to Belfast Board of Guardians, 11 May 1905, P.R.O.N.I., BG/7/BC/38.

outside.[30] After another inmate had been found guilty of throwing a parcel over the workhouse wall in 1917, it was discovered that a workhouse building adjacent to the boundary wall had a small window in the side, something which had clearly offered ample opportunities for this kind of activity over an extended period of time.[31]

Importantly, however, the walls and gates of the workhouse represented a space around which the poor of Belfast very publicly challenged some of the fundamental principles of the Poor Law, drawing public attention to and raising popular awareness of issues surrounding the operation of the Poor Law in the city. During the 1870s, Belfast's newspapers began carrying stories about the harsh treatment being meted out to the city's poor at the hands of the workhouse authorities, focusing in particular on the issue of people having to spend the night on the street outside the workhouse because they had been refused admission having turned up after nine at night. By the end of the decade this had gathered momentum, with letters regularly appearing in the press. In November 1877, the *Belfast News-Letter* reported that a young woman named Anne S. and her child had had to spend all night outside the workhouse gate 'although it was wet and cold' because the porter had refused to admit her on the grounds that she was drunk. One of the guardians commented that this was a regular occurrence.[32] In December of the same year, the guardians received a report from Belfast's Inspector in which he provided a long list of names of people left outside overnight over the past three months, something which was, again, reported in the local press.[33] The issue reached the House of Commons in July 1882 when J.G. Biggar, MP for Cavan, drew the attention of the House to a report in the *Northern Whig* newspaper which stated that Sub-Constable McMahon reported finding three persons lying at the workhouse gate after 11 o'clock at night, one of them an old man 70 years of age, who, at the time of seeking admission, was suffering from a severe attack of haemorrhage, and another 'an infirm old woman sixty-seven years of age' who was also 'kept sitting on the wet, cold, ground, outside the workhouse gate, all night'. The newspaper continued that just the previous week Sub-Constable Burke made a similar complaint against the master for refusing to admit to the workhouse a destitute woman with two young children.[34] The case of Ellen M., reported in the *Belfast News-Letter* the following month, received such public attention that it led to an official inquiry. The paper reported that the 'respectably dressed' married woman and

30  Belfast Board of Guardians minutes, 9 Dec. 1879, P.R.O.N.I., BG/7/A/45.
31  Belfast Board of Guardians, Report of Work Committee, 25 May 1917, P.R.O.N.I., BG/7/A/97.
32  *Belfast News-Letter*, 14 Nov. 1877.
33  Ibid., 12 Dec. 1877.
34  H.C. (28 July 1882), vol. 273, cc. 32–33.

her two children were found outside the workhouse at one in the morning by a police officer who called up the master and demanded that they be admitted at once. The woman explained that her husband, a clerk, had come on hard times and that she had therefore been forced to travel late at night to the workhouse as a desperate last resort.[35]

While the administration's responses in many of these cases simply reflect the general ideas of 'deserving' and 'undeserving' poor that underpinned attitudes towards poor relief throughout the nineteenth century, it is interesting to see the extent to which by the late 1870s these concepts were being challenged, even by those within the system. In the case of Annie S., for example, where the master's justification for refusing her admission rested on the fact that she was drunk, the Board of Guardians' discussions concluded with a motion being passed which expressed the guardians' regret at this treatment of the poor and ruled that in the future the master must admit all women with children at whatever time of the night they appear.[36] The cases described also demonstrate the extent to which the poor themselves exercised agency in the way some of them understood these unspoken rules around deservingness and respectability and used them to gain support. The case of Ellen M. is a case in point. As has been mentioned, her case led to a Local Government Board inquiry. Questioning at the inquiry revealed that Ellen, rather than being married to a clerk and living on the outskirts of the town with their two children as she had previously stated, lived near the workhouse, was the unmarried mother of two illegitimate children and 'supported herself by parting with her clothes'.[37] Presumably Ellen, fully aware of prevailing ideas around 'deservingness', had assumed the kind of character that she knew would be regarded as deserving and thus more likely to be admitted to the workhouse. Her reasons for seeking admission are also interesting – under pressure at the inquiry to explain why she had taken her children out of their home late at night to seek admission to the workhouse, Ellen admitted that she hoped the Poor Law guardians might prosecute the father of her children for failing to support them.[38] Limited as her options were, Ellen was aware of and used the existence of legislation that allowed Poor Law guardians to prosecute negligent fathers rather than letting their families become a burden on the ratepayers.

---

35 *Belfast News-Letter*, 15 Aug. 1882.
36 Ibid., 14 Nov. 1877.
37 *Belfast News-Letter*, 15 Aug. 1882.
38 Ibid. This case is also discussed in Olwen Purdue, 'A gigantic system of casual pauperism: the contested role of the workhouse in late-nineteenth-century Belfast' in Beate Althammer, Andreas Gestrich and Jens Gründler (eds), *The welfare state and the 'deviant poor' in Europe, 1870–1933* (Basingstoke, 2014), pp 42–43 and in Crossman, *Poverty and the Poor Law*, p. 120.

Another contested aspect of workhouse use was that of people using it as somewhere to sleep at night, discharging themselves the following morning and returning again late the same night seeking readmission. This was completely contrary to the idea that, in return for shelter, the able-bodied should spend their day engaged in manual labour. This issue was highlighted after an article in the local press in November 1877 complained that a young woman, Mary S., was found sitting outside the workhouse in the middle of the night having been refused admission. When Mary's case was examined, it emerged that she regularly discharged herself from the workhouse in the morning after having had a place to sleep and a meal of sorts. On this occasion, having left the workhouse that morning she returned late at night in an advanced state of drunkenness, without a relieving officer's admission ticket and, according to the night watchman, clearly in possession of enough money to pay for lodgings.[39] Responding to public criticism of this treatment of the poor, the Chairman of Belfast Board of Guardians, David Taylor, while agreeing that women, especially those with children, should never be left outside the workhouse overnight, again admitted the challenges this presented to the authorities. 'We must', he stated,

> endeavour to devise some means of preventing these inhuman mothers taking their children out of the house and dragging them through the streets of Belfast half-clothed and hungry until they think fit in the middle of the night to come back with them again to the workhouse.[40]

The matter was eventually raised in Parliament, where members were told that one woman had left the workhouse and been readmitted 59 times over a period of several years, just one of the many who came and went on a regular basis. In this contest between the poor of the city and its welfare authorities over the use of the workhouse, it is clear that the authorities were by no means in total control.[41]

The authorities' control over admission to the workhouse was regularly and openly challenged by the poor of the city. So vocal and consistent was this challenge that in January 1900, a resident of the Lisburn Road close to the workhouse requested that the City Commissioner of Police appoint a special patrol for the neighbourhood of the workhouse gate 'as rows are continuously occurring by persons who seek admission to the workhouse'.[42] By the end of

---

39 Belfast Board of Guardians minutes, 27 Nov. 1877, P.R.O.N.I., BG/7/A/42.
40 Ibid.
41 H.C. (1 Sept. 1880), vol. 256, cc. 998–1016.
42 Letter from R.A. Russell, Belfast Board of Guardians minutes, 30 Jan. 1900, P.R.O.N.I., BG/7/A/65.

the nineteenth century, the workhouse gate and wall had become a site of contestation over welfare provision between the city's welfare authorities on the one hand and the poor on the other – a space within which the poor of the city consistently challenged the administration of the workhouse, indeed the very principles of the Poor Law, in a powerful and public way.

## Controlling space within the workhouse

Control of space within the workhouse itself was also being challenged. The steadily increasing numbers of people turning up at the workhouse gate each day requesting admission placed Belfast's workhouse management under severe pressure and threatened to undermine the highly regulated use of space which formed one of the underpinning ideas of the Poor Law. At a basic level the numbers seeking admission occasionally led to a breakdown in the strict registration system on which the Poor Law, like so many nineteenth-century institutions, prided itself. This can be clearly seen in the workhouse registers – from time to time the usual chronological order of the admission registrations becomes confused, while some of the details required to be recorded are missing and spaces left blank. Interestingly, the Board of Guardians minutes for 18 November 1879 contain a sharp reprimand from the House Committee to the officer in charge of the registers for failing to record the full details of inmates being admitted and discharged.[43]

At a more serious level, increasing numbers put severe pressure on space which both represented a threat to the health and safety of the inmates and created problems around the enforcement of the strict segregation which was so fundamental to the idea of the workhouse. Minute books and correspondence from the 1870s onwards reveal a growing anxiety, particularly among the medical staff, about the impact of overcrowding. This anxiety was conveyed to the central Poor Law authority, the Local Government Board for Ireland, who promptly demanded that Belfast's guardians address the problem. A letter sent on 26 May 1879 contained the ultimatum that they must either provide additional accommodation or else start providing outdoor relief, something which Belfast's guardians had consistently opposed.[44] The letter also contained extracts from a recent inspector's report which condemned the workhouse for being 'generally … in an overcrowded state and some parts of it dangerously so'. It went on to quote the report of a committee which had been appointed to consider the cubic space of city workhouses in 1867 which declared that

---

43 Belfast Board of Guardians minutes, 18 Nov. 1879, P.R.O.N.I., BG/7/A/45.
44 Local Government Board for Ireland to Belfast Board of Guardians, 26 May 1879, P.R.O.N.I., BG/7/BC/1.

'there should be allotted to each sick inmate in Metropolitan Workhouses an air space of not less than 850 cubic feet on an average, that there should be a clear space of 6 feet across each bed and that no bed should be placed on the centre of the floor'. The inspector observed that the minimum space allocated to the sick in Belfast workhouse infirmary was only 600 cubic feet and even at that amount there were 272 patients more than there should be. He reiterated the concerns of the workhouse's medical officers

> that ulcers will not heal, that they dread to perform an operation lest erysipelas or some other disease attending on overcrowding would attack the patients. They add that on many occasions they found it necessary to discharge patients before a cure had been accomplished as they had observed that the illness came either to a standstill or retrograded.[45]

By November, there seems to have been little improvement, the master's report for 18 November relaying the concerns of the house committee

> that the crowded state of the Infirmary during the past week has been such, that on an average 30 patients have been obliged to lie on the floor or the passages between the beds, which is manifestly injurious to their health and dangerous to their lives. They therefore press upon the board the urgent necessity of completing the additional Wards as soon as possible.[46]

Despite a Local Government Board directive limiting the total number of inmates to 2,502, many parts of the workhouse continued to be seriously overcrowded, a letter of 16 December 1879 stating that

> 883 patients were under treatment on 13th inst. Of these 72 were obliged from want of space and bedsteads to lie on the Floors and Passages, and they can only repeat what they have already reported to the Board on the 24th November, that such a state of things is manifestly dangerous.[47]

In November 1881, a Poor Law inspector once again reported a considerable increase in the number of inmates, stating that 'with the exception of

---

45  Ibid.
46  Belfast Board of Guardians minutes, 18 Nov. 1879, P.R.O.N.I., BG/7/A/45.
47  Local Government Board for Ireland to Belfast Board of Guardians, 20 Nov. 1879, P.R.O.N.I., BG/7/BC/1; Belfast Board of Guardians minutes, 16 Dec. 1879, P.R.O.N.I., BG/7/A/45.

the fever hospital every part of the workhouse was overcrowded' and that when he visited the workhouse on the night of 14 November the maximum number of inmates established in a limitation order imposed on Belfast workhouse by the Local Government Board was exceeded by 568.[48] Despite the fact that new buildings were constructed and existing ones reconfigured in an attempt to deal with the overcrowding, by the end of the century the control of space, widely accepted as necessary to prevent the spread of infection, was not being adequately maintained. An inspector's report of 20 June 1908 revealed that 'septic' and 'aseptic' patients from the infirmary were using the same bathing facilities, as were syphilitic and non-syphilitic patients in the skin disease wards, while in the male side of the main building there was one bath for 400 men.[49] Interestingly, however, it seems that even at this late stage the control of moral contagion continued to be more of a priority for Poor Law authorities than the control of physical contagion. The report went on to say that,

> classification generally is strictly preserved in accordance with workhouse rules, but owing to the congestion in the infirm departments and body of the house, many of the healthy and infirm classes associate together in the dayrooms.[50]

The suggestion seems to be that while mixing healthy and infirm inmates was considered regrettable but unavoidable, mixing other classes of inmates remained strictly controlled.

Despite the attempts of Belfast's workhouse administration to maintain strict segregation of the classes, by the later decades of the nineteenth century there were suggestions that inmates were subverting the strict rules regarding the use of space. A number of very public accusations were made to the effect that segregation in Belfast workhouse was not being enforced as strictly as the Poor Law demanded, and that the workhouse inmates roamed freely. In March 1879, for example, Revd B. McCann, Roman Catholic chaplain to the workhouse, created quite a sensation by writing to the *Ulster Examiner* to complain about immorality and mismanagement in the workhouse. When asked by the Board of Guardians to explain himself, he replied by referring rather obliquely to 'certain abuses existing in the school building'.[51] Under pressure from the Board of Guardians, McCann clarified that these abuses involved mothers missing mass on a Sunday morning and taking cups of tea

---

48  Local Government Board for Ireland to Belfast Board of Guardians, 18 Jan. 1881, P.R.O.N.I., BG/7/A/45.
49  Report of Local Government Board for Ireland Inspector Mr Agnew, 20 June 1908, P.R.O.N.I., BG/7/BC/38.
50  Ibid.
51  Local Government Board for Ireland to McCann 10 Apr. 1878, P.R.O.N.I., BG/7/BC/1.

– and even the occasional egg – to their children in the schoolroom. McCann added that

> on Sunday last, no later, I counted nearly twenty women giving tea to the children and in some instances eggs were added. My attention was frequently drawn to this matter by those in charge when I had to tell them as superior officers told myself – 'I cannot prevent it'.[52]

While this might be a good example of much being made of very little, it also reveals the extent to which people were actually moving freely within and between the designated spaces of the workhouse. The suggestion that workhouse officials might have been unable to prevent what was seen as an abuse of the system is a refrain that occurs increasingly during this period. More serious claims by McCann that female inmates were falling pregnant in the workhouse – something which would suggest a complete breakdown of supervision and control on the part of the workhouse authorities – were found by a Local Government Board inquiry to be unfounded. The response of the Chairman, David Taylor, revealed the challenges faced by the management of this busy urban workhouse in seeking to maintain strict segregation:

> Everything has been done so far as high walls and locked doors can do to prevent any intercourse between the different classes. The children in the school buildings have no opportunity of mixing with the adults in the house; the hospital and infirmaries are distinct and detached buildings and entirely separated from the body of the house. The aged and infirm class of both sexes live entirely by themselves, the same may be said for those in the Nursery and the apartments for the healthy classes. The separation ward is a building at the rear of the workhouse grounds and is enclosed by a high wall. All unfortunate women and women having two or more illegitimate children are placed in this department; they are kept entirely separate and have no intercourse with other inmates, not even in the general dining hall as their meals are all supplied to them in their own building.[53]

Despite these efforts, however, the inquiry observed that pressure on space meant that spatial regulation was, to an extent, undermined. It observed that:

> the necessities that have from time to time arisen for meeting the increase of inmates of various classes by structural alterations and

---

52 McCann to Local Government Board for Ireland, 18 Apr. 1879, P.R.O.N.I., BG/7/BC/1.
53 Belfast Board of Guardians minutes, 18 Feb. 1879, P.R.O.N.I., BG/7/A/43.

additions ... have complicated the internal arrangement of the House and impaired the simplicity and consequently the efficiency of the provisions for classification which were designed and carried out in the erection of the Irish Workhouses.

While admitting that this had not 'led to grave abuses or offences against morality', the report did conclude that 'the facilities for casual intercourse may serve to render the workhouse less unattractive to the inmates than all experience shows it should be made'.[54]

## Conclusion

The Irish Poor Law, like its English equivalent, was built – figuratively and literally – on the concepts of moral and physical classification and of strict segregation of the classes. Space, and the way in which it was used and controlled, was therefore central to the successful operation of the Poor Law as a means not just of providing welfare for the destitute but of reforming the lower orders in society. The aged and infirm, the young, the deserted and the sick, collectively considered as the 'deserving poor', were to be kept apart and treated differently from the idlers, the profligate and the immoral, the 'undeserving' poor. Fear of physical contagion demanded separate accommodation for the sick; fear of moral contagion necessitated strict segregation of the moral from those who might corrupt the young and the innocent.

This may have been the ideal, but in late-nineteenth-century Belfast it was far from the reality. The maintenance of separate spaces within which people slept, worked, exercised and lived may have been more realistic in rural workhouses with their declining populations. In a workhouse serving an industrial city experiencing phenomenal population growth, a workhouse that saw ever-increasing demand made on available space, and where any extension of space provided always seemed inadequate for the sheer numbers of people being admitted on a daily basis, the strict use of space according to the principles of the Poor Law was impossible to maintain. Pressure on internal spaces and inadequate management led to a breakdown of the strict rules which were considered essential if the aims of the Poor Law were to be achieved.

Furthermore, a study of the records reveals that the poor themselves, considered by many to have been helpless, passive victims of a ruthless system, actually exercised a considerable degree of agency in the ways in which they

---

54 *Copies of minutes of evidence taken at the recent inquiry held at the Belfast Workhouse by Inspectors Bourke and Brodie*, p. 24.

used the workhouse in late-nineteenth-century Belfast. The spaces of welfare in the city were not uniformly spaces of dominance and control but were contested on many levels and in different ways. The workhouse wall, used by some to escape or exploit the system, and by others to demand access to its resources, also highlighted the helplessness of the city's welfare authorities to prevent what was considered by many to be a fundamental abuse of the Poor Law. An outraged editorial in the conservative *Belfast News-Letter* in 1885 declared, 'that in this town there is a gigantic system of casual pauperism never contemplated by the poor laws'. The article went on to state that

> this intolerable practice of tramps and vagrants running in and out at their pleasure and convenience, enjoying themselves outside during the day and returning to be housed and fed by the ratepayers at night must receive a check.

Belfast workhouse was, by the chairman's own admission, 'no longer a workhouse according to the intention of the law'.[55]

Despite the fact that Belfast workhouse was a deeply unpleasant and often stigmatising environment, and deliberately so, it remained a place where the undeserving and those considered deserving, were housed together. Unwilling or incapable of treating the two categories separately, Poor Law records reveal the extent to which the workhouse served a variety of useful functions for sections of the city's poor, not least of which was an element of control in their daily lives. In defiance of the core principles of the Poor Law and despite the repeated attempts on the part of the authorities to control what many considered as a massive abuse of the system, many people used it as a temporary place of shelter on arrival in the city or when there were no alternatives, as somewhere to return to on a regular basis, or as a place to spend the night before heading out into the city during the day. Sometimes through necessity brought about through pressure of numbers, and sometimes through choice, the inmates of Belfast workhouse used its spaces in ways that the architects of the Poor Law never intended. They increasingly made choices, utilised the workhouse as suited them and resisted the attempts of the Poor Law to differentiate between the 'deserving' and the 'undeserving' poor, thus using the spaces of the workhouse in ways that represented a significant challenge to the underpinning principles of welfare in late-nineteenth-century Ireland.

---

55  *Belfast News-Letter*, 9 Mar. 1885.

# 6
# Levelling Up the Lower Deeps: Rural and Suburban Spaces at an Edwardian Asylum

*Gillian Allmond*

## Introduction

[T]he hospital and villas soon to be ready for use, may to the superficial glance seem to aim at a higher standard of hygienic efficiency than is required, especially when compared with the housing of many of the poor in the slums of our great cities. But a little reflection will show the short sightedness of this notion. One of the great social reforms of our time is the effort to solve this very problem of the housing of the poor. We should seek to level up the lower deeps of social life and not to sink down to their degraded and unlovely characteristics.

William Graham, Belfast District Lunatic Asylums, annual report, 1911, pp xi–xii

In this revealing passage from a 1911 annual report, William Graham, the medical superintendent of Purdysburn public asylum for the insane near Belfast (known as Purdysburn Villa Colony), offered a veiled apology for the high level of provision made for the insane poor in a facility which was, after all, financed by the ratepayers and for whose managers and administrators economy was a guiding principle. Graham contrasted the 'hygienic efficiency' of the new buildings with the slums of Britain and Ireland while making an exhortation to 'level up' society, to bring the poor up to the living

---

I would like to acknowledge the assistance of Belfast Health and Social Care Trust, particularly Raymond Hamilton of Knockbracken Healthcare Park, for access to the buildings and archives at Purdysburn.

standards of the better off.[1] At first glance, this passage seems to be little more than a justification for the expense of providing comfortable living conditions for the mentally ill but the dichotomy that is set up here between the 'degraded and unlovely' slums and the 'hygienic efficiency' of the asylum expresses a distinctively Victorian/Edwardian spatial classification, and hints at a cultural context in which the mental, the physical and the moral were closely bound together. This chapter will tease apart some of the resonances of Graham's statement and will begin by setting the public health context in Belfast c.1900 before moving to wider discourses which cast 'the city', and particularly urban slums, as centres of disease and infection to which the rural/agricultural and rural/suburban spaces of the asylum provided a healthful counterpoint. This will be followed by an analysis of the writings of medical superintendent William Graham which will set out the connections he makes between poverty, environment and mental health.[2] Finally, cultural context and materiality will be brought together in an examination of the villa buildings of Purdysburn asylum to determine how they were understood as morally, mentally and physically therapeutic spaces that entailed an elevation of working class practices to meet bourgeois norms.

## Public health and housing in Belfast

In the Victorian and Edwardian periods, Belfast underwent an unprecedented period of industrial expansion accompanied by population growth, driven by the linen, shipbuilding and engineering industries. The city (achieving this status in 1888) expanded from a population of 75,000 people in 1841 to 387,000 in 1911, a fivefold increase. Although this expansion was undoubtedly accompanied by considerable feelings of civic pride, expressed and engendered by the ostentatious new buildings constructed in the city (such as the City Hall constructed between 1898 and 1906), significant concerns remained about the city's infrastructure and material fabric and their relationship to public health.[3]

---

1 'Levelling up' was a term coined in this period in relation to the provision of social housing. Better-off workers were to move into the model dwellings provided by social reform organisations, leaving their former accommodation for poorer workers and thus ultimately improving housing for all. See Richard Dennis, 'The geography of Victorian values: philanthropic housing in London 1840–1900' in *Journal of Historical Geography*, xv, no. 1 (1989), pp 40–54.
2 In Graham's writings, the word 'environment' is used to refer broadly to surroundings, including social surroundings, and lifestyle, rather than simply physical or natural setting, but this chapter will focus on the implications of his understanding of environment for the physical fabric and interior spaces of asylum buildings.
3 *Dictionary of Irish Architects*, available at www.dia.ie (accessed 13 May 2018).

It is generally held that the housing conditions in Belfast were better than in other areas of Britain and Ireland at the end of the nineteenth century and this is thought to be because Belfast's industrial growth came at a relatively late period, when building regulations were already alleviating the housing problems of a previous era.[4] Belfast was in a much better state with regard to housing at the end of the century than Dublin, with only 46 per cent of tenements being of four rooms or fewer (as opposed to 79 per cent in Dublin) and 1 per cent of tenements being of one room (as opposed to 37 per cent in Dublin).[5] Nonetheless, Belfast's rapid growth meant that overcrowding and insanitary conditions were common, and, although newer housing was generally of good quality, older housing in courts and alleyways nearer the city centre was frequently found to be of an unacceptable standard.[6] An 1898 report on the sanitary condition of Belfast records that the city surveyor's department 'has had a great deal to do in the way of destruction, by sweeping away slums and opening out congested areas, and there is no reason to suppose this work is yet at an end'.[7]

The homes of the poor were a concern, not only because they affected the health of the poor, but because they were sources of disease that compromised the health of all. In 1898, the infectious diseases of most concern in Belfast were diphtheria, typhoid and 'phthisis', or pulmonary tuberculosis, Belfast being particularly badly affected by the last two. The belief that typhoid was spread by 'sewer gases' – air escaping from drains – was beginning to subside, but alternative theories, such as the idea that germs were transferred into the atmosphere from infected soil 'saturated with the percolations from defective drains, or pervious ashpits', continued to place fresh, clean air at the heart of public health.[8] The spread of diphtheria was attributed to the crowding together of the 'poorer classes' and the 'lighting, ventilation and overcrowding' regulations with regard to schools were thought to be as yet insufficient. Tuberculosis was considered a disease particularly associated with the dwelling houses of the poor, where spitting

---

4 F.H.A. Aalen, 'Public housing in Ireland, 1880–1921' in *Planning Perspectives*, ii (1987), p. 189.
5 Ruth McManus, 'Suburban and urban housing in the twentieth century' in *Proceedings of the Royal Irish Academy: Archaeology, Culture, History, Literature*, cxi, sect. C, *special issue: domestic life in Ireland* (2011), p. 260.
6 Aalen, 'Public housing in Ireland', p. 189; E. Jones, 'Late Victorian Belfast: 1850–1900' in J.C. Beckett and R.E. Glassock, *Belfast: the origin and growth of an industrial city* (London, 1967), pp 109–19. 'In the Belfast slums' in *British Medical Journal*, i (2 Feb. 1907), p. 283 refers to newspaper reports on Belfast slums which raise feelings of 'disgust, horror, dread, and anger'.
7 F.W. Lockwood, 'The sanitary administration of Belfast (1898)' in *Proceedings of the Institute of Sanitary Engineers* (1898), pp 36–58.
8 Ibid., pp 52–53.

and poor cleaning practices distributed the bacillus, which was best combated by direct sunlight and 'free oxygen'.[9] Discourses of public health located communicable diseases in lower-class housing, attributing their spread, at least partly, to the ignorance and unhygienic practices of the poor. Disease was to be addressed by education of the poor into more cleanly habits and by paternalistic legislation to regulate the spaces in which they lived, worked and were educated.

## Degenerationism, eugenics and social reform

The public health issues that were being addressed in Belfast can be regarded as part of a wider discourse that constituted the urban poor and their environment as centres of disease. In some senses this relationship was painted as symbiotic: the poor were mentally, morally and physically unwell because of their poor environment, and their poor environment was, at least partially, the result of their mental, moral and physical weaknesses. Fears about racial decline and degeneration, excessive reproduction among the working classes and decadence among the upper classes began to achieve coherence in the new racial science of eugenics, which sought to promote the 'best specimens' of every class, those exhibiting 'health, energy, ability, manliness and [a] courteous disposition' and to limit, by social censure, the breeding of less favoured individuals for the good of the 'race as a whole'.[10] However, the proponents of reform in the big cities, coming often from an evangelical perspective, represented a different approach, sometimes complementary to the discourse of degenerationism and eugenics but whose emphasis was on environmental progress. It was hoped that improvements in housing and in the general urban environment would address the problems of poverty, disease, social unrest and crime by improving the health of the poor.

The 1880s, in which degenerationist ideology began to develop, also witnessed a greater urgency in the desire to deal with poverty due to a renewed economic crisis. This coupled with a growth in the tabloid press and increased literacy provided fertile ground for the literature of 'social exploration', which saw adventurers in a colonial mould voyaging into 'unknown territories' to provide the reader with sensationalist and visceral accounts of poverty and moral decline in the slums.[11] The language of the late-nineteenth-century

---

9 Ibid., p. 54.
10 F. Galton, 'Eugenics: its definition, scope and aims' in *American Journal of Sociology*, x, no. 1 (1904), pp 1–25.
11 Sally Ledger and Roger Luckhurst, *The fin de siècle: a reader in cultural history, c.1880–1900* (2000), pp 25–26.

social explorer used some striking imagery to conceptualise the poor and their environment. The slums were stinking, full of 'poisonous and malodorous gases', without air, water or light, where 'the sun never penetrates', they were dirty and 'swarming with vermin'. The buildings were overcrowded and fragile, lacking solidity, tottering, toppling and broken down. Such an environment rendered the inhabitants passive, lacking in energy, miserable, unable to resist the temptations of drink and vice, whether crime, promiscuity, prostitution or incest. The poor were compared to animals that 'herd together', like 'brute beasts', sometimes literally sharing their accommodation with pigs or other creatures.[12] At a time of unprecedented expansion in the British empire, leading to a saturation of culture with the forms and symbols of imperialism, the poor were compared to racialised 'others', at the bottom of a hierarchy which characterised them as 'uncivilised', physically stunted, of unclean habits, animal-like, depressed and despairing. 'Darkest England' was equated with a malarial swamp from which issued foul and fetid air that threatened to infect all around with disease. By contrast, escape was symbolised as emergence from the darkness of an overgrown forest into the light.[13] The rural/urban dyad became, at this period, a cultural trope in which health was correlated with the fresh air and open spaces of the countryside and disease with the industrialisation and slum living of the city.

These two approaches, the eugenicists advocating reproductive control and segregation of the 'unfit' and the social hygienists who linked the physical deterioration of the poor to the unwholesome environment, ultimately came together in strategies of social classification which organised the withdrawal of groups such as the insane and 'mentally defective' to idealised hygienic spaces, in the hope of the subsequent resocialisation of the rehabilitated.[14] Purdysburn Villa Colony, constructed between 1902 and 1913,[15] made tangible the desire to provide a place of light, air and hygiene for the mentally ill, in contrast to the dirt, fumes and darkness of the city, and it is notable that just as Belfast was Ireland's only fully industrialised city it was also the site of its only agricultural colony for the insane.

---

12   Andrew Mearns and London Congregational Union, *The bitter cry of outcast London: an inquiry into the conditions of the abject poor* (1883).
13   William Booth, *In darkest England, and the way out* (1890).
14   Nikolas Rose, *The psychological complex: psychology, politics and society in England 1869–1939* (London, 1985), pp 82–88.
15   Existing buildings on the site were used for patients until the new colony was built. Work began in 1902, and four villas (to designs by Graeme Watt & Tulloch) were completed by 1906. The remaining buildings (a further six villas, a hospital, recreation hall, admin block, laundry, mortuary and churches) were all constructed between 1909 and 1913 to designs by G.T. Hine, Belfast District Lunatic Asylum management committee minutes, (1896–1913) P.R.O.N.I., HOS/28/1/1/6-11.

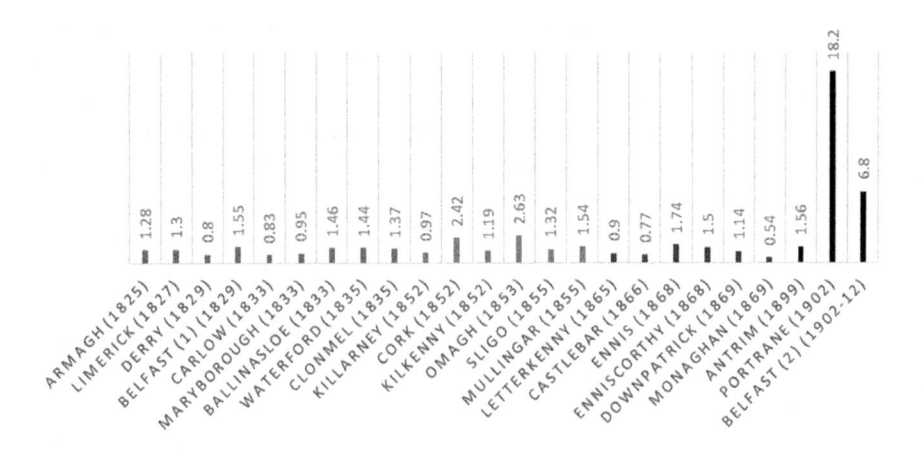

6.1 District Lunatic Asylums in Ireland and their distances
from nearest urban centres
(List of asylums and dates of opening taken from Markus Reuber, 'State and private lunatic asylums in Ireland: medics, fools and maniacs (1600–1900)', Ph.D. thesis, University of Cologne, 1994. Linear distances obtained from Google Maps)

Purdysburn was the second public asylum to be built in Belfast, the first opening in 1829 with accommodation for 104.[16] A series of Acts culminating in the Lunacy (Ireland) Act 1821 initiated the construction of 24 district asylums, which were constructed in three main phases, 1825–35, 1852–55 and 1865–69, with only three built after 1870: Holywell, Portrane and Purdysburn.[17] The majority of asylums were situated a mile or less from the nearest urban centre, within easy walking distance (Cork and Omagh were slightly further, at a mile and a half) (see Figure 6.1). The two great exceptions to this came during the late phase of asylum building after 1900 and are Portrane, which was a new asylum for Dublin, and Purdysburn. Even giving credit for rapid urban expansion during this era in Belfast, the asylum was situated at a considerable distance from the city centre where it was not easily accessible by rail or foot and was beyond the reach of the tram system, in a marked shift from the previous norm.

16 *Dictionary of Irish Architects*. Ireland thus became the first country in Europe to construct a complete public asylum network and was well in advance of England and Scotland which legislated in 1845 and 1857 respectively.
17 Asylums for Lunatic Poor (Ireland) Act 1817 (57 Geo. III c. cvi); Lunatic Asylums (Ireland) Act 1820 (1 Geo. IV c. xcviii); (Lunacy (Ireland) Act 1821 (1 & 2 Geo. IV c. xxxiii).

While most other asylums in Ireland followed the pattern of nineteenth-century 'fringe belt' development,[18] in which hospitals, schools and other institutional buildings were constructed on large plots at a short distance from the town centre where land was cheaper and more freely available, Purdysburn is situated so far from the city that the intervening land has only been developed for housing in the last few decades. Claire Hickman has noted that from at least the early nineteenth century, the contemplation of nature was associated with the elevation of mood, tranquillity, order and virtue and asylums were usually sited with access to the outdoors and to therapeutic views as a prime consideration.[19] However, the location of Purdysburn, relative to earlier asylum sites, suggests the intensification over time of ideology informing the spatial segregation of the insane poor together with an increasing and deepening consciousness of urban spaces as detrimental to physical and mental health. The colony asylum was situated on an estate of around 500 acres, with working farm, dairy and arable fields, another factor that pushed it well into Belfast's rural hinterland, in contrast to the original walled asylum of 1829 which extended to only some 45 acres.[20] The increased acreage per patient, almost doubling in the transfer to Purdysburn, represented a qualitative change, embedding the asylum within a rural/agricultural landscape in which access to the outdoors was intended to form a much more central part in the treatment of mental disease.

## William Graham and Purdysburn Villa Colony

Despite extensions in the 1850s and 1890s, the original Belfast asylum was hopelessly overcrowded by the end of the century, numbers of insane having roughly quadrupled in Ireland since the introduction of the asylum system,[21] and its radial, K-plan, similar to that of a prison, with accommodation arranged in cells and with bars on the windows,[22] had come to seem

---

18 J.W.R. Whitehand, 'British urban morphology: the Conzenian tradition' in *Urban Morphology*, v, no. 2 (2001), pp 103–09.
19 Clare Hickman, 'Cheerful prospects and tranquil restoration: the visual experience of landscape as part of the therapeutic regime of the British asylum, 1800–60' in *History of Psychiatry*, xx, issue 4 (2009), pp 425–41; Clare Hickman, *Therapeutic landscapes: a history of English hospital gardens since 1800* (Manchester, 2013).
20 Belfast District Lunatic Asylum, annual report 1921. The estate when originally purchased consisted of 295 acres but further additions were made to the site over the years as nearby land became available.
21 Damien Brennan, *Irish insanity* (Abingdon, 2014), pp 123–24.
22 'Front elevation and sections of the Belfast District Lunatic Asylum', 12 Mar. 1827, P.R.O.N.I., T1681/1; Image of Belfast Asylum by Robert French, in Lawrence Photograph Collection held by National Museum of Ireland (L_CAB_00048).

outdated.[23] The small amount of land attached to the asylum did not give the opportunities for outdoor recreation and work that were now required and industrial development was creeping ever closer as Belfast expanded. William Graham, the medical superintendent of the asylum, was influenced by reports of German asylums built on a colony principle, in which the layout followed a bourgeois suburban model with separate villas forming the majority of the accommodation, and supplementing central hospital, recreation hall and administration buildings.[24] Environmentalist discourses had informed asylum construction from the first half of the nineteenth century, but these were now given a new emphasis by degenerationist and social reformist thinking which saw light, air and hygiene as guiding principles in the creation of therapeutic facilities. Following Graham's advice, the decision was taken to build a new asylum on the 'villa colony principle' in 1901.[25] Graham was closely involved in the design of the new villa colony, discussing his ideas with the architects on a regular basis.[26] He also published informative accounts of his thinking in relation to the causes and prevention of insanity in the Belfast District Lunatic Asylum annual reports which position him squarely within contemporary discourses on public health.[27]

Numbers of insane increased relentlessly during the second half of the nineteenth century and Graham was not alone in believing that this increase came from the ranks of the poor, stating that mental illness 'increases as we descend the scale of culture'.[28] He stated that the bulk of mental derangement was due to neglect or violation of 'fundamental hygienic laws', because the

23 R. Delargy, 'The history of the Belfast District Lunatic Asylum 1829–1921' (Ph.D. thesis, University of Ulster, 2002). Delargy states incorrectly that Belfast Asylum was not built on a K-plan (p. 33). Purdysburn Villa Colony operated in parallel with the original asylum for some years, but the intention was always that it would be a replacement, and the old asylum was demolished in the 1920s.

24 Belfast District Lunatic Asylum, annual report 1900 – the term 'Villa Colony' adopted by Graham appears to have been first used in a medical context in a report on German and other continental asylums by the Lancashire Asylums Board. See *Report of a deputation appointed to visit asylums on the Continent with recommendations regarding the building of a new (sixth) Lancashire Asylum* (Preston, 1900).

25 Management committee minutes, 11 Feb. 1901.

26 Management committee minutes, 1900–12.

27 Following his medical studies in Belfast in the 1880s, Graham received further medical training in diseases of the mind in Edinburgh possibly under the tutelage of Thomas Smith Clouston, who was clearly a strong influence on Graham's thought concerning heredity and environment. 'Obituary of William Graham' in *Journal of Mental Science*, lxiv (1918), pp 114–15; Margaret S. Thompson, 'The wages of sin: the problem of alcoholism and general paralysis in nineteenth-century Edinburgh' in W.F. Bynum, R. Porter and M. Shepherd (eds), *The anatomy of madness: essays in the history of psychiatry*, iii: *The asylum and its psychiatry* (London, 1988), pp 316–37.

28 Annual report, 1902, p. 10.

poor were seen to live in unhealthy surroundings and to behave in ways which were detrimental to health.[29] Among the poorer classes there had been an ongoing process of degeneration in those whose food and environment were defective, producing the 'thin, stunted, anaemic figures that populate the lower quarters of our great cities'.[30] Graham found that the majority (70 per cent) of the patients who entered the asylum were dirty and unkempt, 'their bodies the happy hunting-ground of a myriad parasites'.[31] He proposed education in the 'predisposing and exciting causes' of madness and also the 'rules and principles of a preventive kind' and suggested that children should be trained in hygienic principles with all schools providing a gymnasium and a swimming-bath so that the body could be developed to a state of efficiency and beauty.[32] Good hygiene included the 'beneficial and invigorating effect of judicious exercise in the open air' which had the additional benefit of allowing the deleterious products of respiration to be removed from buildings by natural ventilation.[33] The connection between the mental and the physical was such that an illness which appeared in one generation as a physical weakness or disease, could reappear in another as an insane predisposition. Graham contended, therefore, that when the guardians of public health addressed themselves to physical diseases such as tuberculosis, they were also addressing themselves to 'ills of the mind'.[34] He saw fatigue and depression as most common 'in our great cities' and held that 'half the existing insanity could be banished or contracted to inconsiderable limits, were the hygienic conditions in the home, the school and the factory what they ought to be'.[35] He suggested that 'the over-crowded tenement houses should be replaced by buildings in which proper hygiene and pure air would enable men and women to live decently' making explicit a link between a healthy environment and morality.[36] Utilitarian work in which the patient was brought into contact with 'reality' was seen to be the best kind of therapy and contact with nature gave steadiness, poise and balance, the soil being 'a permanent source of recreative energy'.[37] Work in the open air was the ideal employment for the mentally disturbed because Nature represented 'solidarity, reality, order and cohesion', expressing the higher rationality that he wished his patients to aspire to.[38] Graham asserted that the villa colony

29 Annual report, 1900, p. 8.
30 Annual report, 1901, p. 11.
31 Annual report, 1901, p. 12.
32 Annual report, 1902, p. 12.
33 Annual report, 1901, p. 19.
34 Annual report, 1910, p. ix.
35 Annual report, 1905, p. xiii; annual report, 1902, p. 11.
36 Annual report, 1905, p. xvii.
37 Annual report, 1908, p. xiii.
38 Annual report, 1911, p. xi.

system brought the patient into the 'healthy currents of normal social life', the inherently sane and healthful practices of bourgeois living lifting the patients above the unhealthy lifestyle of the poor.

### Hygienic efficiency at Purdysburn

In what material ways did the villa colony at Purdysburn exhibit the hygienic efficiency identified by William Graham in 1911? We have seen that contemporary social exploration literature pointed to darkness, odours and lack of ventilation, cramped and overcrowded conditions and dirt as the besetting issues of working-class housing. Turning to two of these issues, darkness and lack of ventilation, an analysis of the villa buildings of Purdysburn colony demonstrates how they exemplified good practice with relation to provision of light and air and therefore provided a wholesome environment for patients from a physical, moral and mental point of view.[39] The villas did not differ greatly, except in scale, from bourgeois domestic houses of the period, and certainly there were no complex ventilation or heating systems of the kind that were sometimes introduced into hospitals.[40] The villa buildings illustrate what was then thought of as a hygienic *domestic* environment and suggest that the 'levelling up' of the lifestyles and daily practices of the poor to more closely resemble bourgeois living conditions was an important part of the therapeutic intention of the villa design.

The 'bird's-eye view' of the asylum in Figure 6.2 was published in an annual report in 1921, nine years after the main phase of asylum building was completed. The picture emphasises, by its perspective, the huge spatial expanse of the asylum estate, with buildings dispersed and broken up into individual residences that resembled a suburban housing estate, rather than the monolithic structures of a traditional asylum, enabling maximum access on all sides to light and air. The almost idyllic pastoral scene of farmland interspersed with hedges and mature trees gives no hint of the nearby city from which most of the patients would have come, and readers were invited to assume that the air is fresh and healthful. The buildings were situated on the high points of the rolling landscape where they would be most likely to benefit from the movement of air, allowing for thorough ventilation.

---

39 Villas 2–9 were built to the same design with a slight variation consisting of the addition of a 'sanitary annexe' to villas 4, 5, 7, 8 and 9. G. Allmond, 'Domesticating the asylum: light and darkness at the Purdysburn Villa Colony' (M.Sc. thesis, Queen's University Belfast, 2012). Villas 10 and 11 differ in design and are not considered here.
40 Notably the plenum system at the Royal Victoria Hospital, Belfast of 1903. Reyner Banham, *The architecture of the well-tempered environment* (London, 1984), pp 75–83.

6.2 Bird's-eye view of Purdysburn villa colony (detail)
(Belfast District Lunatic Asylum annual report, 1921)

The most common wind direction in the north of Ireland is south-westerly, with wind having a westerly component for 50 per cent of the time (wind conditions being still or having an easterly component the remainder of the time).[41] The villa buildings were orientated roughly north to south, making them easy to ventilate by natural means through the opening of windows on both sides of the building. This allowed air to enter on the windward side and exit on the leeward side having brought with it the vitiated air within the room itself. The central dayrooms and dormitories on ground and first floors allowed for maximum benefit from cross-ventilation, the breeze being able to sweep across the room and out the other side (Figure 6.3). In rooms, such as storerooms, which were not occupied by patients, there was generally only one window, cross-ventilation not being thought necessary. The WCs were extremely well-ventilated, with large windows in both outer walls achieving a measure of cross-ventilation, the lack of partitions also assisting with this. However, the rooms ventilated most easily by the prevailing wind were the living and sleeping rooms rather than the WCs, the windows of which face north and east, suggesting that it was the respiration of patients that was the major concern rather than emanations from the sewage pipes. Foul air issuing from the lungs was blamed for numerous ailments including TB and

---

41 'Climatological memorandum 143', *The climate of Northern Ireland* (Bracknell, 1983), pp 14–18.

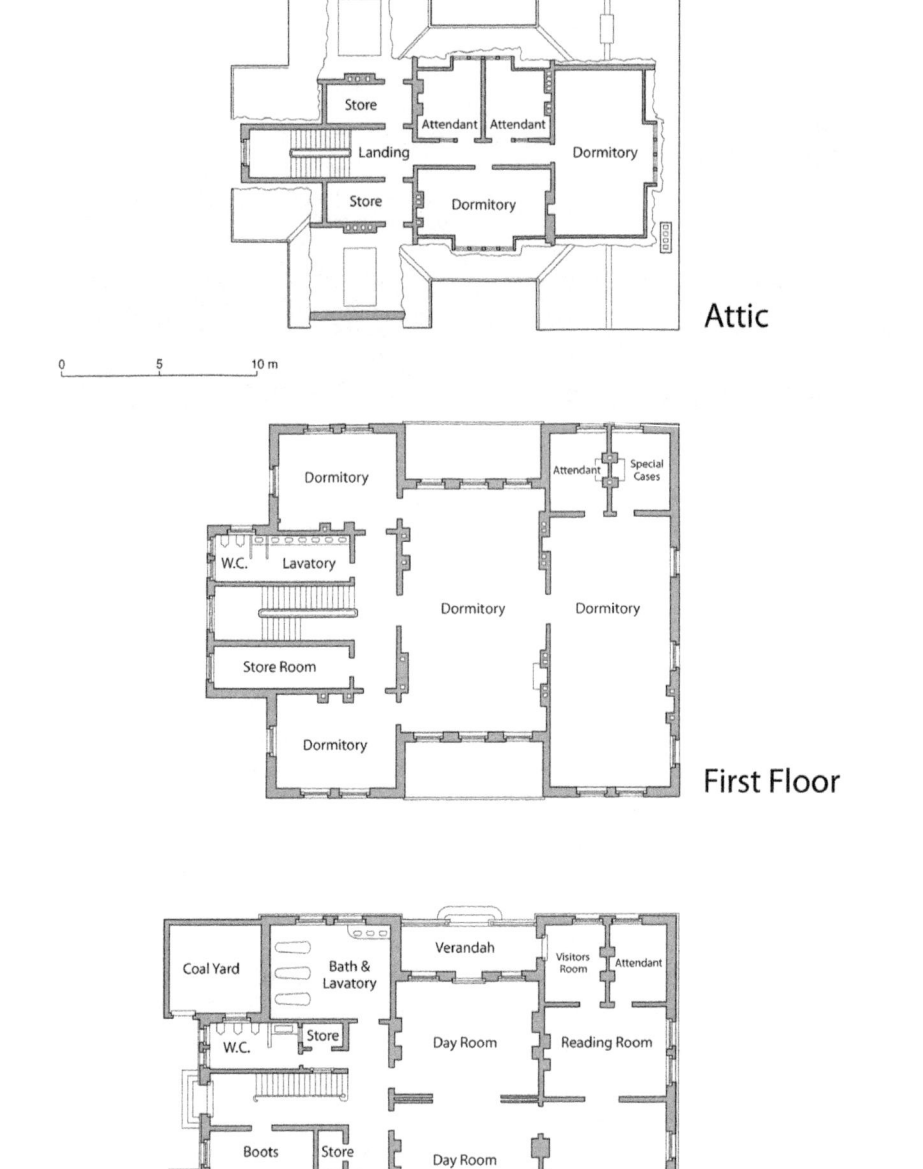

6.3 Ground-, first- and attic-floor plans of Purdysburn villa for chronic/recovering patients (redrawn from original plans)

diphtheria, caused by harmful microbes suspended in the breath or exhaled carbon dioxide.[42]

A sanitary annexe, which was imposed on five out of the first eight villas to be built, against William Graham's wishes, isolated the WCs on both ground and first floors to a greater degree than in the original design and had better cross-ventilation. The sanitary annexe was a standard feature of hospital design and suggests that the management committee remained fearful of the potential for disease to issue from 'sewer gases' while Graham was more concerned about destruction to the architectural symmetry of the building that the annexe entailed, which he felt destroyed the homelike character of the villas.[43] A section diagram of the 'Deluge Adamant' WC that was fitted in the villas,[44] shows a trap and water line that would have prevented any seepage of gases from the pipework back into the building.[45]

The ceilings of the rooms themselves were high (12 feet on ground and first floors, 10 feet in attics) in both living and sleeping areas and allowed for a greater cubic area of air within the rooms and a reservoir of fresh air for the patients below, as the warmed, vitiated air rose. Villa fireplaces were not only a means of heating the asylum but also provided ventilation by sucking foul air out of the chimney and drawing fresh air into the room by convection.[46] Each room was fitted with at least one fireplace and associated flue and the exaggerated height of the external chimneys, reminiscent of tall Tudor chimneystacks, while being a fashionable feature at this period, also demonstrably expels smoke and the vitiated products of human respiration from within the asylum rooms at a height substantially above the level of the building, where it could not cause harm. Villa rooms were further ventilated by means of brass gratings fitted in the upper section of the chimney breast which would take up warm air as it rose within the rooms. No villa had a cellar or basement, as these had begun to seem unhealthy and undesirable,[47] but all the villas were built on a concrete foundation which would have prevented the rise of infected ground air and/or damp into the building. Further ventilation

---

42 G. Townsend, 'Airborne toxins and the American house, 1865–1895' in *Winterthur portfolio*, xxiv (1989), p. 29.
43 Management committee minutes (1902), p. 332.
44 Builder's specification for villas 2 and 3 (1902), P.R.O.N.I., LA/7/29/CB/22.
45 G.H. Bibby, *The planning of lunatic asylums* (London, 1896), p. lix.
46 A popular American magazine commented in 1886 that we would be 'healthier and happier if we heated ourselves with open fires [rather than stoves], and in the course of generations would have appreciably and measurably more perfect forms, more active brains, clearer minds and better morals'. E.Y. Robbins, 'How to warm our houses' in *Popular Science Monthly*, xxx (1886), p. 239, quoted in Townsend, 'Airborne toxins', p. 32.
47 Dr Benjamin Richardson's influential 1876 pamphlet 'Hygeia: a city of health' prescribed that every house should be built on a 'solid bed of concrete' and that cellars should be dispensed with to be replaced by a ventilating space.

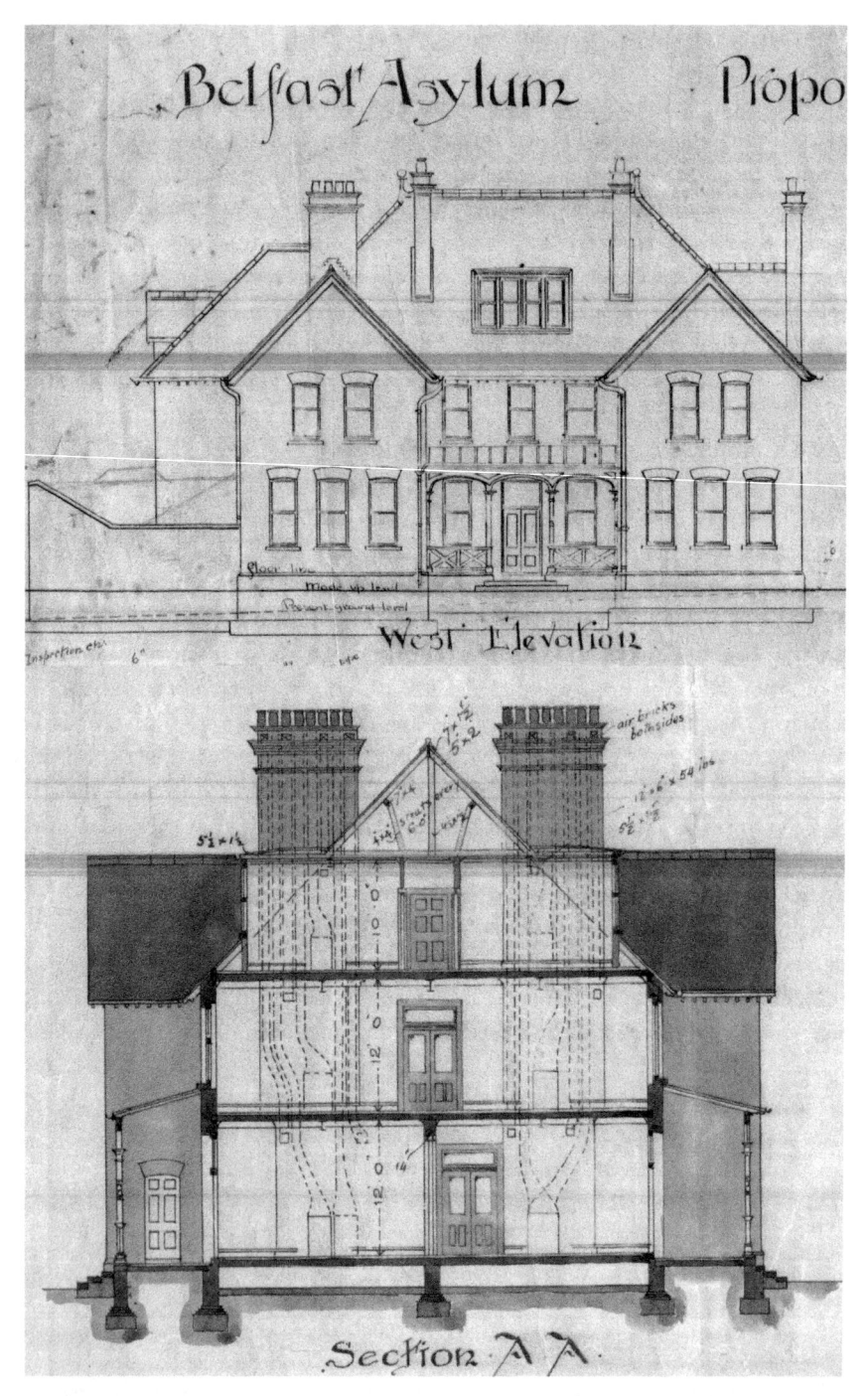

6.4 Elevation and cross-section of Purdysburn villa showing fireplaces and flues. (Estates Department, Knockbracken Healthcare Park)

grilles were placed in the outer walls of the space between foundation and ground floor to allow noxious fumes and damp to escape from this danger area close to the ground. Grilles were also placed on the outer wall at eaves level to ventilate the wall cavity. The drawing at Figure 6.4 illustrates the architects' concern for the proper ventilation of asylum spaces, showing the flues leading from the grilles within the rooms and the fireplaces. Ventilation grilles within the rooms had their own separate flues leading out to the chimneys expelling foul air at as high a level as possible.

The villa buildings at the asylum were also constructed in order to gain maximum benefit from natural light and were fitted with large (8 ft 7 in × 4 ft), sliding sash windows. Because of concerns for patient safety, these windows were fitted with stops that prevented them from being opened more than five inches.[48] The windows were not otherwise distinguishable from their domestic counterparts, although they eschewed the prevailing taste of the period for small-paned/stained glass which may have restricted the entry of light. Although Ireland's climate is generally cloudy, the most usual sky conditions are partial cloud, with natural light coming from the direction of the sun (when the sky is fully overcast, natural light is distributed evenly about the zenith).[49] Villas were double-fronted with glass-roofed verandahs facing west and east in order to receive the benefit of both rising and setting sun. This suggests that the villas were constructed with the daily routine of the patients in mind. As most patients would be out at work during the day, the verandahs were positioned to benefit from the sun during the morning and evening when the patients would return to the villas from their daily work in the workshops, laundry or farm, rather than being south-facing. The facade to the west was privileged over that to the east, with more windows at ground-floor level, and two of the three dayrooms faced in this direction, best lit during the evening when the patients were dining or resting. On average, the proportion of window to floor space, 23 per cent in living rooms, was considerably greater than the building regulations required for domestic houses at this period (10 per cent).[50] The scullery was situated at the west front of the building, where it would be well-lit for preparation of the evening meal, and the washing facilities were at the east side of the building, best lit during the morning ablutions. The attic, which might ordinarily be considered one of the darkest areas of a domestic house, was fitted with very large and wide dormer windows which provided an average proportion of window to floor space of 25 per cent, opening up the attic rooms to light and air. The cistern rooms and

---

48  'Builder's specification for villas 2 and 3' (1902).
49  Ralph Galbraith Hopkinson, P. Petherbridge and James Longmore, *Daylighting* (London, 1966), p. 23.
50  Hermann Muthesius, *The English House*, ed. Dennis Sharp (London, 1979), p. 76.

uninhabited attic spaces beneath the eaves were to be finished with whitewash, a hygienic measure, as they were less well-lit and ventilated and hence likely repositories for dirt, foul air and germs (Figure 6.3).[51] The two main first-floor dormitories were somewhat less well lit (18 per cent), which could be attributed to the stimulating qualities of light, and the need to keep sleeping areas darker particularly during the summer months, the asylum regime calling for patients to retire to bed at 7.30 p.m.[52] Nonetheless, light was also seen as a disinfectant; Florence Nightingale, for example, encouraged the regular 'sunning' of rooms in both hospital and home,[53] and there was no diminution of the size of the dormitory windows, which would also have provided views to raise the spirits of the bed bound.[54]

The villas also show a concern for the passage of light through interior spaces. On the ground and first floors most doors into living and sleeping spaces were half-glazed, with transom lights over, increasing the movement of light between rooms and allowing light to be conducted through the building as the sun moved around the villa. Transom lights and glazed doors also enabled some of the less-well-lit spaces, such as the villa corridor, to receive secondary light. In addition, the transparency of the doors facilitated easier observation of patients, but a primary purpose of interior glazing was to introduce more light into interiors because of its health-giving properties. A corollary of this was that it gave patients a greater sense of freedom, increasing patient contentment and minimising disquiet.[55] The provision of plentiful light within the asylum was seen as an important factor in increasing 'cheerfulness', as light operated on the mentally ill by elevating mood[56] and could eliminate the dark corners and shadows that were troubling to disordered minds.[57]

---

51 'Builder's specification for villas 2 and 3' (1902). The instruction to whitewash garrets was later deleted, although the instruction to whitewash cistern rooms remained.
52 County Borough of Belfast, *Special regulations for the management of Belfast Mental Hospital made in pursuance of the Mental Treatment Act (NI) 1932* (Belfast, 1944). Although these regulations date to a later period, early bedtimes appear to have been a feature of institutional life for many decades.
53 Florence Nightingale, *Notes on nursing: what it is, and what it is not* (London, 1860), p. 16.
54 See Hickman, *Therapeutic landscapes*.
55 Ernest W. White, 'The presidential address, delivered at the sixty-second annual meeting of the Medico-Psychological Association, held in London on July 16th, 1903', *Journal of Mental Science*, xlix (1903), p. 590.
56 Forbes Winslow, *Light: its influence on life and health* (London, 1867), pp 4–5.
57 Dr T.W. McDowall, 'French retrospect', *Journal of Mental Science*, xxxii (1886), pp 108–18; G.H. Bibby, *The housing of pauper lunatics* (London, 1895), pp 97–98.

## Conclusion

As we saw in the opening quotation, the asylum at Purdysburn was explicitly an attempt to improve the living conditions of the insane poor and remove them from an urban context which was thought damaging to their health, mentally, physically and morally. The city was considered threatening because it was dark and dirty, but also because interior and exterior spaces were insufficiently segregated, the proper categorisation of persons giving way to an incestuous jumble that was concealed in the courts and entries which were hidden from the gaze of the proper authorities. Despite Belfast's relatively superior housing stock, the power of the 'festering slums' trope was clearly considerable, and Graham refers continually to 'our great cities' as a concept with almost metaphorical power to act as both a symbol of advanced civilisation and the epitome of unhealthy living and moral depravity. When we analyse the spatial qualities of the asylum he built, its physical positioning and the character and arrangement of internal spaces, the nature of contemporary attitudes to urban/rural, health/illness and to middle class/working class is clarified and we can perceive a number of ways in which these concepts are mapped onto each other. As David Livingstone has pointed out, the aesthetics of hospital spaces 'articulat[e] the core values and beliefs of the medical profession' in a way that cannot always be understood through written sources alone.[58] The spatial segregation of the asylum to a site four miles distant from Belfast constituted a break with the past on two levels. The push into the countryside which had been set off against the asylum's greater inaccessibility suggests that the therapeutic power of rural environments acquired a further dimension in this period, that of sequestering the 'degenerate' insane with their hereditary defects at a safe distance from the city. At the same time, the increase in land available to patients and their greater access to the outdoors, through organised farm labour, recreational activities and separate villa buildings opening directly onto the grounds, suggests that the perception of rural spaces as healing was intensifying at this period. Purdysburn was both pushed into the countryside by fears of contamination associated with a reading of mental illness as hereditary and pulled into the countryside by a long-standing and intensifying understanding of rural spaces as therapeutic and urban spaces as detrimental to health. Chris Philo has queried whether, in England and Wales, 'degenerationist' thinking led to a downgrading of the importance attributed to the environment in the healing of mental illness.[59]

---

58 David N. Livingstone, *Putting science in its place: geographies of scientific knowledge* (Chicago, 2003), p. 66.
59 Chris Philo, *A geographical history of institutional provision for the insane from medieval times to the 1860s in England and Wales* (Lewiston, NY, 2004), p. 71.

However, the 'villa colony' approach to mental illness in Belfast (paralleled by similar developments in Scotland) demonstrates that, in some geographical regions, environment retained its central importance despite the challenges raised by ideologies emphasising the hereditary nature of mental illness.

Segregated from the unhealthy city, the villas at Purdysburn were configured as suburban spaces. At this period, as was typical of nineteenth-century industrial cities, Belfast's middle classes were moving out of the city centre to suburbs which were an 'embodiment of the picturesque with [their] intimations of a domesticated rusticity', leaving an uninhabited central area which was associated with 'monumentalism, modernity and power' and from which slums were to be ruthlessly cleansed.[60] Resembling a bourgeois housing estate of the kind that were springing up around Belfast, the individual villas were simplified versions of middle-class dwelling houses which would have exceeded the aspirations of the majority of the working classes in terms of their hygienic provision, including the relative proportion of window and room space, ceiling heights, concrete-sealed foundations, flushing WCs and plumbed bathrooms, the copious provision of ventilation grilles and fireplaces, the opening up of attic spaces to light and air and the situation and orientation of buildings in order to benefit from natural light and ventilation. Through this spatial configuration, asylum authorities implicitly advanced bourgeois lifestyles as addressing the moral, mental and physical weakness of the working classes, and by suburbanising the insane poor hoped to engender healthy and moral practices.

By contrast with the residents of suburbia, the inhabitants of urban spaces were viewed as animal-like, herding together without thought, listless and unable to resist the temptations of vice. The weakness provoked by their unhealthy environment could lead to transgressive sexual relations or dependency on alcohol or drugs and conversely plentiful air and light could provide the vitality which was the marker of health and gave the fortitude to resist the moral temptation which would lead inexorably to the decay of higher nature and mental decline. To Galton and the eugenicists that followed him, the 'wretched figures – crippled, blind, sick, paupers, lunatics, idiots, criminals – existing in such large proportions in the heart of our great cities were precisely those who manifested that weakness of vital energy which was the sure sign of a degenerate constitution'.[61] The poor were understood to be a source of insanity, which, like an infectious disease, threatened to spread out and contaminate the rest of society. Poverty was a nexus of environment and personal behaviour, and while the poor remained in their unhealthy

---

60 Simon Gunn, *The public culture of the Victorian middle class: ritual and authority in the English industrial city 1840–1914* (Manchester, 2000), pp 38–42.
61 Rose, *The psychological complex*, p. 73.

environment they were liable to be physically sick, morally weak and mentally vulnerable. Graham suggests that acquired weakness could be inherited and that therefore patients who were weakened by environment or immoral behaviour could pass on their insanity to future generations. But he further suggests a utopian get-out clause – that those who followed 'physiological laws' and lived in hygienic circumstances could potentially escape their hereditary fate. The patients who had already succumbed to illness were removed by the asylum system from their unhealthy, immoral, dirty and insanity-provoking urban spaces and were offered at Purdysburn an environment which could act therapeutically by 'levelling up' to a condition of mental health which was itself associated with moral propriety and physical wellness. Those who failed to recover were thereby sequestered from society where their hereditary taint could do no harm. The buildings of the asylum were partially a mute assertion of the dominance – physical, cultural and moral – of asylum authorities over the inhabitants, overwhelmingly of the labouring classes, whose cramped, dark and malodorous dwellings were thought to have contributed to their insanity and lack of moral self-control.[62] The villas were an attempt to inculcate bourgeois values, both aesthetic and hygienic, and bring into the moral light of day the hidden and shameful margins of Edwardian society from their degenerate and festering hiding-places.

Purdysburn asylum presents us with a cultural signpost for contemporary bourgeois fears about the decline and degeneration that were viewed as rife in the cities. The extra-urban spaces of the asylum map these concerns on several levels, sequestering the insane poor outside the city, providing a therapeutic rural/agricultural environment which expressed a level of continuity with earlier conceptions of environment as healing and addressed concerns about moral/mental/physical weakness that were intensifying in the Edwardian period. The rural/agricultural conceit of the asylum maps seamlessly onto the contemporary aspiration towards rural/suburban idealised spaces, allowing the rising middle classes to impress bourgeois norms on a threatening stratum of insane poor while maintaining an arm's-length detachment.

---

62 1911 census of Ireland.

# 7

# Locating Investigations into Suicidal Deaths in Urban Ireland, 1901–1915

## Georgina Laragy

### Introduction

Since medieval times until the early nineteenth century, suicides had been buried outside consecrated ground. This was a spatial expression of their status as outcasts from the community of the honourable dead. By the eighteenth century in England (there is little corresponding information for Ireland) there had been a decline in burials at crossroads and in unconsecrated ground: suicides were increasingly buried within the sacred spaces of the churchyard owing to legal verdicts that found them 'innocent' via temporary insanity.[1] After 1872 and the removal of forfeiture of criminals' goods and chattels, there were no statutory measures available to punish the suicide even though it remained a crime in Ireland until 1993.[2] Despite the fact that it was a crime without punishment, the coroner continued and continues to be responsible for inquiring into the context behind such deaths. A medico-legal process, concluded by a coroner's certificate, was and is required to register a death as suicide. This administrative, governmental process achieved spatial expression when sanitary reform began in earnest and when the office of the coroner became more professionalised.[3] While the coroner continued to be required to 'go to the Place where any be slain, or suddenly dead or wounded', in urban settings by the end of the nineteenth century bodies were often

---

1 G. Laragy, 'Suicide and insanity in post famine Ireland' in C. Cox and M. Luddy (eds), *Cultures of care in Irish medical history, 1750–1970* (Basingstoke, 2010), pp 80–84.
2 Forfeiture Act 1870 (33 & 34 Vict. c. xxiii).
3 Ian A. Burney, *Bodies of evidence: medicine and the politics of the English inquest, 1830–1926* (Baltimore, Md., 2000).

brought to the coroner instead.[4] Between 1901 and 1915, approximately 40 per cent of all inquests on suicides were held at the city morgue in Dublin.[5] The city authorities controlled the movement of certain dead bodies around the city by constructing a scientific and administrative space – the morgue – for the investigation of sudden death in Dublin. The professionalisation of the coroner's office acquired a spatial element. As Ian Burney notes, 'the pub-based inquest served as a kind of rallying point for a campaign to transform the spatial and conceptual grounds for public inquiry into death'.[6]

This chapter explores in detail a sample of suicide cases that occurred in Dublin during the period 1901 to 1915. It will reconstruct the lives and deaths of four suicides from approximately 127 identified using the Dublin Morgue registers and consider the role urban space played in their lives, but more particularly in the legal inquiry into their deaths. We will follow the suicide from their place of death on their various final journeys, via hospitals and morgues, towards their resting place. As Elizabeth Grosz states, 'the city in its particular geographical, architectural, spatializing, municipal arrangements is one particular ingredient in the social constitution of the body'.[7] This chapter examines the way in which the 'geographical, architectural, spatializing, municipal arrangements' constituted the *dead* body, specifically that body which had died by suicide. Using a micro-historical approach, I assess how, in a Victorian urban space, with its mobile and visible police constables, sudden death came to the attention of the authorities. I also question Émile Durkheim's assertion that urban suicides reflect the anonymity of city life, by exploring the social relationships in Irish cities during this period.[8] Finally, I examine where suicide inquests were held, a factor which was a product of existing medical and medico-legal facilities which also reveals attitudes to the dead body and its impact on the living in the Edwardian period.

Focusing on a small number of individual suicide case studies within a broader sample of 127 suicides from Dublin Morgue registers between 1901 and 1915, this chapter attempts what Lindsey Earner-Byrne calls 'A careful (re)construction of [individual stories] … [in order] … to highlight that the individual in history can be resurrected to heighten our historical understanding of broader patterns'.[9] The cases outlined here reveal common personal problems that appeared regularly in the testimony of those who

---

4 Matthew Dutton, *The office and authority of sheriffs, under-sheriffs, duties, county clerks and coroners in Ireland* (Dublin, 1721), p. 6.
5 National Archives of Ireland, Dublin Morgue registers, 1901–15.
6 Burney, *Bodies of evidence*, p. 81.
7 E. Grosz, 'Bodies-cities' in B. Colomina (ed.), *Sexuality and space* (New York, 1992), p. 248.
8 Émile Durkheim, *Suicide; a study in sociology* (London, 2001), p. 70.
9 Lindsey Earner-Byrne, 'The rape of Mary M.: a microhistory of sexual violence and moral

spoke at coroners' inquests on suicides – for example, relationship difficulties (be they marital or inter-generational), professional disappointments and insanity. In the aftermath of a suicide the various spaces between which living individuals as well as dead bodies moved can provide an overall picture of the private, public and scientific spaces that typified the 'contact and friction of city life' in the context of suicide.[10] These spaces include private family homes and various public locations that range from tenement steps and city streets to the more rationalised spaces of hospitals, morgues and cemeteries. In addition, this chapter will examine the role of 'place … [in] the generation of knowledge' through an assessment of the city morgue of Dublin between 1870 and 1915.[11]

## Durkheim, the city and suicide

While suicide remains largely unexplored in the context of Irish history, since the late nineteenth century it has been the subject of sustained sociological investigation, and from the 1980s historians working outside Ireland have explored this difficult subject in a range of contexts. Within these studies, place and space have been critical.[12] According to Durkheim, whose seminal work on suicide at the end of the nineteenth century has strongly influenced the historical and sociological scholarship on the subject to date, 'the social causes of suicide are … closely related to urban civilization and are most intense in these great centres … suicide is much more urban than rural'.[13] Earlier work by the Italian Enrico Morselli concluded that 'cities represent the active and progressive element, the instinct and daring pursuit of novelties, the ardour of scientific investigation by which the intellect is expanded … the contact and friction of city life will alone explain the preponderance of suicides amongst denizens of cities over those amongst country people'.[14] Morselli and Durkheim's work contain important implications for the study of suicide in an urban context, arguing as they do that the anonymity of city life led to social disconnection and isolation which in turn led to anomic suicide; however, neither man dealt with the role of space. City spaces were, for Durkheim and

redemption in 1920s Ireland' in *Journal of the History of Sexuality*, xxiv, no. 1 (2015), p. 78.
10  Enrico Morselli, *Suicide: an essay on comparative moral statistics* (New York, 1882), p. 169.
11  David. N. Livingstone, *Putting science in its place* (Chicago, 2010), p. 11.
12  Olive Anderson, *Suicide in Victorian and Edwardian England* (Oxford, 1987); G. Minois, *History of suicide: voluntary death in western culture* (Baltimore, Md., 1999); S. Morrissey, *Suicide and the body politic in Imperial Russia* (Cambridge, 2006); R. Bell, *We shall be no more* (Cambridge, Mass., 2012).
13  Durkheim, *Suicide*, pp 70, 353.
14  Morselli, *Suicide*, p. 169.

Morselli, merely the context of disconnected social relations, in contrast to the physical proximity in which many thousands of people lived and worked. By interrogating the physicality of urban space and the social characteristics of those spaces at the end of the nineteenth century – congestion, densely populated tenement dwellings, highly visible trading in streets and market squares – we can see perhaps that Grosz's argument is more useful in the context of suicide, that the 'the city can be seen ... as midway between the village and the state, sharing the interpersonal inter-relations of the village (on a neighborhood scale) and the administrative concerns of the state (hence the need for local government)'.[15] The interpersonal inter-relations of the village can be created by the demographic density of the city, space 'shapes physical action by its materiality' and physical proximity on a daily basis leads to knowledge about individuals' habits, movements and relationships.[16] Equally, the administrative concerns of dealing with public health, law and order and decency within the Victorian city led to questions of 'how death should be organised in an urban space'.[17] Grosz's theory of the city as a midway point between the village and the state has important implications when considering Durkheimian theory about urbanisation and suicide. The cases discussed below bear out the point that even large capital cities contained pockets of social and physical intimacy that can be missed by totalising theories about the nature of urban spaces. By considering the physicality of those spaces, we can reconstruct a much more nuanced set of social relations than Durkheim allowed for.[18]

## Dublin city suicides

On 9 January 1911, Eliza McKeon, a 37-year-old Dublin woman, was killed by her army-pensioner husband William after which he turned the knife on himself and committed suicide. Both bodies were found in one of the two

---

15 Grosz, 'Bodies-cities', reprinted in H. J. Nast and S. Pile (eds), *Places through the body* (London, 1998), p. 32.
16 Katrina Navickas, *Protest and the politics of space and place, 1789–1848* (Manchester, 2016), pp 15–16, quoted in Jonathan Jeffrey Wright's chapter, above.
17 A. Brown-May and S. Cooke, 'Death, decency and the dead-house: the city morgue in Colonial Melbourne' in *Provenance: The Journal of Public Record Office Victoria*, iii (2004), available at https://www.prov.vic.gov.au/index.php/explore-collection/provenance-journal/provenance-2004/death-decency-and-dead-house (accessed 27 Oct. 2017).
18 Howard Kushner and Claire Sterk have also disagreed with Durkheim's statement that modernisation automatically led to the social isolation he believed caused suicide. They point to the fact that suicides often occur in groups that are highly integrated into society, such as women and members of the military. Howard I. Kushner and Claire E. Sterk. 'The limits of social capital: Durkheim, suicide, and social cohesion' in *American Journal of Public Health*, xcv, no. 7 (2005), pp 1139–43.

rooms they rented at 9 Mary's Abbey on the north side of the River Liffey in Dublin. The house was listed as a first-class private dwelling, but the 7–9 rooms housed 18 people from six distinct families.[19] The house was next door to three 'ruin[ed]' buildings. In fact, seven out of the nine buildings on the street were 'uninhabited', suggesting a degree of physical decay in this city centre street, one block from the River Liffey. The evidence given at the inquest in January 1911 reveals that three months before the census was taken (March 1911) one of the 'households' or 'families' who lived at that address included Eliza and William McKeon, and Eliza's brother Peter Hughes. Mid-morning on 9 January both Eliza and her brother, who had risen around 4.30 a.m. to begin work at the nearby fish market, took naps. At some point Eliza woke or was woken and her husband had taken a knife to her throat and then his own. When Peter woke he discovered the bodies of his sister and brother-in-law. He alerted a police constable who was then on his beat at Capel Street, immediately adjacent to Mary's Abbey. Once the constable had assessed the scene he called an ambulance and both bodies were transferred to nearby Jervis Street Hospital (two blocks east from their home) 'where it was found that they had passed beyond human aid'.[20] The following day (10 January) an inquest was held at the City Morgue on Store Street by Dr Louis Byrne, City Coroner, where William was found to have been temporarily insane at the time of the tragedy.[21]

Although Paul Fyfe demonstrates that historians and contemporary novelists of England did not trust an inquest to reveal the full story of what happened in cases of violent or sudden death, much can, nevertheless, be learned from what was described by witnesses at these legal inquiries.[22] At the inquest into the deaths of Eliza and William McKeon, the witnesses included: Peter Hughes (Eliza's brother), who found the bodies initially; Constable Walsh, who, on his beat, was brought to the scene by Hughes; Eliza's sister Margaret and her husband Joseph Plunkett; Esther Mitchell, William's mother; the McKeons' neighbour Mary Kearney; and Dr Doherty, the house surgeon at Jervis Street Hospital where the bodies had been taken. All of these people lived or worked less than three blocks away from the McKeons' home at 9 Mary's Abbey. Margaret and Joseph Plunkett lived at 113 Capel Street and testified that Eliza had been staying with them since the previous December during which time she confided that her husband had threatened

19  9 Mary's Abbey, Inns Quay, House and Buildings Return, 1911 census of Ireland, available at www.census.nationalarchives.ie/reels/nai000083947/; Enumerator's abstract, available at www.census.nationalarchives.ie/reels/nai000083944/ (accessed 10 Apr. 2017).
20  *Freeman's Journal*, 10 Jan. 1911.
21  *Freeman's Journal*, 11 Jan. 1911.
22  Paul Fyfe, *By accident or design: writing the Victorian metropolis* (Oxford, 2015), p. 52.

to kill her. Mrs Mitchell, the dead man's mother, also lived at 113 Capel Street and stated that William had attempted to kill his own sister some time previously and that she lived 'in dread of him herself'.[23] The physical proximity of their extended family allowed for shared confidences and key knowledge about the married couple's difficulties and the violent tendencies of William, as well as offering support to Eliza during their temporary separation.

Eliza had lived within a very small area of central Dublin city for much of her life. Born in 1875 on East James Street, she had, by 1901, moved with her family north of the River Liffey to Church Street. In 1903, she married William McKeon at St Michan's Church on Church Street, and both listed their address at the time of marriage as 11 North King Street, suggesting perhaps that they were living together before they married. They moved sometime in the intervening period to Mary's Abbey. This was close to where Eliza, her brother Peter and possibly her sister Margaret (listed as a fish dealer) all worked, on the block between Chancery Street and Mary's Lane, where Dublin's Victorian fish market was located. Eliza's sister Margaret lived very close having been married from 76 Capel Street in 1909 to Joseph Plunkett of Lower Erne Street. In 1911, at the time of Eliza and William's deaths, the Plunketts were living at 113 Capel Street, a tenement building in which six distinct families were listed in April 1911. Three months after the deaths of Eliza and William her sister had taken in their younger brother Peter, with whom Eliza had originally been living. The Plunketts continued to live in the same building as William McKeon's mother Esther Mitchell, along with her daughter Bridget. On the census form of that year it asked women to list the number of children born and the number still living. Mrs Mitchell did not include anything in that column to indicate that she had children living or dead.

William McKeon had been born in the Coombe Hospital on the south side of the city. His parents, William and Esther, lived at 16 Nicholas Street. At some point his father died and his mother remarried in 1893.[24] William was baptised in 1871 at the Church of Saints Michael and John on Lower Exchequer Street. At the inquest, Eliza's neighbour Mary Kearns of 8 Mary's Abbey stated that every Monday Eliza went to mass at that church at 12 noon. This very close, bounded geographic area provides a spatial expression of the close working and familial relationships between Eliza McKeon and her siblings; when her marriage was in trouble Eliza went to live with her sister around the corner, ensuring that she continued to have access to her

---

23 *Freeman's Journal*, 11 Jan. 1911.
24 Marriage certificate of Elizabeth McKeon and Patrick Mitchell, June 1893, available at https://civilrecords.irishgenealogy.ie/churchrecords/images/marriage_returns/marriages_1893/10607/5864448.pdf (accessed 12 Apr. 2017).

job, and some family support. William, on the other hand, had a more difficult relationship with his family, threatening not only his wife but his sister, and making his mother fearful. The reason given at the time was his former life as a soldier in the British Army. He signed up for the army in November 1890 at the age of 18 and listed his mother as his next of kin. As a member of the Prince of Wales's Leinster Regiment he had served in multiple overseas locations: as well as India and South Africa, he had served in Canada and Bermuda. He was invalided out of the army on 31 May 1902 as 'medically unfit' though there were no details listed explaining why; he had not been wounded according to his military service record. It is possible that he suffered from some sort of mental affliction that resulted in his discharge, but nothing serious enough to warrant direct admission into a lunatic asylum.[25] Between 1899 and 1902, 'there were 640 admissions [to lunatic asylums] for mental disease amongst the troops serving in S[outh] Africa' from the British Army as a whole.[26] Unpublished research on Irishmen in the South African War reveals that a significant number of veterans made their way into Richmond District Lunatic Asylum in the years after the conflict ended.[27] When McKeon was invalided out of the army in Dover he intended to return home to 11 Dominick Street (presumably where his mother was living at the time). An illiterate man of 31 who had spent more than a decade travelling the world, he married Eliza thirteen months after he left the army. As we have no indication that Eliza had ever travelled, it is likely that she lived all her life in Dublin; thus, the couple's geographic experiences of the world varied significantly.

The geographic reconstruction of the lives of Eliza and William McKeon demonstrate that Ireland's capital retained strong 'village' elements (as Grosz suggests), while at the same time being strongly connected to far-flung and exotic locations such as Bermuda and South Africa through its position within the British Empire and the fact that it supplied significant numbers of men for service within the army. Eliza's neighbours were knowledgeable about her work, shopping and mass-going habits; proximity undoubtedly helped create this knowledge.[28] Family and friends were also aware of William's soldiering experiences, and perhaps the impact that war had had on his mental state.

Similar issues are observable in other inquest records from the period. In the case of Mary Jane Patterson of 6 Lower Wellington Street, who killed herself in August 1904, a neighbour, Mary Levins, stated, 'I heard the old

25 National Archives, Kew, British Army Service Records, 1760–1913: WO97/5424/70 (accessed via www.findmypast.co.uk 12 Apr. 2017).
26 C. Stanford Read, *Military psychiatry in peace and war* (London, 1920), p. 15.
27 Luke Diver, 'Ireland and the South African war, 1899–1902' (Ph.D. thesis, Maynooth University, 2014), Appendix 11.
28 *Freeman's Journal*, 11 Jan. 1911.

man and woman arguing when she had drink taken'.[29] The two families lived in the same building on a street that had a population density of 3.84 per room, according to the 1901 census.[30] It would have been difficult to maintain privacy in such a crowded street and house: even behind closed doors, noise, words and anger travelled.

The district in which the McKeons lived was well served by Dublin Metropolitan Policemen. In 1901, there were 1,172 members of the force within the city districts.[31] Within a couple of streets there were two barracks from which emanated numerous constables who walked their beats along those streets every day; Green Street Barracks and the Central Bridewell were both very close to the McKeons' rooms. When Peter Hughes left the house on Mary's Abbey he met a policeman within a few minutes. According to his testimony he discovered the bodies at 11.50 a.m. and once the D.M.P. constable viewed the bodies he had them removed to Jervis Street Hospital and the doctor recorded that they were admitted at 12.10 p.m.[32] It was a feature of many Dublin city centre suicide cases that witnesses initially sought the help of either policemen or doctors, and often the former were more readily located probably because of their presence on the streets. In August 1904, Mary Jane Patterson's husband left their home on 6 Lower Wellington Street after she attempted suicide by taking poison. He was going for a doctor a couple of streets away on North Frederick Street when he met a police constable along the way and informed him of what had happened.[33] There is a strong sense of a police presence on the streets of Dublin city centre during this period. This was undoubtedly because of the duties of the D.M.P. constable, who was required to get to know all the parts of his beat – 'the streets, thoroughfares, courts and houses' – and whose movements through the city streets included 'walking at a rate of two-and-a-half English miles per hour, so that any person requiring the aid of a constable, by remaining in the same spot for that length of time, may meet one'.[34] Equally, the diligent constable would make enquiries

---

29  Dublin Inquests, IC.13.11, Inq. No. 149, 18 Aug. 1904. Lower Wellington Street was a series of run-down tenements, classified as second-class houses by the 1901 census enumerators. A number of the houses on this street housed more than one family. The Pattersons lived with two other couples, one of which had an eighteen-year-old daughter living with them. There were seven adults living in a house with six rooms, so the families probably each had two rooms.
30  Calculated from the street entries at www.census.nationalarchives.ie/pages/1901/Dublin/Inns_Quay/Wellington_Street/1281219/ (accessed 16 Jan. 2017).
31  See https://www.tcd.ie/iiis/HNAG/Labour/Police%20force/Dublin%20Metropolitan%20Police%20statistics,%201901.pdf (accessed 14 Apr. 2017).
32  *Freeman's Journal*, 11 Jan. 1911.
33  National Archives of Ireland, Dublin Inquests, IC.13.11, Inq. No. 149, 18 Aug. 1904.
34  Jim Herlihy, *The Dublin Metropolitan Police: a short history and genealogical guide* (Dublin, 2001), p. 104.

when he saw or heard something unusual or untoward. The 'station report', included as evidence in the inquest of Patrick Tynan, who cut his throat at his workplace in Fitzsimon's Timber Yard, noted that 'at 12.50 pm on 17th Inst PC77A Richard Johnston was on duty in Thomas St when he saw the corporation Ambulance passing ... The constable followed and heard some persons in a crowd ... say that a man had committed suicide in the yard'.[35]

It is difficult to imagine that in these circumstances suicide was easily concealed. When William Henderson was passing by 39 Lombard Street as he walked to work he saw 'great commotion and went into the house. I saw a number of people there ... greatly excited. I also saw a man lying on the floor with a number of people about him'. Henderson had no compunction about entering the house of a stranger to discover what was going on, suggesting that where great 'commotion' and 'excitement' occurred a private space transformed into a public space. The man lying on the floor was Louis Newman, a Rabbi who was later said to have been very depressed. His son revealed that the family had taken medical advice and were about to place him in a private institution, but 'were upset at the idea of putting him into an asylum'.[36] Newman was living on a street dominated by Russian-born Jews and their families: over 518 Russian natives lived on Lombard Street according to the 1901 census.[37] Given that the Jewish prohibition against suicide was similar to the Christian one, it is possible that the family may have hoped to conceal or at least keep private the fact of Newman's suicide. We saw earlier how at the inquest of Mary Jane Patterson her neighbour could testify to Patterson's drinking habits and the rows that took place between Mr and Mrs Patterson on occasion. Overcrowding in Dublin's city centre meant that privacy was difficult to achieve. 'Commotion' spilled onto the streets from private homes, renting rooms in tenement dwellings meant that private details of family life were often known to all in the house, and proximity to family and friends reinforced intimacies that were both a support and a strain. All of these factors are pertinent when constructing and reconstructing the contexts behind suicide during this period.

35  National Archives of Ireland, Dublin Inquests, IC.13.11, Inq. No. 149, 17 Aug. 1904. A constable on the corner of Nassau Street and Grafton Street responded to screams on Suffolk Street and on arriving at the scene discovered a man had attempted the murder of his wife and then suicide of himself. *Freeman's Journal*, 16 July 1904.
36  *Freeman's Journal*, 16 July 1904.
37  Census of Ireland http://bit.ly/2hjAzMr (accessed 5 May 2016).

## The morgue and suicides

The morgue is a key site in the process of reconstructing the lives and deaths of suicides in Victorian and Edwardian Dublin. In removing the inquest from public houses and other discreditable locations, reformers attempted to 'rechannel the elements of access and publicity through an acceptable filter of scientific mediation'.[38] By the first two decades of the twentieth century, almost 78 per cent of inquests in Dublin were held in 'medical' locations: morgue, hospital or lunatic asylum. Institutional locations such as prisons and workhouses constituted another 4 per cent of all inquest locations, with the remaining inquests (approximately 16.5 per cent) taking place where the deceased lived (and died) – in military barracks and private homes. (The whereabouts of the other 2 per cent of inquests remains unclear from the records.)[39] The proportion of those going to the morgue over the period in question does not change significantly. A hospital death most probably resulted in a hospital inquest, as in the case of Louis Newman, who died in 1904 and whose inquest was held in the Meath Hospital where he had been brought and subsequently died.[40] Suicide in a military barracks usually resulted in an inquest held at said barracks, as in the cases of William Hunter, Francis McGiven, Harry Gardiner and George Russell, all of whom died by suicide at Richmond Barracks between 1902 and 1912.[41] The only real spatial distinction emerges when we look at place of death in conjunction with class.

Of the seven people whose inquests were held at home, six lived in houses classified as first-class by the censuses in 1901 and 1911, and one address was not traceable in either 1901 or 1911.[42] Of those seven individuals, all were members of the professional classes, or were married to or were the offspring of a professional: Daniel James Wilson was a stockbroker, Beauchamp B. Jameson was a wine merchant and Stephen Catterson Smith was a barrister. Henry McArthur was an auctioneer's son and Alicia White, who died in 1903 from injuries she sustained jumping from a window, was the 55-year-old wife of an organ-keeper who would most likely have been a member of the upper working class.[43]

There appears to be a clear distinction in the post-mortem treatment of the wealthier classes in Dublin in relation to where inquests were held. However,

---

38 Burney, *Bodies of evidence*, p. 83.
39 These statistics are based on 127 suicides found in the Dublin Morgue registers, 1901–15, National Archives of Ireland.
40 *Freeman's Journal*, 17 and 18 Aug. 1904.
41 Dublin Morgue registers, 1901–15.
42 1 Merrion Place, Parkgate House, N.C.R.; 27 York Street; Balmoral Lodge; 5 Ushers Island; 43 Lower Gardiner Street; 110 Donore Terrace; 42 Stephens Green.
43 See www.census.nationalarchives.ie/pages/1901/Dublin/Mansion_House/York_Street/ 1344092/ (accessed 12 Jan. 2017).

the explanation for this is likely to have been more pragmatic than social. In Victorian Hull, 'an inquest required a room big enough to hold some 20 to 25 people; the coroner, jurymen, medical and lay witnesses and, occasionally, representatives of relatives, the deceased, or an insurance company', as well as a police officer. In this respect, the third- or fourth-class accommodations of Dublin's tenement buildings would not have been suitable locations for hosting such gatherings. In Hull, 'the home of the deceased was sometimes the venue ... [but] was restricted to those of some social standing'.[44] It would appear that Dublin was similar to Hull in this regard, and the reasons were likely to be a combination of social and spatial, with the densely populated tenements of the poorer classes being unable to cater for the jury, coroner, witnesses and members of the public.

By the end of the nineteenth century the morgue had come to dominate the spatial setting of inquests into sudden deaths, including suicides, but how did these sites of 'scientific mediation' emerge in the Irish context, and what were the spatial concerns that accompanied their creation?

From the early modern period, anatomy theatres in Padua, Venice and elsewhere throughout Europe were designated spaces for the medical examination of the dead body. The emergence of this phenomenon speaks to the construction of specialised scientific spaces in which the dead body could be used to teach anatomy to medical students. According to Jonathan Sawday, these anatomy 'theatres [also] formed part of the apparatus of punishment which stemmed from the sovereign's power over the bodies of his or her subjects' as those who received this posthumous punishment were generally criminals.[45] By the nineteenth century, anatomical theatres largely became the preserve of medical schools, and from 1830 public dissections of murderers were no longer permitted in London.[46] But there emerged a new space in which the dead body was displayed publicly, not for dissection but for a number of different reasons. From the early nineteenth century, European and American cities, Paris initially, began to bring the unidentified bodies of the urban dead to one central location – the city morgue. In Paris, the morgue became 'a depository for anonymous corpses found in the public domain ... [and] represented the quintessentially urban experience of anonymity with its potential for both increased freedom and alienation'.[47] In the context of

44 Victor Bailey, *'This rash act': suicide across the life-cycle in the Victorian city* (Stanford, Calif., 1998), pp 45–47.
45 J. Sawday, *The body emblazoned: dissection and the human body in Renaissance culture* (London, 1995), p. 189.
46 H. MacDonald, *Human remains: dissection and its histories* (New Haven, Conn., 2005), p. 2.
47 Vanessa R. Schwartz, *Spectacular realities: early mass culture in fin-de-siècle Paris* (Berkeley, Calif., 1998), p. 46.

urban space, Vanessa Schwartz argues that a morgue was almost a microcosm of the anonymity of the urban experience during this period. However, there was also a pragmatic intent behind this centralised deposit of dead bodies in the nineteenth century. It can be linked to newer administrative concerns of the modern state, chiefly the legibility and identification of its citizens, even in death.[48] Identifying citizens in an urban environment could be difficult: a large, mobile and often migrant population meant that bodies found dead on the streets or in rivers were 'problematic for the authorities'.[49] From 1804, in Paris, crowds gathered to view unidentified corpses through purpose-built windows which made a public spectacle of the dead body.[50] However, such public spectacles were not characteristic of the municipal morgues that emerged in Irish cities from the 1870s. The Irish city morgues functioned more as a centralised location where people knew the unidentified dead might be housed. While it was open to the public during times of inquests and upon request, in Dublin the morgue was less about public spectacle and more about public service.

It was not until 1871 that Ireland's capital city had a morgue for the reception of the unidentified dead, housed at No. 3 Marlborough Street, close to the River Liffey. In Belfast, the city morgue was housed initially at Police Square (which subsequently became Victoria Square). Cork's morgue was opened at some point in the early 1870s also, though it has proven difficult to establish exactly when.[51] The Sanitary Act 1866 appears to have given impetus to the creation of city morgues in Ireland during this period. The Act stated:

> Any Nuisance Authority may provide a proper place ... for the reception of dead bodies for and during the time required to conduct any *post-mortem* examination ordered by the Coroner of the district or other constituted authority, and may make such regulations as they may deem fit for the maintenance, support, and management of such place.[52]

The text of the Act makes it clear that the concerns of British parliament were less about identification of the dead per se and more about conducting medico-legal examinations, i.e., identifying cause of death as well as controlling public health 'nuisances'. The attachment of the coroner's court to the morgues

---

48 James C. Scott, *Seeing like a state: how certain schemes to improve the human condition have failed* (New Haven, Conn., 1998), pp 53–83; Patrick Carroll, *Science, culture and modern state formation* (Berkeley, Calif., 2006), pp 113–42.
49 Schwartz, *Spectacular realities*, p. 46.
50 Ibid., p. 47.
51 For early mention of the Belfast Morgue, see *Freeman's Journal*, 19 Aug. 1870.
52 Sanitary Act 1866 (29 & 30 Vict. c. xc), sect. 28.

in Dublin and Cork demonstrates the twofold purpose of the morgue in the Irish context: it was the duty of the coroner to investigate the deaths of all those who died suddenly.[53] However, it is clear that in Irish cities the morgue would also cater for 'the unnamed and unknown dead [who] may obtain a temporary repose'.[54] The health implications of dead bodies, alongside the Victorian concern with decent disposal of the dead, meant that the morgue catered for multiple anxieties raised by the presence of dead bodies in urban spaces.[55] During public debates about locations for Irish morgues, largely played out in newspapers, a number of spatial concerns emerged: first, the location of the morgue within built-up areas; secondly, the organisation of the internal spaces of the morgue itself.

While the lack of a morgue in Dublin was flagged as early as the 1850s, it was not until the 1870s that the Public Health Committee of the Dublin Corporation was tasked with finding a suitable location for the city's morgue, which would function as a 'decent receptacle' for housing the dead prior to identification and investigation.[56] Until 1871, when the morgue finally opened, the bodies of 'suicides and other unfortunate persons' were brought to a 'discreditable den in a filthy stable lane'.[57] Public discussion surrounding the location of the morgue at the identified site on 3 Marlborough Street emerged in the newspapers; the *Irish Times* criticised the committee's choice because it was a built-up, highly populated area. The characteristics of Victorian urban space ensured that finding a suitable place for a new morgue 'presented a novel problem' for municipal authorities.[58] Furthermore, the transportation of dead bodies from the surrounding city streets and the river Liffey would have a detrimental impact on the value of property in the area, and any 'mercantile' operations nearby. The Editorial argued that 'the site for a Morgue should be separate and detached, with no buildings in its immediate vicinity. There should be ample space around … and the road to it should pass by as few residences as possible'.[59] Converting a private dwelling in a 'crowded neighbourhood' was unsuitable for this new administrative and sanitary enterprise by the Corporation. Those most likely to be temporarily housed there were the 'unnamed and unknown', 'suicides' and 'the murdered'; however, before they 'are hidden out of sight forever', the *Irish Times* argued,

53 *Irish Times*, 18 June 1870 (Dublin); *Irish Examiner*, 18 Jan. 1873 (Cork).
54 *Irish Times*, 9 June 1870.
55 Brown-May and Cooke, 'Death, decency and the dead-house'.
56 When an unidentified body was dragged from the Liffey in 1851, the lack of a morgue was bemoaned in the newspapers. *Freeman's Journal*, 2 Sept. 1851; *Irish Times*, 9 June 1870.
57 *Irish Times*, 24 May 1870.
58 Brown-May and Cooke, 'Death, decency and the dead-house'.
59 *Irish Times*, 9 June 1870.

they deserved 'a fit building on a proper site'.[60] It is clear from the negative impacts outlined in the piece that it was not consideration for the dead that was of most concern but the wealth and comfort of the living. Despite these protestations, the first city morgue was opened on Marlborough Street in September 1871 and remained there until a new, purpose-built morgue was established in 1901.

The same concerns were evident in Queenstown, County Cork in 1872, when discussions about where to place a morgue in this important port town became the subject of frequent, if intermittent, correspondence in the *Cork Examiner*. The proposed site for that 'benevolent object' was on the 'highway from the town to the railway station', a regularly used route that would host visitors, and locals, as well as the British Royal Navy. Having a morgue on such a prominent road into town was problematic, not only for 'ladies', but, equally, 'men of the strongest nerves would hesitate before passing through an atmosphere laden with the deadly gases given out by a corpse in the last stage of decomposition'.[61] The letter-writer, Town Commissioner Joseph Fitzgerald, believed it would diminish the value of the property in the area, which included the railway company and the Royal Cork Yacht Club, which had been located in a beautiful old Italianate building since 1854 and which was a meeting place for Cork society.[62] The leisure functions of this seaside town included yachting and cycling and, according to Fitzgerald, the 'evening walk along the lower road' would be ruined by the presence of a morgue. The Lower Road in Queenstown was the site of many 'impressive high-gabled villas'.[63] It appears that the presence of this new type of public building, housing the unidentified dead, would create spatial dissonance in the area, juxtaposing 'odorous decompos[ing]' dead bodies alongside the healthful sea air that was lauded by the Victorians.[64] Equally (if not more) significant were the social and economic impacts.

The economic impact of a morgue on local business and property values evident in the 1870s in discussions about the Dublin and Queenstown

---

60 Ibid.
61 *Cork Examiner*, 11 Dec. 1872.
62 An Ordnance Survey map of 1876 demonstrates clearly the types of houses that featured on the Lower Road in Queenstown, pointing to a wealthy, middle-class presence in the vicinity of the proposed site of the morgue. See 'Town of Queenstown: County Cork, sheet 17', available at http://archiseek.com/2014/1854-royal-cork-yacht-club-cobh-co-cork/ (accessed 31 Oct. 2017).
63 Liam Nolan and John E. Nolan, *Secret victory: Ireland and the war at sea, 1914–1918* (Cork, 2009), p. 260.
64 B. Griffin, 'Bad roads will absolutely nip in the bud the new development': cycling tourism in Ireland in the late nineteenth and early twentieth centuries' in L. Lane and W. Murphy (eds), *Leisure and the Irish in the nineteenth century* (Liverpool, 2016), p. 189; John Hassan, *The seaside, health and the environment in England and Wales since 1800* (Aldershot, 2003).

morgues was again mentioned in the 1880s and 1890s during discussions about the presence of the Belfast City Morgue in Victoria Square. Economic and cultural transformation in 'the capital of Ulster' meant that Victoria Square, while once thought a suitable location for a morgue, was by 1887 'the business and fashionable centre of ... [this] populous and improving town' and therefore the morgue posed a 'very serious and objectionable nuisance'.[65] Residents and those having commercial property in the area were constantly confronted with 'the almost daily occurrence of the bodies of the dead, some of them in a state of putrefaction, being laid and landed even at their very doors'. Accompanying the dead were 'sensational crowds of friends and copious lamentations of the relatives of the deceased'.[66] Nevertheless, it is worth noting that the commercial and fashionable district of Belfast developed around the centrally located morgue in spite of its presence, challenging somewhat the objections of various 'Merchants' and 'Electors' who wrote into the *Belfast News-Letter* during the last decades of the nineteenth century.

While the geographic site of the morgue within an urban space was an issue, equally important were the internal spatial arrangements of this new municipal building. There were multiple important aspects to the spatial design of a morgue. First, it had to be adequately arranged to allow for proper scientific investigations – that is, there had to be sufficient light, space and equipment for the performance of a post-mortem examination. It also had to be well ventilated and be in no way off-putting to those citizens who were compelled to act as jurors at inquests. There were practical, scientific, political and sensory concerns at play in the organisation of internal space in municipal morgues.

The 'discreditable den' which had functioned as Dublin's morgue until 1871 was described as 'dark and dirty ... [with] not even light and conveniences for performing *post mortem* operations'. The sensory impact of the space was also not conducive to the performance of scientific and legal investigations: 'the air is stifling and odorous, hanging about the walls laden with the effluvia of a charnel house'.[67] When arguing for the relocation of the Belfast City Morgue from Victoria Square in 1887, a correspondent to the *Belfast News-Letter* stated that voters should be asked to 'draw an outline, in their imagination, of the interior of the building in which they may be called upon to serve as jurors'.[68] Election candidates should consider this of personal interest to their electors and act accordingly. The internal arrangements of

65 *Belfast News-Letter*, 25 Nov. 1887; 14 Nov. 1887; 24 Aug. 1887.
66 *Belfast News-Letter*, 6 July 1894.
67 *Irish Times*, 24 May 1870; 9 June 1870.
68 *Belfast News-Letter*, 14 Nov. 1887.

the city morgue were politicised, with reference to electors, but also to the wider community. There was no accommodation for jurors, witnesses or the public who may wish to attend an inquest. The correspondent described the morgue as an 'abominable cage of foul air' that emanated into the local neighbourhood and created an environmental and economic nuisance to householders and property owners alike.[69]

At an inquiry into Dublin Corporation's request for various loans from the Local Government Board, city architect Charles McCarthy noted that the late city coroner Nicholas C. Whyte had been complaining for some time about the 'insanitary conditions of the present morgue'.[70] The major problem was the situation of the mortuaries and post-mortem room which were separated from the courtroom above only by wooden floorboards. 'The odor from below, especially in warm weather, was almost unbearable'.[71] There was an identifiable need for two new mortuaries, adequately separated from the court room, the coroner and his jury. The new morgue should also have a microscope room for the investigations into cases of poison, and 'an office on the ground floor where the books of the establishment could be kept'.[72] When it was opened in 1902, the new morgue contained a court, including a gallery for public attendance, a jury box, retiring rooms and a waiting room for witnesses. The mortuaries and post-mortem room were separate and to the back of the building, 'completely isolated from the court and from all the surrounding buildings'.[73] And, in a final act of separating the living from the dead, 'the viewing lobby ... [was] separated from the mortuaries by glass screens, so that jurors and others called on to view the bodies on which inquests are being held may observe them perfectly without being under the necessity of entering the mortuaries'.[74] The jurors therefore became more reliant on medical professionals acting as intermediaries between them and the dead body, recasting the boundaries 'between the lay person and the medical expert'.[75] Through physical and proximate investigation of the dead body, doctors used their specialised access and subsequent knowledge to augment their expertise, elevating their professional status within the judicial system.[76] In this regard, Dublin gained what Livingstone has referred to as a 'venue ... of science', among venues that

---

69 Ibid.
70 *Irish Times*, 15 Aug. 1900.
71 Ibid.
72 Ibid.
73 *Irish Times*, 29 Mar. 1902.
74 Ibid.
75 Burney, *Bodies of evidence*, p. 81.
76 Ibid., pp 107–36; Michael J. Clarke, 'General Practice and Coroners' Practice: medico-legal work and the Irish medical profession, c.1830–c.1890' in C. Cox and M. Luddy (eds), *Cultures of care in Irish medical history, 1750–1950* (Basingstoke, 2010), pp 37–56.

included laboratories, asylums, zoological gardens and ships, as well as the physical body of the individual itself.[77] The morgue was a space where the practice of investigating deaths took place and where scientific knowledge about the cause of death was constructed. In this regard, we can identify the morgue specifically as a 'space of diagnosis'.[78]

The physical proximity of dead bodies to the living was problematic in cities for many reasons, including public health, sensory comfort and social and economic realities. In separating the living from the dead during medico-legal investigation the authorities were revealing official attitudes, and those of the wider community, to the dead in urban centres.

## Conclusion

The way urban space impacted on legal inquiry into suicides provides a telling insight into, first, the impact of urban space on individuals' relationships; secondly, the relationship between class and space in an urban context; and finally, the relationship between science and space in the urban context. Case studies of individual suicides that appear in legal records and newspaper reports disrupt the wider, metanarrative of modernisation that Durkheim deployed in his work and which has had such a seminal influence on the history of suicide subsequently. By exploring the micro-history of urban suicides, we see that the physical proximity and emotional ties, that Durkheim suggested were less likely to coexist in urban centres, do emerge as features of Irish urban life. Anonymous and anomic suicides may have existed in Irish cities, but this was not the only type of suicide that occurred: the cases that emerge in the Dublin Morgue registers, 1901–15 suggest that social isolation was not a feature of all urban suicides. The appearance of suicides by members of immigrant communities and the military, both of which tended to have high levels of social integration within their own community or 'neighbourhood', provides further evidence that social isolation was not a feature of all urban suicides. The suicide of a Jewish rabbi in a large, tightly knit group of Russian emigrants is also not indicative of social isolation, though the suicide of his fellow Russian Jew Samuel Smulovitch who had only recently emigrated is perhaps more explicable in these terms.[79] The cases of William McKeon and Louis Newman reveal individuals who were deeply embedded within their families and neighbourhoods. William's experience in the British Army

---

77 Livingstone, *Putting science in its place*, pp 17–86.
78 Ibid., pp 45, 62.
79 Smulovitch arrived in the country approximately two years before his death and lived in Tralee but moved to Dublin five weeks before his died. *Kerry Evening Post*, 11 Nov. 1905.

reflected a wider incidence of military suicides during the period in question: 12 of the 126 cases were soldiers or ex-soldiers, including William himself.

In terms of the relationship between science and urban space, we can see that certain scientific endeavours, such as the sanitary management of corpses, led to the emergence of distinct scientific spaces within the city. The establishment of a purpose-built city morgue in 1902 was a source of civic pride for the Corporation, and a means by which they could properly acknowledge and provide for Dublin's citizens who contributed to medico-legal investigation by appearing as witnesses and jury members. Ensuring their safety and comfort was of paramount importance, while also ensuring that death was partially sequestered.

Equally important was the creation of geographic knowledge about the many processes involved in dealing with the dead. Since the early nineteenth century, British governments had been taking a decennial census, locating the population in time and place across the British Isles. Although mortality statistics had been part of the Irish census since 1841 under the governance of Sir William Wilde, it was only in 1864, when the General Registry Office was created, that locating 'place of death' was important. Further information, such as 'where found' and 'where disposed' can be found in the morgue registers themselves, adding an extra geographical layer to the knowledge we have about the dead. In between life, death and burial there were multiple movements of the body through time and space that demonstrate both agency and passivity, as well as the spatial realities of social class.

# 8

## Visualising the City: Images of Ireland's Urban World, c.1790–1820

*Mary Jane Boland*

From the muted calmness of Johannes Vermeer's views of seventeenth-century Delft to the vibrancy of Claude Monet's impressions of Victorian London, the activities and routines of the urban world have fascinated artists for centuries. In Ireland, things have been no different in this respect: market towns and cities, as well as the busy lives of those that inhabit them, have continually been the subject of artistic attention.

From the late eighteenth century, one of the most prolific chroniclers of the urban world was the Cork-born artist Nathaniel Grogan (c.1740–1808), who created an array of images that celebrated the enterprise and vibrancy of his local city. For instance, in his etching *North Gate Bridge* (c.1794) (Figure 8.1) the viewer is presented with a diverse slice of life beneath the looming structure of Cork's northern gatehouse (which also served as a jail). In the foreground, bricklayers with a wheelbarrow and trowel can be seen building part of a stone wall, behind them a man is begging, whilst other labourers (both male and female) can be seen throughout the picture carrying heavy loads, baskets and selling wares. On the other side of the bridge, a soldier (or constable) is just visible as he patrols the street in front of the jail with a rifle over his shoulder. In contrast to these activities, an elegant carriage, which possibly carries Richard Barry, the Earl of Barrymore, traverses the crowded scene.[1] The lack of a narrative sequence here means that the etching reads like a detailed portrait of a city and its people – an illustration of a mundane 'day in the life' in the city of Cork. However, the variety of activity and the diversity

---

1 Peter Murray, 'Nathaniel Grogan: North Gate Bridge, Cat. 11' in Peter Murray (ed.), *A question of attribution: the Arcadian landscapes of Nathaniel Grogan and John Butts* (Cork, 2012), pp 128–29.

of the crowd immediately indicate that this is not just a picture of the ordinary lives of a singular group within Irish society; rather, it introduces the daily routines of both the industrious workers and the leisurely elites – a collective *everyday* that encompasses many aspects of Irish urban life.

Visualisations of the urban environment like this one have had a recognisable function within Irish studies to date. Pictures like *North Gate Bridge*, or others of markets, busy ports and street scenes, have been used by historians and art historians to illustrate findings on material culture, as frontispieces for economic histories or to 'offer significant new evidence about the lives of a silenced population'.[2] Scholars have seldom acknowledged that these *social records* are first and foremost works of art, and belong to a long tradition of painting urban life in European art history.

While it is certainly true that images like *North Gate Bridge* can be useful as visual evidence of early-nineteenth-century commerce and social habits, this chapter will argue that these readings are only interpreting part of the story. Indeed, the meaning of an image lies both in its content and in how it is presented to the viewer. Rather than producing something that would accurately record Irish society at a certain moment in time, Grogan, William Turner de Lond (*fl.* 1820–26) and other artists of the urban space were creating pictures with a recognisable European visual language that would captivate their audience and appeal to their patrons. The majority of the images discussed in this chapter were never shown at contemporary exhibitions outside Ireland.[3] From this point of view, it is clear that Irish artists were primarily creating their images of the urban world with the intention (or hope) of selling them to local patrons and should be analysed accordingly.

Recent art historical scholarship on the visualisation of the urban environment has argued that the city is a 'spatial, symbolical and ideological construct that needs to be simultaneously decoded on these different levels'.[4] With this in mind, my approach in this chapter is indebted to Henri Lefebvre and his theories on both urban space and everyday life, as argued in

---

2 Vera Kreilkamp, 'Introduction' in Vera Kreilkamp (ed.), *Rural Ireland: the inside story* (Boston, 2012), p. 7. For instance, one of William Turner de Lond's images of life in Limerick is used as the frontispiece to R. Gillespie and R.F. Foster (eds), *Irish provincial cultures in the long eighteenth century: essays for Toby Barnard* (Dublin, 2012).
3 For example, there is no known evidence to suggest that any of the images by Turner de Lond discussed in this chapter were publicly exhibited during the artist's lifetime anywhere other than in Limerick in 1821.
4 Katrien Lichtert, Jan Dumolyn and Maximillian P.J. Martens, 'Images, maps, texts: reading the meanings of the later medieval and early modern city' in Katrien Lichtert, Jan Dumolyn and Maximillian P.J. Martens (eds), *Portraits of the city: representing urban space in later medieval and early modern Europe* (Tournhout, 2014), p. 3.

8.1 Nathaniel (the Elder) Grogan (c.1740–1808), *North Gate Bridge* (c.1794), etching, 35.5 cm × 27 cm (Crawford Art Gallery, Cork)

*Production of space* (1974) and his three-volume *Critique de la vie quotidienne* (1947–81).[5] In the latter, he tries to establish 'whether the critical analysis of everyday life can serve as a guiding thread for knowledge of society as a whole and its inflection in a particular direction, in order to give it meaning'.[6] Accordingly, a central element in Lefebvre's theoretical endeavour is that *space* is both physical and ideological. Thus, he argues that both the everyday and the urban environment are conceived with ideological objectives. From this perspective, visual representations of the quotidian city-space have a series of constructed meanings, from propagating values of political or military power, to functioning as part of a strategy of social distinction.

In light of this, instead of revealing something new about the material culture of the urban world, or communicating something about the lives of the artists, this chapter will underline how an image like *North Gate Bridge* could be used to propagate the fundamental values and ideologies of those that were consuming it. By examining these pictures as art objects that were created for a specific group of local buyers, this chapter will question why elite patrons of the arts were interested in hanging everyday images of Irish city life on their walls.

Throughout the eighteenth century in English art, the urban world was often perceived as an emblem, or a setting, of lost innocence and crime. In fact, specific locations within London's urban sprawl had distinct social and historical associations of their own; certain backdrops, like Covent Garden or Charing Cross, could heighten an image's moral message or narrative.[7] This is best exemplified in the work of William Hogarth, who satirically portrayed London and its disreputable inhabits as a sort of vortex that swallowed up naive country folk. These negative associations of the city can particularly be found in Hogarth's narrative series *A Harlot's Progress* (1732), which tells the simple story of a young girl from the country who comes to London, falls into immoral ways, embarks on a road to ruin and eventually catches a fatal dose of the pox and dies. In each of the six images in the series, London – from Cheapside to the Bridewell Prison – is as much a character in the story as the young girl herself. The *Progress*, then, is also a literal journey through the allegorical geography of the capital.[8] However, rather than presenting topographical accuracy, Mark Hallett has argued that Hogarth created 'topographical satires', or in other words, 'satirical illustrations … which

---

5 Henri Lefebvre, *La production de l'espace* (Paris, 1974); Henri Lefebvre, *Critique of everyday life*, trans. Gregory Elliott and John Moore (3 vols, London, 2014).
6 Lefebvre, *Critique of everyday life*, iii, 2.
7 Roy Porter, 'Capital art: Hogarth's London' in Frédéric Ogée (ed.), *The dumb show: image and society in the works of William Hogarth* (Oxford, 1997), p. 49.
8 Ibid., p. 61.

focused on the different sectors of the city, and which collectively depicted the metropolis as a labyrinthine succession of corrupted spaces, swarming with dubious and deceitful characters'.[9] Hallett continues to explain that Hogarth succeeded in creating a pictorial language that helped to condition the visual experience of the cityscape for the affluent print or picture-buying urbanite, becoming a point of reference in their everyday encounter with the urban world.[10]

It should be noted that Hogarth was well represented in private collections in Ireland from the mid-eighteenth century. Paintings and prints by the British artist could often be found in the homes of elite collectors and were consistently on sale in Dublin from the 1790s onwards.[11] As well as this, surviving auction catalogues reveal that illustrated collections of Hogarth's writings on aesthetic theory were available for consumption countrywide by the nineteenth century.[12] Indeed, perspectives on his work, and on the urban landscape in eighteenth- and nineteenth-century English art in general, can be helpful in understanding the visualisation of the city in Ireland during the period covered in this chapter. Aesthetic trends from Britain were widely imitated and even manipulated by peripheral artists and art dealers in Dublin, Cork and Limerick in order to attract potential patrons and buyers.

The practice of modelling one's work on sought-after British and European artists seems to have been widespread among artists in Ireland at this time. Indeed, part of the popularity Grogan enjoyed, during his own lifetime and posthumously, was as a result of his similarity to artists like Hogarth. It is perhaps unsurprising then that several of Grogan's pictures of Irish life borrow directly from the Hogarthian aesthetic – something that did not go unnoticed by contemporary observers.[13] For example, in 1822, more than a decade after the artist's death, Maria Edgeworth noted that she had seen 'Two curious pictures ... done by an Irish boy, or man, of the name of Grogan, of

9 Mark Hallett, 'The view across the city: William Hogarth and the visual culture of eighteenth-century London' in David Bindman, Frédéric Ogée and Peter Wagner (eds), *Hogarth: representing nature's machine* (Manchester, 2001), p. 149.
10 Ibid., p. 160.
11 Sales catalogue entries, 'Hogarth in Ireland' (Getty Provenance Index online, no longer available). For a discussion of Hogarth in private collections, see Fintan Cullen, *Ireland on show: art, union and nationhood* (Farnham, 2012), p. 8. Works by Hogarth can also be found in the inventory of furnishings in Mount Bellew, Co. Galway, N.L.I., Fragment of inventory of art collection of the Bellew family of Mount Bellew, 1825, MS 31,992, p. 4.
12 For instance, see *Catalogue of a valuable collection of books, manuscripts, and Irish History, the library of the late celebrated Irish historian, General Charles Vallancey, sold by auction, on Thursday 18th February, and following days, by Thomas Jones, at his sale-room, No. 6 Eustace Street, Dublin, 1815*, N.L.I., pamphlets collection, P124 (24).
13 For instance, figures in Grogan's painting *The Itinerant Preacher* (1783) appear to be copied directly from Hogarth's earlier print *The Sleeping Congregation* (1736).

Cork ... of the Wilkie, or better still, of the Hogarth style', while staying in Convamore House on the estate of her friends Lord and Lady Listowel.[14] Similarly, in 1827, *Bolster's Quarterly Magazine* published an article on Irish art that suggested Grogan shared a 'curious coincidence of thought' with David Wilkie and even with Edward Rippingille, both of whom he 'seems to have anticipated'.[15]

It seems then that when looking at images like *North Gate Bridge*, it would be short-sighted to ignore the strong European artistic inheritance that it displays; the humorous characterisations are certainly reminiscent of Hogarth, while the visual comparisons between young and old, rich and poor, industrious and leisurely bring to mind similar devices in Dutch and Flemish seventeenth-century genre scenes. Within these contexts, the attraction of this mundane view of the city to an elite audience seems more comprehensible – first and foremost, here is an image of a familiar urban space painted in a fashionable, international aesthetic language – and in owning or admiring it the viewer could prove his (or her) status as an informed purveyor of taste.

However, while an examination of the influence of outside forces is important, it still only tells part of the story. In a recent discussion on the appropriation of English art by artists in Europe, Christiana Payne has argued that studies of the shared histories of artistic practice should go 'beyond the simple question of "influence"' and should instead 'consider the ways in which models and conventions developed in Britain (and elsewhere) were adapted, appropriated or resisted' by those further afield.[16] From this point of view, the more interrogative question to ask here is how (or why) artists of the urban world in Ireland actually modified British and European traditions in order to suit the demands of their local patrons. Does a type of urban imagery emerge that is specific to Ireland? And what can such imagery reveal about the fundamental values of those that were commissioning, viewing and buying these works of art?

Some possible answers can be found by returning again to *North Gate Bridge*. Various copies and versions of this print exist, which indicates that it was popular and well known with patrons throughout the locality.[17] While the image clearly references the urban imagery of Hogarth and others, it

---

14 Maria Edgeworth, *A memoir of Maria Edgeworth, with a selection from her letters, edited by her children* (London, 1867), p. 179.
15 Anon., 'Irish art and artists' in *Bolster's Quarterly Magazine*, no. 5, vol. 2 (1827), p. 59.
16 Christiana Payne, 'Introduction: international cross-currents in an age of nationalism' in Christiana Payne and William Vaughan (eds) *English accents: interactions with British art c.1776–1855* (Aldershot, 2004), p. 2.
17 A reproduction of the print can be found in *Cork Historical and Archaeological Journal*, ser. 2, vol. 5 (1899). Other, rather poor, extant copies after the print indicate it was popular enough to be imitated (and/or pirated).

also communicates a series of ideologies specific to the city it represents: the guarded jail intimates a strong judicial framework; the presence of the stonemasons suggests urban development that requires expansion; the pauper begging in the shadow of three fashionable females implies a distinct urban social hierarchy, while the distant sails indicate a busy trading port.

Indeed, in each of his works of art that reference the city of Cork, Grogan presents the viewer with an urban world that is energetic and expanding, with the River Lee as its industrious nerve centre. Specific architectural and spatial features invariably mark the identity of the city – and in Grogan's work this demarcation is provided by the river, and particularly by its status as a sort of commercial in-road from the harbour. For many of Cork's citizens the harbour was a paradigm of local prosperity and a source of great pride. For example, in 1810, William West argued that the harbour was of singular importance in the increasing development of the city: 'whatever advantages its environs may possess, or whatever improvements may take place in this city, the source of all must be found in its safe and capacious harbour'.[18] It is unsurprising then, that when Grogan published a set of twelve aquatinted views of Cork and its environs in the 1790s, all but one of them included some reference to the river and the harbour.[19] In many ways, these views bring to mind similar devices in Hogarth's much earlier work – from *A Harlot's Progress* to *Four Times of the Day* (1736) – as Grogan also takes his viewer on a visual journey (or progress) around the city and encounters a diverse mixture of local life along the way. Marginal vignettes in each scene, from both the daytime and the night-time, show people working: labourers appear quarrying, farming, fishing, trading and unloading cargo from the River Lee.

In *Patrick's Bridge* (Figure 8.2), Grogan is in the midst of the action, at the heart of the city itself, so that the viewer too becomes an active participant in what is happening in this busy urban space. The river stretches across the foreground, indicating that the viewpoint may be from a vessel that is just about to land. The sight ahead is what visitors to the city (or returning travellers) could expect to see upon arrival. Sails of trading vessels and smoke from distant chimneys give a sense of burgeoning industry and the newly built bridge itself, which had only been completed several years previously in 1791,[20] underlines the feeling of progression and improvement that emanates from the scene.

---

18   William West, *A directory and picture of Cork and its environs* (Cork, 1810), p. 74.
19   Grogan's *Views of the River Lee and Cork Harbour* (1796) include: Patrick's Bridge; Glanmire Church; Passage West; Carrigrohane; Monkstown; Haulbowline; Glanmire Village; Blarney Castle; Lower Glanmire Road; River Lee, opposite Tivoli; Glanmire Church; Blackrock.
20   David Dickson, *Old world colony: Cork and south Munster, 1630–1830* (Cork, 2005), p. 422.

IMAGES OF IRELAND'S URBAN WORLD 169

8.2 Nathaniel (the Elder) Grogan (c.1740–1808), *Patrick's Bridge* (c.1796), aquatint, 36 cm × 46 cm (private collection)

8.3 Nathaniel (the Elder) Grogan (c.1740–1808), *Boats on the River Lee below Tivoli* (c.1790), oil on canvas, 94.3 cm × 168 cm (National Gallery of Ireland, NGI 4074)

While it is possible to suggest that these images take the viewer on a geographical progress around the cityscape, they lack the grittiness and especially the moral undertone of Hogarth's work. There is no sense of didacticism, nor is there a central character or narrative to connect the scenes to each other. Instead, they provide a series of picturesque views – a portfolio that emphasises the order and prosperity of the region; the viewer here is not being taught a lesson, they are being reassured.

This is also the case in Grogan's most highly finished visualisation of Cork: *Boats on the River Lee below Tivoli* (*c*.1790) (Figure 8.3). This image was most probably commissioned by James Morrison (Lord Mayor of Cork in 1784) to decorate his residence at Tivoli House, a Palladian mansion that is visible on the hillside.[21] In the scene, the city space is but a haze on the horizon and can only be glimpsed by following the boats up ahead as they wind their way into the port. The sense of mobility between the centre and its hinterland is underlined, and the presence of travellers in carts, as well as the busy roadside and even the blacksmith's forge, where a labourer can be seen shoeing a horse, further emphasise this idea.

Indeed, it seems that Grogan has deliberately placed the blacksmith's forge under the watchful eye of the Palladian house on the hillside, as if to emphasise (or perhaps advocate) the inherent social order that existed in Ireland in the late eighteenth century: busy labourers maintain the commercial success of the nation's second city under the watchful eye of an elevated elite. Morrison was part of an educated middle-class elite that emerged in Cork city and its surrounding areas from the middle of the eighteenth century. Much scholarship has been undertaken into the lives of this group, which was made up of wealthy businessmen that had become hugely successful as a result of strong trading links between Cork, Britain and North America.[22] Many of these professionals also erected grand mansions along the banks of the River Lee to house their expanding collections of art and literature; in fact the site of Grogan's *Boats on the River Lee below Tivoli* became something of a suburban, maritime avenue in the closing decades of the eighteenth century.[23] In his directory of Cork, West describes how, just outside the city, 'there are a number of Genteel Houses, the Country retreats of the Gentry,

---

21 Brendan Rooney, 'Boats on the River Lee near Tivoli' in Elizabeth Mayes (ed.), *Irish paintings in the National Gallery of Ireland* (Dublin, 2001), p. 245.
22 For a discussion of this group of merchant and professional classes, see J.P McCarthy, 'In search of Cork's collecting traditions: from Kilcrea's library to the Boole library of today' in *Journal of the Cork Historical and Archaeological Society*, no. 100 (1995), pp 29–46 and Dickson, *Old world colony*.
23 These include Lota, Woodhill, Summerhill, Tivoli and Lotamore. McCarthy discusses West's descriptions of these from 1810 in 'In search of Cork's collecting traditions', pp 29–46.

and Professional and Commercial characters. They are all most pleasantly situated, mostly with neat Gardens, both in front and rear, which are kept in neat order, and similar to those of the outlets of London'.[24] While many of these houses were decorated with works by Old Masters of the Dutch and Italian schools, a substantial number of them also included artworks by Grogan – an accomplished local artist who, as has already been argued, could help his patrons emulate what was fashionable in artistic centres like London and Paris.

It should be noted at this point that Grogan's output as an artist was incredibly diverse; he created everything from shop signs to classical murals. Writing in 1833, Thomas Crofton Croker recollected that '[Grogan] was a figure, landscape, cattle and flower painter *as required*'.[25] According to Croker, the artist took opportunities as and when they arose – something that was perhaps driven by his responsibility for 19 children.[26] During his lifetime, there were no public exhibitions or sales of fine art in Cork. Although he did travel to London and exhibit four landscapes at the Free Society of Artists in 1782, it is probable that he was wholly reliant on commissions and the support of elite patrons for his livelihood.[27] As a result, it is fair to assume that he was driven by an opportunism typical of his time and would construct his works of art according to the demands of his commissioning patrons. Were local collectors attracted (at least in part) to Grogan's images of the urban space because they portrayed both the city and its inhabitants as prosperous, autonomous and reputable? Was this how elite urbanites (and patrons of the arts) wanted to be identified?

Unfortunately, the provenance of much of Grogan's work remains a mystery; although, in 'Recollections of Cork', Croker did make a list of the main proprietors of his work at the time of the artist's death in 1808. Among the recognisable names mentioned here are the Newenhams of Summerhill and the Penroses of Woodhill.[28] Extant exhibition catalogues from the Cork Society for Promoting Fine Arts (C.S.P.F.A.) annual exhibitions of 1815–22 also give some insight into the elite group that furnished their homes with images of urban life by Grogan. For instance, most of the pictures by Grogan

---

24 West, *Directory and picture of Cork and its environs*, p. 59.
25 'Recollections of Cork by Crofton Croker, 1825' (Trinity College Dublin, MS 136, p. 136). The emphasis on 'as required' is this author's.
26 Croker tells us that Grogan had 19 children, all of whom died of consumption – 16 of these before the artist himself. See 'Recollections of Cork by Crofton Croker', p. 137.
27 Algernon Graves, *The Society of Artists of Great Britain (1760–1791); The Free Society of Artists (1761–1783): a complete dictionary of contributors and their works from the foundation of the societies to 1791* (London, 1907), p. 107. The first public exhibition of fine art in Cork did not take place until 1815 (seven years after Grogan's death).
28 'Recollections of Cork by Crofton Croker', p. 137.

that were exhibited (posthumously) at the C.S.P.F.A. in 1820 were in the collection of the local banker, James Roche (1770–1853).[29]

The type of collector interested in Grogan's work also tended to be actively involved in the promotion of culture and the arts in the city: for instance, Grogan's patron George Newenham became renowned as 'an encourager and cultivator of the arts'[30] and his home at Summerhill boasted a collection that included works by Richard Wilson, Canaletto and Grogan.[31] Summerhill became an important focal point for artistic activity well into the nineteenth century, as did the homes of other patrons like Cooper Penrose.

Investigations into the habits and attitudes of these figures can reveal a great deal about the ideological underpinnings of Grogan's images of the city: not only was this group involved in the economic and commercial advancement of their region, they were also interested in the promotion of culture and in the refinement of public taste. Thus, images of the urban environment like *Boats on the River Lee below Tivoli* and *North Gate Bridge* take on deeper ideological connotations and aspirations when viewed with these patrons in mind. What better way to express such dedication to the citizenry than in an image that shows all members of society going about their day-to-day business? This is certainly the picture presented in *North Gate Bridge* where beggars and labourers mingle with fashionable elites and horse-drawn carriages, thus projecting an image of civic order and cooperation between the various ranks in society. As well as this, throughout each of Grogan's visualisations of Cork, there is a tone of genuine affection for the idiosyncrasies of life in the city – from gossipy women and mischievous street urchins, to local fishermen and hard-working quarrymen. Each of these elements combine to give an overall feeling of community spirit and empathy towards the hard-working labourers – something that can only have provoked feelings of contentment and pride from the wealthy middle-class beholders of the images.

Of course, as mentioned previously, aesthetic considerations must also be taken into account when assessing the attraction of these images to patrons like Newenham, Penrose and Roche. As well as the aforementioned similarity to Hogarth, there is certainly an adherence to contemporary European artistic ideas and trends: *Boats on the River Lee below Tivoli* borrows heavily from the aesthetic of Aelbert Cuyp (1629–91) and other northern European painters that were in vogue at the time. Consequently, on the one hand, Grogan's

---

29 Exhibition catalogues for the Cork Society for Promoting the Fine Arts (C.S.P.F.A.) annual exhibitions from 1816 to 1820 list the proprietor with each artwork (Royal Irish Academy, HP-1094/15).
30 West, *Directory and picture of Cork and its environs*, p. 20.
31 Newenham loaned works by all of these artists to the C.S.P.F.A. in 1819. See 'Cork Society for Promoting the Fine Arts, 1819, fourth exhibition, Cork, 1819', Royal Irish Academy, HP-1094/15.

images of the city could give collectors in Cork a feeling of accomplishment in knowing they were up-to-date with what was happening in the artistic centre of London. On the other hand, because Grogan was a Cork-based artist, his oeuvre incorporated a sense of regional and local identity that was missing in the work of 'foreign' artists like Teniers or Hogarth; spectators in Cork could look at an image like *Boats on the River Lee below Tivoli* and see their *own* locality painted by one of their *own* artists. In addition to this, they could see the benefits of industry and improvement that they themselves had made and see the day-to-day routines of the ordinary urban space that they believed they were helping. Thus, Grogan's work would appeal to regional collectors in the city for a variety of reasons: through the use of a recognisable and highly regarded visual language, his pictures not only projected regional identities and ideas of improvement, they also satisfied cultural ideologies and aesthetic agendas.

However, it is important to remember that these images are selective in the daily life that they include and, indeed, omit. Unlike their British counterparts, the urban spaces in each of Grogan's images do not hide a threatening undercurrent, nor do they present a realm effected by the social and economic realities of the period. There is little evidence of the overcrowding and unsanitary living conditions that were affecting Irish cities by the early nineteenth century, nor is there any indication of the unrest that was dominating life in rural areas. Instead, the viewer is presented with a detached reality, in which the dominant trope is social cohesion. From this point of view, many of the images discussed in this chapter present an illusion rather than an actuality, and mainly serve to reassure potential patrons and elite audiences, rather than provide accurate records of daily urban life.

This continued to be the case in the first two decades of the nineteenth century. Patronage remained the most significant influencer of artistic practice and output in Ireland; artists were driven by market forces and deviated towards subjects and themes that would be attractive and popular with audiences. Consequently, the underlying tones of the early-nineteenth-century urban aesthetic continued to be ones of progression, order and social cohesion.

This is certainly the case in the work of William Turner de Lond, whose engagement with regional centres like Ennis (*Market Place and Courthouse at Ennis*, c.1821) (Figure 8.4) follows the civilised tradition established by Grogan. Throughout the Ennis scene, the artist presents a series of vignettes that lead the viewer through the commercial centre and down the street in the distance. The compositional arrangement of the artwork means the urban space is presented as a stage-like setting and the spectator is placed in the role of bystander – a somewhat distant observer that watches the social habits of an anonymous group of people, all of whom are unaware of the fact that they are

IMAGES OF IRELAND'S URBAN WORLD

8.4 William Turner de Lond (*fl.* 1820–26), *Market Place and Courthouse at Ennis* (*c.*1821), oil on canvas, 75.6 cm × 106 cm (Merrion Hotel, Dublin)

being watched. This distancing strategy creates a certain degree of ambiguity and control between the painting's audience (as observer or spectator) and the participants in the life that is portrayed. The elite exhibition-goer is not immersed in the hustle and bustle of the action itself – instead, the viewer safely surveys what is happening from afar.

It is market day and the energy and excitement of the weekly event has been heightened by the arrival of a mail coach in the centre of the scene. Its advertised destinations reveal that it is travelling between Cork, Killarney, Ennis and Limerick, and therefore must have been part of the stagecoach network that had been recently improved in 1815, when Charles Bianconi introduced more advanced passenger lines. Horses and donkeys dispersed through the crowd allude to the fact that people from the surrounding hinterland have travelled specifically to the city for the event – and thus provide a reminder here of how reliant the urban economy was on the rural population. The image also includes the key characteristics of an 'improved' urban centre: widened streets, regularly planned open spaces and vistas geometrically framed with public buildings such as court houses, market houses and churches.[32]

With these contexts in mind, the backdrop of the urban space, from the courthouse to the market square, and even the road on which the coach travels, gives the image a progressive dimension. As was the case with Grogan's images of Cork, local improvement and social cohesion seem to be a key themes then – urbanisation and the spread of metropolitan ideas to this local centre are being welcomed. This mail coach is bringing passengers, news, post (and ultimately change) to the regional outpost of Ennis.

Indeed, it was probably one of these very coaches that brought Turner de Lond himself to the south west, having travelled to Ireland from Britain sometime prior to 1821.[33] Unfortunately, very little is known about the artist before he came to Ireland, but it is most likely that he travelled over from Britain on a speculative venture, hoping, it would seem, to find a new market for his works of art. He exhibited 25 paintings at the *Exhibition of Works by Old Masters, Artists and Amateurs* in Limerick in autumn 1821, which ranged from views of Killarney and Bunratty Castle to a portrait of Bonaparte, a crucifixion scene and the portrait of a horse at Newcastle racecourse.[34] All of these works were for sale at the time of the well-advertised exhibition, which took place at Mr. O' Connor's temporarily erected Exhibition Room, in Swinburne's Ball

---

32 Susan Hood, 'The significance of the villages and small towns in rural Ireland during the eighteenth and nineteenth centuries' in Peter Borsay and Lindsay Proudfoot (eds), *Provincial towns in early modern England and Ireland* (Oxford, 2002), p. 251.

33 See Ann M. Stewart, *Irish art loan exhibitions 1765–1927: index of artists* (3 vols, Dublin, 1990), ii, 722–23.

34 Ibid.

Room on Brunswick Street.[35] The fact that Turner de Lond exhibited scenes from County Kerry, County Clare and County Limerick at the same exhibition means he must have travelled extensively during his sojourn in the country.

In particular, the urban world seems to have interested him; all of his surviving paintings are of urban spaces like the one seen in *Market Place and Courthouse at Ennis*. The most ambitious of these are a series of images that commemorate the arrival of King George IV at Dublin (and his departure) in August 1821[36] – a momentous occasion that attracted the attention of many artists.[37] This was probably due, in part, to a competition that was run by the Royal Institution for the Promotion of Fine Arts in Ireland, which offered £500 for 'the best painting of his Majesty's landing in this country by an Irish artist'.[38] Turner de Lond may have entered the competition but he did not win, as his *George IV, King of England, entering Dublin* (Figure 8.5) was for sale when exhibited at Swinburne's in October 1821 and even then it remained in the artist's possession until the following summer.[39]

The scene focuses on the pomp and ceremony of the king's arrival, rather than on the monarch himself, who stands in the distance facing the viewer in his gilded carriage, directly under a temporary triumphal arch that was erected specifically for the occasion. The Royal cavalcade, made of up of numerous horses and various regiments and squadrons, are led at the front by a young black soldier. This image then, presents a microcosm of the vast empire, in all its grandeur, ascending on Dublin and being met with crowds of well-dressed urbanites, many of whom wave banners declaring *céad míle fáilte*.

The painting also serves to demonstrate how visualisations of the urban space could function in a variety of ways for elite viewers at this time. The urban space here becomes a site of controlled celebration for a specific type of individual – an arena for urbanites to gather in a familiar environment and experience something out of the ordinary.

All the figures in the foreground stand with their backs to the picture's audience, making the composition rather curious, and emphasising that the focal point should be the parade taking place in the centre. In contrast to the

---

35  This exhibition was advertised in the *Limerick Chronicle*, 13 Oct. 1821.
36  There are multiple paintings of the king's entrance into Dublin in 1821 by Turner de Lond. Two of these, formerly from the collection at Glin Castle, were sold at Christie's, London on 7 May 2009. Another version is in the collection of the National Gallery of Ireland and is illustrated in Anne Crookshank and the Knight of Glin, *Ireland's painters, 1600–1940* (London, 2002), p. 232.
37  Extant printed images, watercolours and oils of the event, by both known and anonymous artists, attest to its popularity with contemporary artists. For instance, a watercolour by Joseph Patrick Haverty entitled *King George IV's Triumphal Entry into Dublin, 17 August 1821* exists in the collection of the British Embassy in Dublin.
38  This competition was advertised in the *Limerick Chronicle*, 15 Aug. 1821.
39  See adverts in the *Limerick Chronicle*, 18 May 1822; 29 June 1822.

8.5 William Turner de Lond (*fl.* 1820–26), *George IV, King of England, entering Dublin* (c.1821), oil on canvas, 171 cm × 279 cm (National Gallery of Ireland, NGI 1148)

Ennis scene, this compositional device suggests that Turner de Lond wanted its potential buyer to feel as though they were also part of the civilised crowd, facing towards the king with the rest of the welcoming committee. When looking at the image, the viewer could revel in the sumptuous detail and enjoy a prime position from which to watch the theatrical events unfold on the city stage. Indeed, the strong emphasis on the crowd here hints at the kind of buyer Turner de Lond hoped to find for the image. When it was advertised by the artist in 1821 he specifically targeted 'the admirers of the FINE ARTS'[40] and later, in 1822, alerted the 'the Nobility, Gentry and respectable inhabitants' that it was still for sale. In this image, then, Turner de Lond may have been pandering to the patriotism of a local Peer, keen to experience – or to remember – what it was like to be part of the event and to be among the crowd that saw the king wind his way through the streets of Dublin.

The commemorative function of Turner de Lond's images of the urban world is further exemplified in *The Chairing of Thomas Spring Rice* (Figure 8.6), which pictures a triumphant moment in Limerick's political history. In fact, in both composition and theme, this painting could almost be a sister image to *George IV, King of England, entering Dublin*. However, its subject matter sets it apart and makes it one of the most unique images of early-nineteenth-century Ireland in existence. It focuses on the figure of Thomas Spring Rice, who was controversially defeated by the conservative Major John Prendergast Vereker when he stood for office in 1820. However, on petition to parliament, all the votes of the non-resident freemen were disallowed, and Spring Rice was successfully elected.[41]

This was a particularly noteworthy victory for the Independent Citizens of Limerick and Rice's arrival back to the city from Dublin was widely celebrated and reported on in the local newspapers. According to the *Limerick Evening Post*, there were more than 80,000 people involved in the procession.[42] Turner de Lond portrays the politician under an arched canopy of festooned silk, entwined with shamrocks and gilt laurel leaves, as the procession halts at the Commercial Buildings. Beside him on the stage are prominent Limerick citizens and members of the Chamber of Commerce. The windows are filled with handkerchiefs, banners and extremely detailed renderings of the flags from local guilds, including the butchers, shoemakers, hatters, coopers, millers and bakers.[43]

---

40  *Limerick Chronicle*, 13 Oct. 1821.
41  Bridget Hourican, 'Rice, Thomas Spring 1st Baron Monteagle' in James McGuire and James Quinn (eds), *Dictionary of Irish biography* (Cambridge, 2009), available at http://dib.cambridge.org/viewReadPage.do?articleId=a7661-A (accessed 30 May 2014).
42  *Limerick Evening Post*, 24 July 1820.
43  Robert Herbert, 'The chairing of Thomas Spring Rice' in *North Munster Antiquarian Journal*, iv, no. 4 (1945), pp 136–41.

8.6 William Turner de Lond (fl. 1820–26), *The Chairing of Thomas Spring Rice* (c.1821), oil on canvas (Limerick Chamber of Commerce)

As with *George IV, King of England, entering Dublin*, both the compositional arrangement and the meticulous attention to detail in this image provide the viewer with an eyewitness account of proceedings. The city – both space and inhabitants – are orderly and civilised and exude a sense of togetherness. It is unclear whether Spring Rice, a group of his supporters or members of the Chamber of Commerce commissioned the work, or whether Turner de Lond's decision to paint it was purely speculative. Its current poor condition makes it more difficult to analyse, but the discrepancies in perspective (some figures are vastly larger than others) and the poor application of the medium indicate that Turner de Lond created it rapidly, possibly in the hope of making a quick sale while the event was still fresh in the public memory. In any case, it was not sold at Swinburne's in October 1821 and appeared on the market again in July 1822, when the following advert was published in *The Limerick Chronicle*:

> The Grand Picture representing the Chairing of Mr. Rice, painted to commemorate and transmit to succeeding generations the universal enthusiasm which animated every Independent on the successful termination of the most arduous struggle ... Mr. Turner's departure for Edinburgh being near, begs to offer to the Independents the above Picture, either individually or collectively, for purchase at one-half its intrinsic value ... and feels confident that so great and powerful a body as the Independents will not be indifferent to the merits of an individual who has exhausted his substance and talents, or suffer him to depart without an endeavour to give him at least a partial remuneration, for his time.[44]

This advert reveals a great deal about Turner de Lond's underlying motivations in painting the scene. It also communicates something about how he intended the urban space to be read by his consumers from an ideological point of view. He uses a specific moment in the city's contemporary history, a specific place within its topography and a specific set of recognisable urbanites to underline the civic harmony of the event, to 'commemorate and transmit [it] to succeeding generations' and thus ensure its lasting posterity. This construct of the urban world, both city and people, is a platform for an ordered community gathering and mutual celebration, but also a commemorative object.

In what ways, then, do the images produced by Grogan and Turner de Lond conform to Lefebvre's conceptualisation of urban space as something both physical and ideological mentioned in the introduction? During the period covered in this chapter the rural world was increasingly becoming a point of anxiety – a place (and a people) that were both physically and

44 *Limerick Chronicle*, 21 July 1822.

ideologically distant from urban patrons and 'admirers of the Fine Arts' that artists like Grogan and Turner de Lond were targeting.[45] Images of the city space might attract patrons because they presented recognisable places that were safe and far removed from the volatility of the unfamiliar countryside. From this perspective, and in contrast to the work of British artists like Hogarth, perhaps visualisations of the urban world in Ireland functioned as emblems of security.

Certainly, this chapter has argued that men like Newenham, Cooper Penrose and even the Independent Citizens of Limerick used visualisations of the urban world to communicate their aspirations of how life in Ireland could be (or what they imagined it might be): hard working, prosperous and refined. As well as that, an image like *Boats on the River Lee below Tivoli* or *The Chairing of Thomas Spring Rice* would reassure and confirm their audience's affinity with (and understanding of) the variety of the city's people, their pride in their local community and, most importantly, their own place within the urban – and indeed, the national – social system. Thus, rather than providing a snapshot of the actuality of daily life in the Irish urban space during this period, these images shed new light on the ideologies and values of the urban dwellers that were looking at them.

45 *Limerick Chronicle*, 13 Oct. 1821.

# 9
# Forging a Shared Identity: Irish Migrants and Steel Cities, 1850–1900

*Oliver Betts*

Ruminations on the spaces of Irish history have been increasingly widespread in recent years. In a recent essay in the *Dublin Review of Books*, Breandán Mac Suibhne discussed those 'patches' of the U.S.A. in the nineteenth and twentieth centuries in which Irish culture had resonated. Originally a term that denoted a 'cluster of shacks on a colliery', patches came to represent so much more. They were, Mac Suibhne argued, spaces where the fiddle held sway, and the wise woman and the keener of much older cultural traditions practised their arts.[1] In a similar vein, in a contemplative article in the *Journal of American Ethnic History*, published in 2009, Timothy Meagher mused over the question, 'How much more is there to learn about Irish Americans?' The problem, Meagher determined, was one of scope. Too many studies of Irish migrants in the U.S.A. were clustered on the urban centres of the Eastern Seaboard in the latter two-thirds of the nineteenth century. The 'really exciting' possibilities lay, he concluded, in the broadening out of these areas of investigation, through extending studies either into the centuries preceding and following the intense period of post-famine migration or into wider geographical comparatives as exemplified by Malcolm Campbell's *Ireland's new worlds*.[2] Campbell's work, comparing Irish migration to the Pacific Coast of America and to Australia, was an attempt to question the often unintentional explanation of Irish immigrant experiences 'in terms

---

1 Brendán Mac Suibhne, '"Them poor Irish lads" in Pennsylvania' in *Dublin Review of Books*, lxiv (2015), available at www.drb.ie/essays/%27them-poor-irish-lads%27-in-pennsylvania (accessed 20 July 2015).
2 Timothy J. Meagher, 'From the world to the village' in *Journal of American Ethnic History*, xxviii, no. 4 (2009), pp 118–24.

of their *Irishness*, as though this constitutes a homogenous, coherent, and constant phenomenon'. Irish experiences, Campbell observed, extended well beyond the Eastern Seaboard of the U.S.A., encompassing a variety of urban and rural settings. Each of these spaces shaped the nature of Irish migration in different ways.[3]

Selecting which spaces to examine, however, is more difficult. The issue has been particularly relevant in the developing field of transnational history. Connecting the different scales involved in such an enterprise, from the oceanic to the neighbourhood, is complex and challenging.[4] The move away from the nation state as a unit of analysis has left historians with a 'container concept' mentality, as Michael Müller and Cornelius Torp have argued; one that still exhibits a preference for the defined and lasting space as a unit of analysis. Moving beyond established borders, despite established historical tradition, is a hard task. '[A]ll historical phenomena have to be studied within their own geographical frameworks',[5] allowing a more organic approach to transnational history. Adapting this to an Irish historical focus, following on from the discussion of Meagher and Campbell, clearly indicates that a much more nuanced approach must be taken to those spaces considered somehow 'Irish'.

This chapter has taken the reverse approach to the one outlined by Müller and Torp; instead of allowing 'the selection of a given topic with its particular historical analysis' to define which spaces must be scrutinised, this study began with a series of comparative contexts and from there entered into a consideration of Irish transnational history.[6] This was, however, more by accident than design. The study did not begin life with a determination to seek out Irish history; instead, it began life as an initial investigation into conditions of life in steel cities in the Anglophone world. Enormous hubs of industry, steel cities have rarely featured in histories that go beyond the national, the intensely individual or, from an economic perspective, the corporate.[7] Despite the clear lines of connection that extend between them, historians have been reluctant to place these titans of the modern industrial world in a related context, and this chapter represents an attempt to remedy

---

3 Malcolm Campbell, *Ireland's new worlds: immigrants, politics and society in the United States and Australia* (Madison, Wis., 2008), pp vii–viii.
4 Jan Rüger, 'OXO: or, the challenges of Transnational History' in *European History Quarterly*, xl, no. 4 (2010), p. 660.
5 Michael G. Müller and Cornelius Torp, 'Conceptualising transnational spaces in history' in *European Review of History*, xvi, no. 5 (Oct. 2009), pp 610–11.
6 Ibid., p. 611.
7 See, for example, Daniel Headrick, *Tentacles of progress: technology transfer in the Age of Imperialism, 1850–1940* (Oxford, 1988), pp 276–87; David Brody, *Steelworkers in America: the non-union era* (Cambridge, Mass., 1960); Minoru Yasumoto, *The rise of a Victorian ironopolis: Middlesbrough and regional industrialization* (Woodbridge, 2011).

this historical neglect. Research into three prominent steel cities in Britain and the U.S.A. revealed that Irish migrant populations formed a sizeable and important part of all of them. It therefore seemed fitting that Irish experience and identities within these urban spaces should form the preliminary element of this wider examination of steel cities in the Anglophone world.

Steel cities were defined by their industry like no other. Vast industrial conurbations, many were single-company towns, and all were solely dependent on the steel industry for their existence. By the late nineteenth century, when large-scale technical shifts in the production of and demand for steel were beginning dramatically to reshape the industry, the entire civic identity of steel cities was firmly bound up in the production of steel. Middlesbrough, on the north-east coast of England, was so widely known as Ironopolis that for many years one of the city's two football teams was *Middlesbrough Ironopolis*. By 1911, Pittsburgh, colloquially known as 'Steel City', was churning out almost half of all U.S.-produced steel. This chapter examines Irish communities in three urban spaces outside of Ireland. These are the steel cities of Coatbridge, in North Lanarkshire in Scotland, Middlesbrough, on the north-east Teesside coast of England, and Pittsburgh in Pennsylvania, U.S.A. Selected because of their significance to national and international steel production in the period of industrial growth and upheaval between 1870 and 1940, within the context of a study of Irish transnational history these cities offer particular spaces worth investigating.

Throughout the nineteenth century, all three cities played host to Irish migrant populations who were subject to the intense social, cultural, economic and environmental conditions created by the near-exclusive focus on the steel industry in each city. All three groups, moreover, were caught, as Campbell has put it, between both the 'fervent demands' of their new societies to adapt and the 'global power of nationalism [that] provided the motivation and opportunity for Irish immigrants and those of Irish descent to argue more assertively in support of Irish national aspirations'.[8] Moving from male migrant experience to female migrant experience and then, finally, to wider civic experiences of the migrants themselves, this chapter will show that these steel cities did become, at least in part, Irish urban spaces. Drawing upon these cities as contexts allows for a greater exploration of the smaller spaces where Irish identities resonated. As this study will show, these spaces, emphasised by many as vital to the 'change of question and of explanation' that transnational histories encourage, reflected ideas about Irish identity on smaller levels.[9] Thrust into the blast

---

8 Campbell, *Ireland's new worlds*, pp 134–35.
9 Bernhard Struck, Kate Ferris and Jacques Revel, 'Introduction: space and scale in transnational history' in *International History Review*, xxxiii, no. 4 (Dec. 2011), p. 580. See also Müller and Torp, 'Conceptualising transnational spaces', p. 614.

furnaces, the back-street slums and the expansive and contested civic streets of modern industrial society, Irish migrants formed particular identities that were wrought both by themselves and by their surroundings.

## Work, danger and masculine identity

Contemporary accounts of steel cities frequently began with a journey to the city from the peripheries, from where their true industrial impact could be gauged. 'Twilight and night are the conditions under which to see an Iron-making town', Lady Florence Bell urged in her 1907 study of Middlesbrough, 'the pillars of cloud by day, the pillars of fire by night'.[10] Upon entering the city the sensory assault became more profound. In 1845, one visitor to Coatbridge captured the scene in dramatic style:

> At night the groups of blast furnaces on all sides might be imagined to be blazing volcanoes ... From the town comes a continual row of heavy machinery ... the pounding of many steam hammers seemed to make the very ground vibrate under one's feet. Fire, smoke and soot with the roar and rattle of machinery are its leading characteristics.[11]

None of the three cities in question produced steel exclusively. Middlesbrough was also home to shipbuilding, coal miners set off each day from Coatbridge for the surrounding hills and in Pittsburgh coal and glass lay alongside steel as key industries. All three, though, were considered in their own right as steel cities, defined by this one heavy industry.

By extension, the metal workers of the steel cities were seen, and saw themselves, as part of this sole all-consuming industry. Blast furnaces, lit all day and all night, hungered for labour and Ireland was one of the key locations, in all three cases, that provided a stream of young male workers. Minoru Yasumoto has calculated that 9.2 per cent of migrants in Middlesbrough in 1871 were from Ireland, a higher percentage than any other industrial town in England that year, apart from Liverpool. Almost all, moreover, were newcomers, he has observed, and many could not be traced from one census to the next, hinting at residential instability on the part of these young male migrants, although it is worth noting that the proportion of second- and third-generation families that considered themselves Irish continued to grow in certain neighbourhoods.[12] Coatbridge was likewise swollen by Irish migration,

---

10 Lady Florence Bell, *At the works: a study of a manufacturing town* (London, 1985), p. 12.
11 Peter Drummond and James Smith, *Coatbridge: three centuries of change* (Glasgow, 1982).
12 Yasumoto, *The rise of a Victorian ironopolis*, pp 65, 129–31.

with, even before the Famine, Irish households comprising roughly 10 per cent of the population in 1841.[13] Pittsburgh, with foreign-born migrants comprising a third of the city's population in 1850, told a similar story.[14] Young, male, Irish migrants were clustered throughout these industrial work spaces.

The work of steel production was long, hard and intensely dangerous in the nineteenth century, and workers of all backgrounds and origins took pride in being part of it. 'Blast-furnace men', a Coatbridge doctor pointed out in 1864, 'have always been easily distinguishable from the rest of the community by the peculiar red and scorched appearance of their faces'.[15] Indeed, in the later *Pittsburgh survey*, the faces of steel workers from different backgrounds and companies, marked by the soot and the heat of the blast furnace, grin out at the reader.[16] Much of the labour around the blast furnaces, working with molten metal at huge temperatures without any safety equipment, was intensely dangerous. The pouring of the metal from the furnaces into moulds or grooves on the ground could subject men to splashes or scalds from the heat. Lady Bell recounted, in her 1908 work, one particularly harrowing incident in which the cap of a blast furnace was being replaced when a sudden expulsion of fumes caused the wooden work-way above to collapse, plunging two workmen into the 'glowing mass beneath'. 'Then followed', she wrote, 'two hours of horror for those who … tried to recover the remains'.[17] Men were repeatedly scalded, splashed or crushed at the works but employers rarely struggled to find new recruits.

The ready pool of labour for the blast furnaces was, whether Irish or not, overwhelmingly young, single and ready to risk huge dangers for the potential of huge rewards. Steel works operated, in all three cities, on a hierarchy of labour, and if wages might have been unimpressive at the bottom of the scale, they were certainly not at the top. Out of 1,270 men paid in a given week, Bell calculated, the wages received ranged between 10s. (for the 'boys') and £4 for key personnel. The vast majority were taking home somewhere between £1 and £3 a week – sums that, in many cases, easily exceeded the poverty line of £1 1s. 8d. set by the social investigator Seebohm Rowntree in 1901.[18]

---

13  John Foster, Muir Houston and Chris Madigan, 'Irish immigrants in Scotland's shipyards and coalfields: employment relations, sectarianism and class formation' in *Historical Research*, vol. lxxxiv, no. 226 (2011), pp 659–60.
14  Roy Lubove (ed.), *Pittsburgh* (New York, 1976), p. 2.
15  Andrew Miller, *The rise and progress of Coatbridge and surrounding neighbourhood* (Glasgow, [1864]), chapter 25.
16  See, for instance, the pictures included in Paul U. Kellogg (ed.), *The Pittsburgh survey* (6 vols, New York, 1910–14), vol. iv.
17  Bell, *At the works*, p. 102.
18  Ibid., p. 48; B. Seebohm Rowntree, *Poverty: a study of town life* (York, 2000), pp 132–34.

So tantalising were the wages in Middlesbrough, Bell concluded, that young men would not even contemplate alternative sources of employment. 'Between the ages of thirteen and sixteen', she argued, boys were 'simply turned loose', caught between the ending of compulsory schooling and the necessary wait to turn the required age for employment at the works. Whilst Bell worried about the consequences of such a lack of direction for young men on the cusp of adult life, she could not deny the powerful appeal of the high-wage world of the works.[19] Even during times of fluctuation, especially in America, where wages in the steel industry were less stable than elsewhere, workers remained keenly aware of their *potential* for higher earnings.[20] News, in 1880, that steel workers in nearby Motherwell had successfully negotiated a higher wage brought Coatbridge men out in force.[21] Performing dangerous work, men employed at the steel works in all three cities felt entitled to a reward equal to the task.

It was a model of masculinity that, rather than supplant ethnicity, instead could sit alongside it. The technical shift from iron to steel in this period focused attention on the bodies and physical labour of the steel workers.[22] Hard spaces produced hard men, and many Irish migrants claimed, at least, to relish the test of strength that work at the foundry brought. 'Mighty few men have stood what I have', John Griswold, a 'Scottish-Irish' worker, told the investigators of the *Pittsburgh survey*. At the time of the survey, Griswold was a furnace boss with responsibility for a number of men and furnaces. 'I've been twenty years at the furnaces and been workin' a twelve-hour day all that time, seven days a week', he proudly informed his interviewers.[23] For Irishmen like Griswold and their descendants the working spaces of steel cities functioned as arenas in which a powerful and lasting vision of masculinity could be enacted day by day, shift by shift, moment by dangerous moment. Yet these were also spaces where the socio-cultural identity of being an *Irish* man was reinforced.

Irish masculinity drew upon the camaraderie and physicality of the works but expressed its distinctly Irish nature outside of the industrial centres of production. It was the public arena of the streets and squares of all three cities that saw Irish masculinity manifest itself on a day-to-day basis, through an everyday violence linked to extant cultural and religious practices and celebrations. One Saturday evening in August 1875, the *Glasgow Herald* noted, the decision to hold a public meeting in favour of Home Rule in Coatbridge led to a 'Fiery Cross' being paraded through both the town and

19 Bell, *At the works*, pp 138–41.
20 Brody, *Steelworkers in America*, pp 42–43.
21 *Glasgow Herald*, 12 Jan. 1880.
22 Edward Slavishak, *Bodies of work: civic display and labour in industrial Pittsburgh* (Durham, N.C., 2008), p. 20.
23 Kellogg, *Pittsburgh survey*, iii, 11.

the nearby villages to summon supporters. Violence followed in its wake, with scuffles throughout Coatbridge and a parade of 300 Orange Order supporters waiting for the Motherwell contingent upon their return.[24] Home-Rulers and Anti Home-Rulers clashed in Pittsburgh in the spring of 1914, a running brawl taking up much of the Woods Run district of the city. 'When several Ulster sympathizers took issue with the Brannigans', who the *Chicago Tribune* described as 'ardent Home Rulers', a fight began, 'and soon all the residents in the immediate neighbourhood became involved'.[25] These were distinct from the orderly parades of Irish identity that Paul O'Leary has observed; yet whilst often eschewing order they still represented a shared desire temporarily to appropriate public space to advance a particular notion (or in this case conflicting notions) of Irish identity.[26] The streets, ultimately, were the arena where the physical demonstrations of Irish male identity were played out.

Such violent expressions of patriotic fervour, however, should be treated with caution. For one thing, violent expressions of masculine identity did not always need a national veneer to make sense to participants. As David Taylor has observed in the case of Middlesbrough, whilst it is true that for much of the nineteenth century 'Englishmen fought Irishmen' in the town, it is also true that 'Irishmen (and women) fought each other ... and finally, men and women, Irish and English, attacked the police'.[27] Secondly, and crucially in light of Campbell's critique of historians resting simply on supposed notions of Irishness, such scant sources as there are on workplace-related expressions of masculinity rarely speak to specifically national cultures. Only in the pages of the monumental *Pittsburgh survey* of 1907–08 were the voices of Irish migrant labourers on this subject captured in any detail. By the end of the nineteenth century, Pittsburgh was host to a second wave of migration from southern and eastern Europe as well as African Americans from the South. 'The day labourer in the mills today is a Slav', the survey authoritatively concluded, and Irish men like Griswold were instead propelled into supervisory roles over them.[28] The 'Hunkies', as Griswold and others termed them, 'repelled' the more-established English, Irish and German migrant communities.[29] 'They don't seem like men to me hardly', Griswold complained to the researchers, 'They can't talk United States'.[30] Only in moments of clear racial or religious

24 *Glasgow Herald*, 18 Aug. 1875.
25 *Chicago Tribune*, 7 Apr. 1914.
26 Paul O'Leary, 'Networking respectability: class, gender, and ethnicity among the Irish in south Wales, 1845–1914' in *Immigrants and Minorities*, xxiii, nos. 2–3 (2005), p. 264.
27 David Taylor, 'Conquering the British Ballarat: the policing of Victorian Middlesbrough' in *Journal of Social History*, xxxvii, no. 3 (2004), p. 759.
28 Peter Roberts, 'The immigrant worker', quoted in Lubove, *Pittsburgh*, pp 44–45.
29 Brody, *Steelworkers in America*, p. 119.
30 Kellogg, *Pittsburgh survey*, iii, 11–12.

conflict did the blast furnace floor become a space of comparison and the physical masculinity of Irish male migrants take on a particularly national character in steel cities. Taken on their own, such flashpoints do not move the historian closer to a definitive picture of what Irishness was in situ. A wider approach to space is required.

### Home, street and female identity

It is vital to turn to the other element of the Irish presence in steel cities – the female migrants – truly to examine cultural practices in each location. Unlike male migrants, able to throw themselves into an established culture of work, women in steel cities were cut off – by their gender – from the defining economic identity. The census returns from 1871 to 1911, for example, record the vast majority of women in the Marsh Ward of Middlesbrough, a nexus of Irish settlement, as having no listed occupation.[31] Bell observes that beyond brief periods in domestic service, it was shops and small workshops for unmarried girls; 'organized women's labour' simply did not exist in the town.[32] Even in Pittsburgh, where, unlike in Middlesbrough and Coatbridge, there was some smaller light industry and the service sector, the work was predominantly short-lived and in the hands of young unmarried women.[33] The majority of Irish women in the three cities, whether married or simply cohabiting, were drawn instead to urban spaces beyond the world of work: the home, the street and the church. 'We must know', the *Pittsburgh survey* urged, 'the homes and lodging places … settlements and clubs'.[34] These were for many contemporaries the truly Irish spaces of the city.

'Irish' homes were able to be identified as such because, in all three cities, Irish migrants clustered into areas that gained reputations as 'Irish' neighbourhoods. As Paul O'Leary admits, whilst the phenomenon of Little Irelands is overplayed in both contemporary middle-class and current historical discourse, it is difficult to deny the strength of such an image of residential clustering.[35] In Coatbridge, as John Foster, Muir Houston and Chris Madigan have demonstrated in their joint study of Irish sectarianism and class formation, 'even within small neighbourhoods adjacent streets can sometimes show quite different outcomes'.[36] Coatbridge, they argue, became intensely divided between Catholic and Protestant Irish groups on a street-

---

31 1871–1911 censuses of England.
32 Bell, *At the works*, pp 179–80.
33 Kellogg, *Pittsburgh survey*, i, 17–30.
34 Ibid., p. 318.
35 O'Leary, 'Networking respectability', p. 258.
36 Foster *et al.*, 'Irish immigrants', p. 662.

by-street level.[37] Often, as Richard Dennis has observed, such clustering could be on an intensely micro-scale.[38] Households containing Irish-born residents were by no means a majority in Middlesbrough's Marsh Ward, a few ruler-straight streets of poorer housing north of the centre, but nevertheless maintained a sizeable minority in streets at the heart of this district.[39] Even in more racially mixed Pittsburgh, with its successive waves of immigration, areas maintained a distinctly Irish hue. The Lawrenceville section of the city, investigators noted, hosted 'Poles[,] Greeks and Assyrians ... but the characteristic nationality is Irish'.[40] Irish was a clearly observable and understandable group identity that could be easily applied in spatial terms for outsiders.

Residential clustering placed the home at the centre of Irish life and identity formation by helping to maintain those migration chains that Meagher has argued represent an exciting, yet understudied, aspect of Irish American history.[41] Migrants in both Middlesbrough and Coatbridge did not have to travel far from Ireland to arrive in their new steel city environment. 'Crossing the Irish Sea did not cost much', Geraldine Vaughan has observed in her study of the Irish in Western Scotland, and consequently migration pathways saw travel back and forth throughout the period.[42] Likewise, those migrants who travelled to Middlesbrough were rarely persistent over the long term, and the Teeside area clearly existed on a wider network of migration pathways.[43] This led, particularly in Middlesbrough, to a widely developed informal economy of lodging newly arrived migrants. Several registered lodging houses dotted the Marsh Ward catering to an overwhelmingly young, single and male stream of newly arrived Irish migrants and run by more-established Irish migrant families. It was not only registered lodging houses that flourished in the Marsh Ward, the Medical Officer of Health noted, but more informal affairs run from individual dwellings.[44] In some cases it could be an exceedingly short-term arrangement. The residents of 2 Back Nile Street, housing one lodger in addition to their family of five, admitted to census-takers that 'two lodgers slept here on Sunday but they [the residents] did not get the names'.[45] Bernard and Eliza O'Niel, Irish

---

37 Ibid., pp 663–65.
38 Richard Dennis, *English industrial cities of the nineteenth century: a social geography* (Cambridge, 1986), pp 223–24.
39 1871–1901 census of Ireland.
40 Kellogg, *Pittsburgh survey*, i, 319.
41 Meagher, 'From the world to the village', p. 120.
42 Geraldine Vaughan, *The 'local' Irish in the west of Scotland 1851–1921* (London, 2013), pp 36–37.
43 Yasumoto, *The rise of a Victorian ironopolis*, pp 99–105.
44 Report to the sanitary committee, 5 Dec. 1899, 7, Teeside Archives, Middlesbrough, CB/M/H/1.
45 1871 census returns, Middlesbrough, District 12, RG 10/4891, 12.

migrants settled in Coatbridge, may not have been directly connected to their five lodgers, four of whom were Irish, yet they were clearly, intentionally or otherwise, part of a wider network of migration.[46]

Taking in lodgers served a twofold purpose for many Irish families in Middlesbrough and Coatbridge. On a material level, it helped ensure, through the exchange of space in the home for rent money, the economic survival of the family unit. On a social level, however, the widespread lodging network helped support those who arrived without clear connections. Whilst families frequently did take in close kith and kin as lodgers, the census returns for both towns point to a lodging house culture that was much wider than such clear-cut connections alone would explain. As Vicky Holmes has recently emphasised in an English context, it is important to remember that 'informal financial arrangements' were as common as obvious rental divisions in such households, and that for the poor the presence of the unrelated lodger was nowhere near the 'shocking and unacceptable' practice middle-class diatribes made it out to be.[47] It was not just newly arrived young labourers who found lodgings with fellow Irish migrants. Over the course of the second half of the nineteenth century, a growing proportion of lodgers in Middlesbrough's Marsh Ward were older men and women. For elderly men, Bell noted, if security could not be found in the homes of relatives, especially for those older migrants who never married, private lodgings were vastly preferable to the workhouse.[48] Scattered across Irish households on census returns between 1871 and 1911 are elderly relatives and strangers lodging in private houses. Multi-generational household units were by no means an exclusively Irish phenomenon in the industrial city of the nineteenth century, but they nevertheless enabled cultural connections to be sustained, particularly for residents who were the children of immigrants and had not been born in Ireland itself.

The children of migrants were one of the chief beneficiaries of the cultural practices of Irishness that emanated from the home. Working-class children in both Britain and America, in the late nineteenth century, were subject to an array of influences as they navigated urban spaces that ranged from the schoolroom and workplace to home and street.[49] Yet the peculiar economic make-up of steel cities, which denied long-term work opportunities to women

---

46  1871 census returns, Old Monkland, District 17, 33, 1, CSSCT1871_149.
47  Vicky Holmes, 'Accommodating the lodger: the domestic arrangements of lodgers in working-class dwellings in a Victorian provincial town' in *Journal of Victorian Culture*, xix, 3 (2014), pp 330–31.
48  Bell, *At the works*, p. 110.
49  Howard Chudacoff, *Children at play: an American history* (New York, 2007), pp 4–5; Anna Davin, *Growing up poor: home, school and street in London 1870–1914* (London, 1995), pp 160–61.

and also prohibited entry into the steel industry for young men until they reached a certain age, left youths of both genders with fewer alternative influences beyond the home. Irish children, moreover, were often notorious for skipping school in steel cities. Whilst the *Pittsburgh survey* at the start of the twentieth century might be able to report with enthusiastic surprise that a growing number of Irish children were not only completing compulsory education but moving beyond it, it also featured a little of the older stereotype as well.[50] 'Truant Officers?' one Irish mother in Pittsburgh's Skunk-Hollow asked the investigators as a knot of children played in her yard, 'What are they?'[51] With limited opportunities in which to develop long-term working identities, and with a reluctant relationship with the guidance of school, the family and the home, personified by mother, remained chief influences over the lives of Irish children in steel cities.

One of the most significant manifestations of the influence mothers had over their offspring was a religious identity. The 'social distance' between Protestants and Catholics embodied, as the authors of the Coatbridge study have observed, in the housing patterns of Irish migrants, was reinforced throughout childhood.[52] Growing up in either Protestant or Catholic households, Irish children in all three cities were presented with the active practice of religion, and its attendant undertakings, as a cornerstone of cultural identity. In Middlesbrough, where authorities were preoccupied with the heavy drinking culture amongst male workers, observers were astounded by the sheer numbers of Irish children taking the temperance pledge and attending the Catholic League of the Cross each Sunday.[53] Teetotalism may have been, as Victor Walsh has suggested in the case of Pittsburgh, a 'middling-sort' of movement, stoutly resisted by Irish groups in the impoverished Skunk-Hollow and Point districts, but it was just one manifestation of cultural activity that revolved around religion.[54] From Sunday School to Church to festival days, be they Catholic or Protestant, for Irish migrants and their offspring religion was an enacted part of culture that played out across an urban stage.

It was in these urban spaces that Irish culture, in its manifest forms, was defined and reinforced. These were the ethnic spheres that Louise Miskell has observed in her work on South Wales, but ones that contracted and expanded through a variety of smaller spaces *within* steel cities as well as encompassing

50 Kellogg, *Pittsburgh survey*, v, 31–32.
51 Ibid., p. 126.
52 Foster *et al.*, 'Irish immigrants', p. 666.
53 Anon., *Middlesbrough year book* (Middlesbrough, 1901).
54 Victor A. Walsh, '"Drowning the shamrock": drink, teetotalism, and the Irish Catholics of gilded-age Pittsburgh' in *Journal of American Ethnic History*, x, no. 1/2, 'The Irish in America' (Fall 1990–Winter 1991), pp 68–70.

them.[55] Each house, in each street, could be a nexus for both the outward display and inward reinforcement of culture. This was achieved through a myriad of small, everyday set-pieces and practices that both harked back to older traditions and involved widespread community participation. Wakes for the dead, whilst not an exclusively Irish cultural event, nevertheless formed small moments in which the homes of Irish residents could be opened up to friends, family and wider connections. Investigating a smallpox outbreak in Middlesbrough in 1898, the Medical Officer of Health traced the event back to a wake in an Irish household. His report painted a vivid picture of the open house event: 'As is very common amongst the lower class of Irish people, a wake was held in the house on two successive days over the body. Hundreds of people, I am told, passed in and out of the house'.[56] Nor was it the only instance where homes played host to wider communal gatherings during the epidemic. The Medical Officer of Health also noted that a sick child in the Ryan family had, for about 14 days of illness, been visited by a host of well-wishers. 'Most of the next cases', he pointed out, 'were amongst people who ... called at the house'.[57] Neither opening up the house nor the custom of displaying the dead for public commemoration was solely the preserve of the Irish. Yet they were, for both Irish migrants and outside observers such as the Medical Officer of Health, regarded as expressions of Irish culture.

## Urban spaces and Irishness

Identity cannot exist in a vacuum. 'Otherness is an essential component of identity', Vaughan has pointed out. In examining the Irish in West Scotland, she concludes that 'Irishness was ... constructed by the immigrants themselves and also by Irish gazing into the Scottish mirror'.[58] This is well observed, yet a mirror is an imperfect metaphor. For what it was to be Irish in Coatbridge and, by extension, in other steel cities, depended not just on the actions and reflections of the migrants themselves but also on the views of non-Irish outsiders. The mirror was, in essence, two-way: identities could be reinforced or rejected by others beyond the group. Whilst the perceptions of others were by no means as powerful as internal individual or group relationships amongst migrants, in the urban spaces of steel cities the images and reputations of

---

55 Louise Miskell, '"Operating in the ethnic sphere": Irish migrant networks and the question of respectability in nineteenth-century south Wales' in *Immigrants and Minorities*, xxiii, 2–3 (2005), p. 247.
56 Charles Dingle, 'The story of the Middlesbrough small-pox epidemic and some of its lessons' in *Public Health*, xi (1898–1899), p. 175.
57 Ibid.
58 Vaughan, *The 'local' Irish*, p. 37.

'the Irish' were significant. Steel cities, so newly expanded and with such monomaniacal focus on their chief industry, were also blank urban canvases upon which group identities could be projected. Three small instances, one from each of the cities in question, illustrate just how Irish migrants, and perceptions of them, shaped the civic face of these steel cities.

Coatbridge, which expanded into steel a little earlier than Middlesbrough or Pittsburgh, saw the reputation of Irish migrants shift back and forth throughout the period. Listing the population of Coatbridge in her poem 'Oor Location', Janet Hamilton, writing in the mid-nineteenth century, described:

> Navvies, miners, keepers, fillers,
> puddlers, rollers, iron millers,
> reestit, reekit, raggit laddies,
> Firemen, enginemen an' Paddies.[59]

The *Leeds Mercury*, reporting on a murder in the district, went further. A violent death had ensued, it informed its readers, after a 'melee' which was 'one of those occurrences which is too frequent in the neighbourhood, namely a "navvie row"'.[60] Whereas Hamilton's poem merely associated the Irish with manual labour, this report clearly linked violence to the areas inhabited by the migrants. However, at the same time as such close associations between the Irish, menial wage labour and violence were being penned, the Coatbridge Mechanics' Institute was opening. In November 1850, at the official dedication ceremony, the *Glasgow Herald* reported that the 'Academy was crowded to excess by a respectable and intelligent auditory'.[61]

Such inconsistent images reflect the fragmented nature in which the Irish in the town appear to the historian filtered through the Victorian fourth estate. The press dwelt on stories of sectarian conflict in steel cities. This did happen, of course, as previous examples have indicated, but such violent flashes represent only one small facet of Irish identity. Individual Irish migrants had enormous, and varied, impacts on the urban spaces of Coatbridge, yet remained marginal figures in the news reports, often only visible now to the historian through the medium of electronic searches that throw up every brief and disparate mention of their names and urban haunts. Two of such fleeting characters were the Revd John Hughes and Dr Charles O'Neill. The obituary in the *Irish Times* points out that Hughes had shaped the Catholic nature of Coatbridge dramatically. In 1899, he had erected a new church at

---

59  Janet Hamilton, *Poems and essays of a miscellaneous character on subjects of general interest* (Glasgow, 1863).
60  *Leeds Mercury*, 14 Sept. 1850.
61  *Glasgow Herald*, 22 Nov. 1850.

a cost of £10,000 and strived to establish secondary education institutions in the district. 'One of the most popular priests in the West of Scotland', he had, it must be assumed, exercised considerable influence over the Catholic community in the town.[62] Dr O'Neill, by contrast, made his mark on other Irish spaces, namely in South Armagh, where in 1909 he stood for election as an Irish Nationalist MP. A respected physician in Coatbridge, O'Neill had been radicalised by his time in the town amidst the sectarian tensions of the late nineteenth century and carried this radicalism back to Ireland along with considerable donations to the cause raised in Coatbridge itself.[63] Both men shaped, and were shaped by, the urban spaces of Coatbridge as they pursued parallel yet distinct 'Irish' causes.

In Middlesbrough, the official face of Irish identity, despite the sizeable population of Protestant Irish and a myriad of other associational groups, was the Catholic Church. 'Roman Catholicism could not be other than conspicuous', Malcolm Chase has pointed out, with the establishment of a Catholic Bishopric in the town in 1879. By the 1870s, civic spaces throughout Middlesbrough were given over to celebrations of Irish Catholic identity on significant calendar moments.[64] The displays were given particular prominence, however, by the intermittent presence of key figures of national interest. Chief amongst these was Cardinal Henry Manning. Manning, who by the 1870s had been elevated to both the Archdiocese of Westminster and the College of Cardinals, came to Middlesbrough at least twice in the final decades of the nineteenth century.

On both occasions he spoke about temperance. Manning's sermons, carried in the local papers verbatim, were a powerful tirade against drink. In 1881, haranguing a packed congregation in St Mary's Cathedral, he drew not just on the spiritual ruin of drink but the health impact. Holding up the evidence of a visiting doctor at the London Hospitals he told the congregation:

> So convinced was Dr. Clarke of the great evils of drinking that he was doubtful whether it would not be wiser to give up the practice of medicine and devote the whole of his life to trying to prevail upon people to abstain.[65]

Drink was a significant issue at the Iron Works in Middlesbrough. Lady Bell, like many reformers, felt that the issue was most acute at home, and argued that whilst few men drank on their way to their shifts, the vast majority did

---

62 *Irish Times*, 16 Aug. 1900.
63 *Irish Times*, 16 May 1908; 4 Nov. 1909.
64 Malcolm Chase, 'The Teeside Irish in the nineteenth century' in *Cleveland History: The Bulletin of the Cleveland and Teeside Local History Society*, lxix (1995), p. 5.
65 *Northern Echo*, 7 Sept. 1881.

on the way home.⁶⁶ Yet drinking at work, especially during breaks, was equally common and even workers hired by the city corporation to build a new fever hospital were paid, in part, with whiskey.⁶⁷ It was a reputation that particularly attached itself to the Irish and one that was fuelled, in part, by their participation in the hard-working and hard-drinking culture of the works. Manning would have been well aware of this complicated relationship. An earlier sermon, delivered in 1878, compared the town to the depiction of Corinth in Corinthians. They too, he argued, had been renowned for their 'wonderful workmanship in metals' but were also full to corruption with 'self-indulgence and … vain-glory'. Sermon delivered, Manning concluded his tour with a visit to St Mary's School to meet 1,500 children and be presented with an address and bouquet.⁶⁸ In his visits to the town Manning embodied the dual nature of the Irish in Middlesbrough. They were, as his railing against drink and excess in this vast Ironopolis made clear, subject to the same pressures of industrial life as their fellow cohabitants. Yet the cultural mechanisms they called upon to respond to these pressures were, fundamentally, distinct from those of their English or Welsh neighbours. Temperance rhetoric, religious celebration and the involvement of schoolchildren in the pageantry of the anti-drink movement was cast in a distinctly Catholic (which for the vast majority of residents in the period corresponded with Irish) hue.

The final of the three examples, the last chronologically, relates to the political Catholicism of Irish migrants to Pittsburgh in the 1920s. 'Where are your Irish?' one social investigator asked a factory foreman in Pittsburgh in 1911. 'Go to the city hall and the police station', was the answer, 'you'll find them there'.⁶⁹ As the *Pittsburgh survey* authors noted, by the end of the nineteenth century, Pittsburgh's Irish residents were no longer the bottom of the labour pile. With southern and eastern European and Middle Eastern migrants moving in from abroad, and African American immigrants arriving from the south, those Irish who remained in the industry found themselves increasingly in supervisory roles. Griswold, the Irish foreman interviewed extensively by the investigators, was increasingly depressed about the situation. There had been 50 other Irishmen working with him 16 years ago, he noted, but now they were elsewhere. 'I meet 'em sometimes around the city, ridin' in carriages and all of them wearin' white shirts', he concluded morosely, 'and here I am with the Hunkies'.⁷⁰ By the 1900s, it was the newer arrivals who were facing the lower wages and higher risks of the unskilled labour

66  Bell, *At the works*, pp 246–51.
67  H. Gilzean-Reid, *The story of the smallpox epidemic in Middlesbrough* (Middlesbrough, 1898), pp 8–9.
68  *Daily Gazette*, 22 Aug. 1878.
69  Quoted in Lubove, *Pittsburgh*, p. 44.
70  Kellogg, *Pittsburgh survey*, iii, 11–12.

market at the steel mills.[71] Many of these newer arrivals, especially from the Hungarian, Polish and Italian communities, were also Catholics. Yet it was the Catholicism of the Irish migrants, particularly, that was stressed when the urban spaces of Pittsburgh were singled out for a political challenge.

That challenge came from the Ku Klux Klan. Whilst originally a rural and southern phenomenon, with its roots in the post-bellum anxieties of the Reconstruction south, by the 1920s the Klan had resurfaced as a decidedly anti-immigrant, anti-Catholic and urban force. In this period, as Kenneth Jackson has shown, it gathered hundreds of thousands in the north-east to its banner. 'To many native-born Protestants', Jackson argues, 'the threat of Catholic and Jewish immigration was greater than the menace of hooded Americanism'.[72] Yet the organisation struggled to gain a clear foothold in Pittsburgh. A show of force, it was determined by Klan leadership, would help bring the silent majority they assumed were there onside and into the open. Thus, on the evening of 25 August 1923, 10,000 Klansmen gathered on a hill overlooking the suburb of Carnegie to begin a march into the centre of town.

It was an attempt directly to challenge ownership of the public space of the steel city and was met with outright hostility. 'Klan and deputies battle: marcher slain, many hurt at Pittsburgh!' ran the headline the following morning in the *Chicago Tribune*.[73] Denied a permit at the last minute by the Mayor, in a well-intentioned but ultimately futile attempt on his part to stave off the impending violence, the Klansmen had marched anyway, only to be met by a monster counter-demonstration intent of contesting this intrusion into the public space of the suburb. One Klan marcher was shot and killed, and the arrest of four Carnegie men two days later with the surnames of McDermott, Flaherty, Joyce and Kimmel left the papers in no doubt as to the identities of many in the opposing crowd.[74] It was a blow from which the Klan was never to recover in the Pittsburgh area. Whilst it made headway, during its brief upsurge in the 1920s, in other parts of the urban north-east, the Klan remained wary about Pittsburgh itself. '[We decided] it would be impossible', one leader demurred, 'to do much more than influence ward politics so we didn't try'.[75] Indeed, many individual members chose henceforth to conceal their membership when active in the public life of the city.[76] Although the open political spaces of Pittsburgh had lain before the Klan, they had been effectively beaten back in their attempt

---

71 John Bodnar, Roger Simon and Michael P. Weber, *Lives of their own: blacks, Italians, and Poles in Pittsburgh, 1900–1960* (Chicago, 1983), pp 17–18.
72 Kenneth Jackson, *The Ku Klux Klan in the city 1915–1930* (Chicago, 1992), p. 170.
73 *Chicago Tribune*, 26 Aug. 1923.
74 *Chicago Tribune*, 27 Aug. 1923.
75 Jackson, *Ku Klux Klan*, p. 173.
76 Thomas R. Pengram, *One hundred percent American: the rebirth and decline of the Klu Klux Klan in the 1920s* (Lanham, Md., 2011), p. 195.

to enter into them. It was the Irish, along with other Catholics and anti-Klan groups, who were able more effectively to mobilise in defence of these urban spaces. It was an explicit challenge to a group which had come to the steel city to emphasise that the Irish did not belong.

## Conclusion

By the start of the twentieth century, a strong Irish presence in all three steel cities was confirmed. The reputations of Pittsburgh, Middlesbrough and Coatbridge as centres of Irish migration echoed through the political, cultural and religious mediums of the period. The defeat of an independent socialist candidate in Middlesbrough, for instance, in 1906, was largely put down to the relationship between the sitting Liberal MP and the Catholic Electoral Association.[77] Coatbridge's Irish heritage has been the subject of growing interest from across the Irish Sea, with a 2008 RTÉ television documentary covering the 'Irish experience' of the town.[78] Pittsburgh, meanwhile, has long been a site of active engagement with Irish migrant experiences. *Irish Pittsburgh*, part of the popular *Images of America* heritage collection, drew the memories and family histories of many residents together along with donated photographs and facsimiles.[79] Irish migrants had adapted to the varied spaces these steel cities comprised, securing lasting places within the urban landscape. Homes, workplaces and public spaces were all arenas where Irish identity could be established and reinforced.

Steel city spaces were more durable than the ephemeral and transient migrant spaces Torp and Müller have argued demand historical attention, but they were, as Irish migrants found, open to exploitation.[80] The steady stream of migrants, largely from the south and east of Europe, did little to dent their utilisation of space. As Mac Suibhne noted in relation to the coalfields of the U.S.A., 'having come for so long, Boyles and Breslins ... Shovlins and Sweeneys remained ubiquitous' in these spaces.[81] In Pittsburgh, clearly, the presence of newer arrivals seems to have solidified Irish identities as spaces became shared and Irish workers became surer of their own masculine senses of self in the face of Hungarian or Italian competition. Such was the 'clannishness' of the workforce, the authors of the *Pittsburgh survey* recorded, efforts at unionisation amongst the workers were rife with 'dissension'.[82] The effects of such solidifi-

77 Chase, 'The Teeside Irish', p. 19.
78 *The Irish experience*, RTÉ television documentary broadcast 19 Dec. 2008.
79 Patricia McElligott, *Irish Pittsburgh* (Charleston, S.C., 2013), p. 6.
80 Müller and Torp, 'Conceptualising transnational spaces', p. 614.
81 Mac Suibhne, 'Those poor Irish lads'.
82 Kellogg, *Pittsburgh survey*, iii, 98.

cation was not always welcome to others in the urban milieu (such as the Chief Constable of Middlesbrough who proclaimed the law utterly unable to stop the 'Irish Rowdyism' that occurred 'when different factions came together' in the streets) but they were lasting.[83] Diverse spaces throughout these three steel cities allowed for the establishment and reinforcement of migrant culture. So focused were these environments on one industry, so rapidly built and in need of male labour, that they were open spaces ready to adapt and be adapted by the identities of migrant groups such as the Irish.

What emerges from this albeit brief study is that steel cities were by no means melting pots of urban life. Irish migrants succeeded in establishing clear, culturally reinforcing spaces because these cities were, particularly in the case of the British ones, blank canvases. To journalists from Middlesbrough's *Daily Gazette* in 1878, however, it seemed only natural that they should. 'There are possibly 12,000 or 13,000 Irish in Middlesbrough', the paper reported, 'many of whom are consistent Catholics, and it is only right and proper that they should provide for themselves church and school accommodation'.[84] Whilst this may appear a crystallisation of Patrick Joyce's theory of the nurturing of neighbourhood 'self-control' by civic authorities in the period, it is perhaps closer to the observations Dennis has made regarding public spaces and practices in the modern city.[85] Dennis has argued that barriers and internal divisions meant that wider demonstrations of identity and purpose, such as labour marches, needed to move beyond the confines of their original neighbourhoods and intrude into the wider public spaces to 'advertise their cause'.[86] The same was true for Irish identity in these three steel cities. It was able to lay down roots in the houses and streets, workplaces and foundries of the steel city, but it was also an identity that was expressed through public practice. These staging spaces of Irish residence served, on special occasions such as the visit of Cardinal Manning to Middlesbrough or the challenge of the Klan march on Pittsburgh, to feed residents into the wider public spaces of the city. There, on the broad canvas of industrial cities fuelled by migrant groups such as themselves, Irish celebrations were played out. Unlike labour demonstrations they did not aim at gathering new converts but were instead public affirmations of the faithful: reinforcements of cultural identity in these spaces so far from Ireland.

83  *Newcastle Courant*, 25 Oct. 1878.
84  *Daily Gazette*, 21 Aug. 1878.
85  Patrick Joyce, *The rule of freedom: liberalism and the modern city* (London, 2003), pp 87–89.
86  Richard Dennis, *Cities in modernity: representations and productions of metropolitan space, 1840–1930* (Cambridge, 2008), p. 116.

# Index

Abbott, John (author) 90
alcohol 151, 188, 193, 196–97
anatomy theatres 154
Archer, John (historian) 22
architects and architecture 35, 40, 41, 64
Armagh 3, 66
art
    as commemorative 181
    reflecting illusion rather than reality 174
    as visual evidence 163
associational culture 190
Athlone, Co. Westmeath 3
Australia 47

Ball, Mother Frances Mary Teresa (founder of Loreto Order) 91–96
Ballsbridge (Dublin) 31
    Haddington Road 31
    Pembroke Road 31
Ballyshannon, Co. Donegal 3
Bandon 3
Barcroft, Jeffrey (builder/developer) 26, 31, 33
Barrymore, Earl of (Richard Barry) 162
Bath (England) 7, 22, 35, 40
    Royal Crescent 22, 40
Beaufort, Reverend Daniel (geographer) 64
begging 162, 168
Belfast 2, 3, 8–9, 52, 53, 54, 56, 61–83, 155
    Belfast Academical Institution 62, 74

Belfast Castle 69
Belfast City Hall 8
Belfast Corporation 50, 72
Belfast District Lunatic Asylum 130–34, 135
Belfast Law Society 74
*Belfast News-Letter* 68, 76, 80, 81, 82, 83
Belfast Society for Promoting Knowledge 74–75, 76
Belfast Workhouse 106–24
Belfast Working Men's Institute and Temperance Hall 81
Botanic Gardens 74, 76–77
College Square 73
Commercial Buildings 62
dispute with Newry 66
Donegall House 71
Donegall Place 63, 69–70, 71, 72, 73, 83
Donegall Square 63, 69, 71, 72, 73, 83
Exchange and Assembly Rooms 61–62
First Belfast Presbyterian Church 62
Frederick Street 62
General Hospital 62
Glengall Street 73
growth of 61–62, 111–12, 126–27
High Street 62
housing in 56, 127–28, 131, 134, 141–42
Joy's Paper Mill 75
Linen Hall Library 74–75, 76

Linen Hall Street 71
Nelson Club 73
Ormeau House 71
Police Square Morgue 155
Poor House 62, 65
public health 126–28
St George's Church 62
social conditions in 111, 126–28
South Parade 71, 72
The Flags 71
The Mall 75
Victoria Square (previously Police Square) 155, 158
Victoria Square Morgue 158
Waring Street 62
Wellington Place 73
Welwood Place 73
*see also* White Linen Hall
Bell, Lady Florence (writer) 186, 187–88, 190, 192, 196
Benn, George (historian) 64, 70, 76, 78
Bermuda 150
Bianconi, Charles (transport entrepreneur) 176
Biggar, J.G. (politician) 116
Birmingham, George A. (writer) 75
*Pleasant Places* 75
Blackrock (Dublin) 42, 51, 54
Blackrock House 28
Blackrock Urban District Council 50
Boards of Guardians 49
Belfast 110, 112, 115–22
Donegal 55
Bonaparte, Napoleon 176
Borsay, Peter (historian) 62, 63, 70
bourgeoisie/embourgeoisement 44–45, 57–59, 60, 85–86, 87–88, 97
Bradley, John (archaeologist) 3
Bradley, Thomas (builder/developer) 30, 31, 33, 34, 35, 36, 37
Bray, Co. Wicklow 3
Brighton (England) 15, 27, 40
British Army 150, 160
British Royal Navy 157
builders and building 22–23, 26, 30, 31, 34, 35–36, 37, 38, 39, 47, 55
Bunratty Castle, Co. Clare 176

Cahir, Co. Tipperary 3
Canada 150
Canaletto (artist) 173
Cannadine, David (historian) 13
Carlingford, Co. Louth 3
Carr, Christine (historian) 13
Carrickfergus, Co. Antrim 3
Carroll, Martin H. (surveyor) 35
Cashel, Co. Tipperary 3
Catholic League of the Cross 193
Catholics/Catholicism 61, 190, 193, 198
Cavan (town) 3
cemeteries 146
censuses (England) 186, 190
of 1871 191, 192
censuses (Ireland) 161
of 1881 52
of 1901 151, 152, 153
of 1911 50, 148, 149, 153
Chichester, Arthur (fifth earl of Donegall, later first marquis of Donegall) 64, 65, 69–70
Chichester, George Augustus (second marquis of Donegall) 70–72
childhood
constructions of 87–88
femininity 103
gender and schools 85–86
children 10, 12, 32n54, 76, 85–90, 93, 94, 97, 100–02, 104, 122, 149, 172, 192–93, 197
(at) home 88
(in) cities 88–91
(in) danger 89–90
education of 122, 193
health 99, 101–02, 104, 105, 133
illegitimate 110, 122
legislation pertaining to 89
(of) migrants 192
orphans 98
poor 99
(in) space/spaces 88
(in) workhouses 109, 111, 113, 116, 117, 118
working 95
working class children 192
churches 18

# INDEX

cities
    characteristics of 147
    as civilising spaces 11
    compared with rural areas 181–82
    connections with British Empire 9, 150, 177
    and decay 11
    and disease 110–11, 120–21, 126–29, 137, 142, 150
    and health 141–43
    and their hinterlands 171, 176
    ideological spaces 182
    improvements in urban landscape 176
    relationship to regional towns 176
    as setting of crime 165
    social cohesion 173, 181
city streets
    daily routines 163
    as sites of 'commotion' 152
    as sites of display 177, 179, 189
    visual representations of 163
class 14, 19, 23, 32, 40
    and education 93–96, 104–05
    middle class/classes 10, 11, 44, 58, 63, 65
    upper class/classes 58
    working class/classes 8, 43, 44, 45, 56, 57, 60, 77, 153, 168, 173, 192
Clements, Nathaniel (politician) 99
Cloncurry, Lord (Irish peer) 28, 29
Clonmel, Co. Tipperary 3
Coatbridge (Scotland) 12, 185, 186–87, 190, 191, 192, 194, 195–96, 199
    Coatbridge Mechanics Institute 195
    Commissioners for National Education in Ireland 89, 100–01
commuting 32, 38
Connolly, Sean (historian) 61, 62
Conservative Party 47
Convamore House, Ballyhooly (Co. Cork) 167
Cooper, Austin (antiquary) 15
Copeland, Charles (banker) 32–33
Corbin, Alain (historian) 15
Cork (city) 3, 41, 45, 46, 50, 51, 53, 54, 56, 59, 155, 162, 166

Cork Corporation 50, 56, 57
Cork Harbour 168
Cork Improved Dwellings Company 49
Cork Jail 162, 168
Cork Morgue 155, 156
Cork Society for Promoting Fine Arts (C.S.P.F.A.) 172–73
    Royal Cork Yacht Club 157
    Tivoli House, Cork, 171
Cork (County) 162
coroners 11, 144
    inquests 146
country 14
Craig, Mary 76
Crawford, W.H. (historian) 66, 67
crescents 15
Crofton Croker, Thomas (writer) 172
Cuyp, Albert (Artist) 173

D'Alton, John (writer) 13, 41
Darley, Gillian (historian) 13
Dease, Teresa (founder, Loreto Order in Canada) 96
de Certeau, Michel (historian) 5
degenerationism 128–31
Delft 162
Derry/Londonderry 3
    Corporation 55
developers 14, 26, 30, 31
de Vesci family 7
    Vesey, Thomas (1st Viscount de Vesci) 14
    Vesey, John (2nd Viscount de Vesci) 14, 16, 27, 29, 36
    Vesey, Thomas (3rd Viscount de Vesci) 38, 39
Diver, Patrick (builder) 55
diphtheria 127, 137
Donegal (Town) 55
Donegal Rural District Council 55
Donegall family 8
    residences of 71
    and White Linen Hall/Donegall Place 70–73
    *see also* Arthur and George Chichester

Downpatrick, Co. Down 3
Drennan, William (patriot) 71–72
Drogheda, Co. Louth 3, 42, 51, 53, 54, 55
Drogheda Corporation 50, 55
Dublin (city) 2, 3, 10, 13, 14, 15, 22, 40, 42, 45, 49, 50–54, 56, 57, 59, 73, 81, 179, 145, 148, 155, 156
   arrival of George IV at 177
   Ballsbridge 59
   Blue Coat Hospital 98
   Capel Street 148
   Catholic bourgeoisie in 85–86, 87–88, 97
   Chancery Street 149
   Church Street 149
   Coombe Street Hospital 149
   Dominick Street 150
   Dublin Artisan Dwelling Company 57, 59
   Dublin Corporation 50, 55, 56, 156, 159, 161
   Dublin Corporation Public Health Committee 156
   Dublin Industrial Tenements Company 49
   Dublin to Kingstown Railway 27–28, 29, 30, 32–33
   Dublin Linen Board 66, 80
   Dublin Metropolitan Police 145, 151
   Dublin and Suburban Workmen's Dwelling Company 50
   Dublin Port 14
   Dublin Townships 53, 55, 56
   Erne Street (Lower) 149
   Exchequer Street (Lower) 149
   Fitzsimon's Timber Yard 152
   Frederick Street (North) 151
   Harcourt Street Day School 94
   housing in 127
   Iveagh Buildings 59
   Jervis Street Hospital 148
   King Street (North) 149
   Kevin Street 59
   Lombard Street 152
   Loreto Convent School, Rathfarnham 9, 84–85, 91–97, 95, 97
   Loreto House, St Stephen's Green 92, 95
   Maretimo 28
   Marlborough Street Morgue 11, 155, 156, 157
   Mary's Abbey 148
   Mary's Lane 149
   Nicholas Street 149
   North Denmark Street School 94
   Phoenix Park 9, 85–86, 97–100, 102
   Rathfarnham 9, 84–86, 91–96
   Richmond Barracks 153
   Richmond District Lunatic Asylum (Dublin) 150
   Rotunda Hospital 87
   St Stephen's Green boarding school 94–95
   Sandymount 59
   schools in 84–105
   Stonybatter 57, 59
   Store Street Morgue 148
   Thomas Street 152
   Victorian Fish Market 149
   Wellington Street (Lower) 150
   White Church Protestant school 95
   White Linen Hall 8, 66
   *see also* Ballsbridge; Blackrock; Dunleary; Kingstown Monkstown; Rathmines-Rathgar; Pembroke; Salthill
Dunbar, Charles (estate owner, Monkstown) 14n5
Duncan, William (map maker) 27
Dundalk, Co. Louth 3
Dungannon, Co. Tyrone 3
Dunleary (Dublin) 14, 15, 18, 19, 20, 22, 34, 35
Dunleary Creek 14
   harbour 18
   new harbour 23, 28, 35
   Salt Hill House 18
Durkheim, Emile (sociologist) 11, 145–47
Dutch school 172
Dyos, H.J. (historian) 13

Edgeworth, Maria (writer) 166
Edinburgh (Scotland) 35, 73

# INDEX

education 87
    and class 93–96, 104–05
    compulsory 87, 188, 193
    elite 87, 93–94, 104
    female 85–86, 90–95, 103–04
    male 101–03
    and gender 85–86, 88, 93, 97, 102, 103–05
    spaces 9
Elliott, Marianne (historian) 65
Ennis, Co Clare 3, 174–76, 179
Estate plans 23, 24, 30
    *see also* surveys and surveying; maps and mapping
eugenics 128

Fabbrini, Gaetano (artist) 74
female education 85–86, 90–95, 103–04
Fethard, Co. Tipperary 3
Fishman, Robert (historian) 13, 14, 19
Fitzgerald, Joseph (Town Commissioner) 157
Florence Nightingale (social reformer, nurse) 140
Foucault, Michel (philosopher) 5, 6, 43
Fraser, Murray (historian) 43, 60
    *John Bull's other homes* 43
Free Society of Artists 172
*Freeman's Journal* 27
freemasonry 68

Gaffikin Thomas (linen merchant) 77
Galway (town) 3, 42, 45, 51, 52, 53, 54, 56, 59
    Galway Town Commissioners 50, 55
Gamble, John (writer) 61, 75, 76
gardens 23, 38, 39
gender 9–10, 12
    and childhood 88
    constructions of 88–89
    and education 85–86, 88, 93, 100–05
    responsibilities 90
    and space 88n18
General Registry Office 161

Gill, Conrad (historian) 78
Gillespie, Raymond (historian) 62
Glasgow (Scotland) 81
Gleig, Rev George R. (Inspector General of Military Schools) 102
Glin Castle, Co. Limerick 177n36
governmentality/governmentalisation 43, 44, 60
Graham, William (Resident Medical Superintendent, Belfast Asylum) 125, 126, 131–43
Green Coat Hospital, Cork 98
Griffith, Sir Richard (surveyor) 53
Griffith Valuation 53
Grogan, Nathaniel (artist) 11, 162, 163, 166, 168, 171–72, 181
    *Boat's on the River Lee below Tivoli* (c.1790) 170, 171, 173, 182
    *North Gate Bridge* (c.1794) 162–63, 164, 165, 167, 173
    *Patrick's Bridge* (Figure 8.2) 168, 169
Guinness/Iveagh Trust 49–50, 59
Gunn, Simon (historian) 5, 6

Hamilton, Janet (poet) 195
Harding, Vanessa (historian) 4
Hardy, P.D. (author) 75n72, 76
Harrison, James (soldier) 34
Haverty, Joseph Patrick (artist) 177n37
    *King George IV's Triumphal Entry into Dublin*
Harvey, David (anthropologist) 5
health 15, 43
    and air 10, 99, 133, 134, 157
    alcohol 196
    in the asylum
    children's 99, 101–02, 104, 105
    and the city 85, 141
    and dead bodies 11, 156, 157
    Dublin Corporation Public Health Committee of 156
    and leisure 7
    and masculinity 102
    mental 131
    moral 85, 101, 105
    physical 85, 101, 105

of the poor 87, 126, 132–33, 134, 141
public health 126–28, 132, 147
Public Health Act (1878) 44
and space 99, 101, 119
in workhouse 109, 111, 119, 120, 121, 122
Hibernian Society 98–100
Hill, John (map-maker) 23, 24
Hogarth, William 11, 165–66, 167, 168, 173, 174
   *A Harlot's Progress* (1732) 165
   *Four Times of The Day* (1736) 168
   in Irish homes 166
Home Rule 8, 47, 188–89
house types
   cottages 18, 22, 23, 26, 41, 46, 47, 48, 55
   crescents 15, 19, 22, 23, 24, 26, 27, 31, 40, 41
   detached 13, 17, 18
   semi-detached 13, 23, 24, 26
   slum housing 8, 10, 45, 48
   tenements 45, 46, 49, 57, 152, 154
   terraces 15, 19, 22, 23, 24, 27, 30, 32, 35, 39, 40, 41
   villas 13, 15, 17, 19, 26, 41, 58
housing 8, 42–60, 125–28, 131, 134, 141–42, 191, 193
   census categories of 52–53
   in Dublin 127
   healthy/unhealthy characteristics 137, 140
   slums 8, 125–29, 141–42, 186
   spatial arrangement of 57–59, 137, 140
   social symbolism of 70
   *see also* social housing; house types
Hove (England) 15
Hull (England) 154

immigration 12, 183, 184, 189, 191, 193, 199
   immigrants and suicide 160
   networks of 192
India 46, 150
industry/industrialisation 44

inquests 148, 149, 150, 151, 152
   locations of 145, 153–54
   in morgues 155, 158, 159
   verdicts 144
insanity 132, 133, 142, 143, 146
   'temporary insanity' verdicts 144
Institute of the Blessed Virgin Mary 91–92
Irish America/Irish-Americans 183
Irish district asylums 130
Irish Historic Towns Atlas (Royal Irish Academy) 2–3
Irish Modern Urban History Group 3
Irish Parliamentary Party 8, 47, 54, 56–57, 60
Irish Poor Law 10, 106–12, 114–24
Irish Transport and General Workers' Union 47
Irish Volunteers 67
Irishness 190, 194–99
Italian school 172

Jerram, Leif (historian) 5–6, 63
Jews 152, 160, 198
   in Dublin 152
   Russian 160
Johnston, Francis (architect) 97

Kells, Co. Meath 3
Kerry (County) 176
Kildare 3
   Kildare Place Society 89
Kilkenny (town) 3, 42, 51, 52, 53, 54, 56
Kilkenny Corporation 50
Killarney, Co Kerry 176
Kincaid, Joseph (railway company director) 32n54, 35, 36, 39
King George IV 23, 73, 177
Kingstown (Dublin) 23, 27, 28, 35, 41, 42, 51, 54, 59
   Gresham Terrace 35
   Kingstown Urban District Council 50
   Mariners Church 32n54
Kohl, John George (travel writer) 78
Ku Klux Klan 198

# INDEX

labour 47, 56, 57
Labour Party (Ireland) 47, 55, 56
labourers 162
Land acts 49
Larkin, James (trade unionist) 47
Leamington Spa (England) 15
leases/leasing 31
Lee, James (engineer) 80
Lees, Sir Harcourt (clergyman, pamphleteer) 28, 29
Lefebvre, Henri (philosopher) 5, 15, 85, 163, 165, 181
leisure 7, 14, 15, 18, 23, 28, 63, 74–77, 90, 157, 163, 167
Lewis, Samuel (publisher) 74
Limerick (city) 3, 42, 45, 46, 50, 51, 52, 53, 54, 55, 56, 58, 176, 179
    Chamber of Commerce 179
    Church Street, King's Island 58
    Independent Citizens of Limerick 182
    Limerick Corporation 50, 55, 58
    Limerick Labourer's Dwelling Company 50
    O'Dwyer Villas, Thomondgate 58
    Thomond Artisans Dwellings Company 50
linen trade 66, 77–81
Listowel, Lord and Lady (peers) 167
Liverpool (England) 186
Livingstone, David N. (geographer) 5
Lodging Houses 49, 112–14, 191–92
London (England) 22, 30, 35, 73, 81, 154, 162, 165, 172, 196
    Blackheath 22
    Bridewell Prison 165
    Charing Cross 165
    Covent Garden 165
    Kent Road 22
    London to Greenwich Line 28
Londonderry/Derry 3
    Corporation 55
Londonderry, Marchioness of (peer) 82
Longford (town) 3
Longford de Vesci Estate 14, 15, 16, 19, 23, 24, 26, 27, 29, 31, 32n54, 33, 36, 40, 41

Loughrea, Co Galway 3
lunacy
    legislation pertaining to 130
lunatic asylums 10
    design of 139–41
    materiality of 10, 126
    military service as cause of admission 150
    Richmond District Lunatic Asylum (Dublin) 150
    ventilation of 139

Maguire, W.A. (historian) 71
Manchester (England) 81
Manning, Cardinal Henry (Archbishop of Westminster) 196, 197, 200
maps and mapping 16–17, 18, 20, 24, 25, 28, 31, 37, 38, 39, 69n41, 75n77, 95n44, 130, 157n62, 163n4
Marx, Karl 44
material culture 163
Maynooth Co. Kildare 3
McCann, Revd B. (Belfast workhouse Catholic chaplain) 121–22
McCarthy, Charles (Dublin City Architect) 159
McDonagh, Máirtín Mór (politician) 55
McGuire, Chester (urban economist) 42
McKellar, Elizabeth (historian) 13, 15
McIvor, Peter (historian) 67, 68, 79
McTier, Martha (letter-writer) 71–72
Meath Hospital 153
Medical Officer of Health, Middlesbrough 194
medical schools 154
men 133, 185
    education and masculinity 102–03
    health and masculinity 102
    'irish' masculinity 12, 188
    masculine identity 186–90
    and physical labour 188
Middlesbrough (England) 12, 185, 186, 187, 189, 190, 191, 194, 195, 196, 199, 200
migrants 12, 112, 155, 191
military barracks 153
Monet, Claude (artist) 162

Monkstown (Dublin) 7, 13, 14, 15, 16, 18, 22, 23, 27, 28, 30, 31, 32, 40, 41
   Albany Avenue 27
   Belgrave Square 27
   Brighton Terrace 27
   Clifton Terrace 23, 27
   De Vesci Terrace 31, 35, 41
   Longford Terrace 23, 24, 27, 28, 30, 31, 32, 33, 34, 35, 37, 38, 39, 40, 41
   Monkstown Avenue 17
   Monkstown Church 17–18, 19, 22, 23, 24
   Monkstown Crescent 19, 23, 26, 27, 31, 41
   Monkstown Road 18, 19, 22
   New Brighton 27
   Pakenham Road 22
   Royal Paragon 19, 20, 22, 23, 30, 40
   Royal Paragon Avenue 22
   Seafield Avenue 27
   The Hill 41
   Vesey Place 31, 35, 41
Moore, Frederick Frankfort (journalist) 76
moral contagion 9, 10, 109, 121, 123
morgues 144, 153–60
   in Belfast 155, 158
   in Cork city 155, 156
   in Dublin city 145, 148, 155, 156, 157
   Dublin Morgue registers 145
   economic impact of 156–57
   internal arrangements 158–60
   locations of 158
   as location for inquests 153
morphology 4, 7, 40, 85
Morrison, James (Lord Mayor of Cork, 1784) 171
Morselli, Enrico (physician) 146, 147
Motherwell (Scotland) 188, 189
Moyers, George (architect) 39
Moyers, William (builder) 31, 35, 36, 37, 38, 39
Mulholland, Roger 65
Mullingar, Co. Westmeath 3

Mulvany, John Skipton (architect) 28, 34, 35, 36, 40
municipal government 44, 46, 47, 48, 49, 50–57, 59
   legislation pertaining to 47, 49, 68
municipal socialism 46, 49, 50
Murray, Daniel, Archbishop of Dublin 91

Naas, Co. Kildare 3
National Gallery of Ireland 177n36
nationalists/nationalism 55, 56, 68
   *see also* Irish Parliamentary Party
Navan, Co. Meath 46
Navickas, Katrina (historian) 5–6, 63, 65
Nelson, Horatio (British Navy Admiral) 73
New Brighton Company 27
New Ross, Co. Wexford 46
New Zealand 47
Newenham, George (patron) 172, 173, 182
Newry, Co. Down 3, 66
Nicholls, George (Poor Law Commissioner) 108
Nicholls, Dr John (surgeon general of British Army) 99, 108
Northern Ireland 55

Ó Floinn, Críostóir (author) 58
O'Flynn, Richard and Elizabeth (O'Floinn's parents) 58
Orange Order/Orangeism 68, 69, 189
overcrowding 152, 174

Padua (Italy) 154
Pakenham family 7
   Pakenham, Edward Michael (2nd Baron Longford) 14
   Pakenham, Elizabeth 32n54
   Pakenham, Thomas (2nd Earl of Longford) 14, 16, 27, 29
Papworth, George (architect) 34
Paris (France) 81, 154
Parnell split 47
Pearce, Sir Edward Lovett (architect) 91

# INDEX

Pembroke (Dublin) 42, 51, 54, 59
    Pembroke Urban District Council 50
Pembroke estate 30
Penrose, Cooper (patron) 172, 173, 182
Philadelphia (U.S.A.) 81
philanthropy/philanthropic companies 43, 44, 47, 49–50, 52, 54
'phthisis' 127
Pilson, James Adair (author) 73
Pittsburgh (U.S.A.) 12, 185, 187, 189, 190, 191, 193, 197, 198–99, 200
place, as distinct from space 5–6, 63
police 145, 189
poverty and the poor
    agency of the poor 10, 107, 111, 114–19
    deserving poor, 112, 117
    health 87, 126, 132–33, 134, 141
    Poor Law Commissioners 110, 112
    Poor Law Inspectors 106, 116, 119–21
Power, Anne (sociologist) 2
Power, Chief Commissioner 109
Prince of Wales' Leinster Regiment 150
prisons 153, 165
professional classes 153–54, 172, 173
Protestants/Protestantism 190, 198
public dissection 154
public health 46, 126–28, 132–33, 147, 154, 155–56, 160, 194
public houses 145, 153
Purdysburn Villa Colony 10, 125–43
    hygiene 129, 132–33
    light 132, 134, 139–42
    spaces of 126, 129, 140–41
    ventilation 127, 133–35, 137–39, 142

Queen Caroline 73
Queen Victoria 44, 80–81
Queenstown/Cobh, Co. Cork 157

railways 27–28, 29, 30, 32–33, 45
Rathmines-Rathgar (Dublin) 42, 51, 54, 59
    Rathmines and Rathgar Urban District Council 50

Reid, Forrest (novelist) 75
    *Apostate*, 75
Rice, Thomas Spring (1st Baron Monteagle of Brandon, politician) 179–81
Rippingille, Edward (artist) 167
River Lee 168
River Liffey 148, 149, 155, 156
Roberts, Abigail (author) 89
Roscommon (town) 3
Rowntree, Seebohm (social reformer) 187
Royal Commission on the Housing of the Working Classes 45, 46
Royal Hibernian military academy 9, 85–86, 97–101
    female pupils of 100–04
    military parades in 101–02
Royal Institution for the Promotion of Fine Arts in Ireland 177
Royal Irish Academy 2–3
Royle, Stephen A. (geographer) 70
rural space 181
    rural/urban dyad 129
Russell, Thomas (United Irishman) 75
Russia 46

Saint, Andrew (author) 18, 30
Salthill (Dublin) 13, 23, 27, 28, 29, 30, 41
    baths 28
    railway station 28, 38
    Salthill Hotel 28
sanitation 30, 43, 46, 63
    legislation pertaining to 155
schools
    boarding 84–103
    free 95
    military 9, 85–87, 97–104
    religion and 104
    segregation 103–04
    supervision of 89, 101
seaside resorts 15, 18, 19, 23, 27, 28, 40
sectarianism 190, 195–96
Semple, John (architect) 18

Sherrard, Brassington & Greene
   (surveyors) 19, 10
shipbuilding 185, 186
shops and shopping 63, 73–74
Sinn Féin 47
Sligo (town) 3
smallpox 194
Soane, Sir John (architect) 62
social housing 8, 42–60
   building of 49–50
   legislation pertaining to 48, 49
   municipal authorities provision of
      50–57, 59–60
socialism 57
Soja, Edward (geographer) 5
South Africa 150
   war (1899–1902) 150
space/spatial 4, 28
   childhood 87–90, 95–99, 102, 104
   construction of 5
   delineation of 97, 104, 107
   domestic space 8, 12, 58
   gendered 12, 88, 103–04
   hygenic 129
   institutional 9–10, 86
   materiality of 5–6, 63, 147
   not neutral 5
   performative 102
   peripheral space 7, 13
   place (as distinct from) 5–6, 63
   production of 85–86
   public and private space 23, 44, 60,
      88, 97, 104
   regulation of 18, 96, 98, 100–01, 107,
      109, 119–23, 128
   segregation 9, 10, 95–96, 103–04,
      106–08, 110, 119, 121–23, 192,
      131, 141
   spatial arrangement of housing
      57–59
   therapeutic 126
   unhealthy 132–33
   White Linen Hall and Donegall
      Place (Belfast) as 73–83
'spatial turn' 4–5
Spillane, William (Mayor of Limerick)
   45

squares 15, 40, 44, 69
'steel cities' 184, 186
Stewart and Kincaid (agents of
   Longford and de Vesci estate) 14n7,
   27, 29, 32n54, 33, 34, 36, 38
Stewart, A.T.Q. (historian) 68
Stewart, Henry (resident, Longford
   Terrace) 32n54
Stewart, James Robert (resident,
   Longford Terrace) 32n54, 36
Stobart, John (historian) 66
Stokes, G.T. (historian) 15
suburban development and Suburbia 7,
   13, 14, 18, 22, 24, 25, 30, 32, 40,
   59
Suffern, John 79–80
suicide 11, 144–61
   anomic suicides 145, 160
   causes of 145–46
   decriminalisation of in Ireland
      (1993) 144
   legislation pertaining to 144
   marital trouble and 149
   in the military 153, 161
   urbanisation as a cause of 146–47
surveys and surveying 16–17, 19–22,
   26, 27, 35, 40

Taylor, David (Chairman, Belfast Board
   of Guardians) 118, 122
telegraph 79
temperance 81, 193, 196
Thompson, F.M.L. (historian) 13
Thurles, Co. Tipperary
   The Mall 57
   Town Hall Commissioners 57
Tipperary 57
Tivoli House, Cork 171
Tone, Theobald Wolfe (United
   Irishman) 75
Trafalgar 73
Tralee, Co. Kerry 3
transnational history 184
Trim, Co. Meath 3
Tuam, Co. Galway 3
tuberculosis 127, 133
Tullamore, Co. Offaly 3

Turner de Lond, William (artist) 11, 163, 174, 176, 179, 181
    *George IV, King of England, entering Dublin* 177–78, 179, 181
    *Market Place and Courhouse at Ennis,* c.1821) 174–77
    *The Chairing of Thomas Spring Rice* 179–80, 182
typhoid 127

Ulster 44, 47
unionisation 199, 200
unionists/unionism 54–55, 68–69
United States of America 43, 47
    cities in 154
urban history 1
urban planning 15, 19, 22–23, 26–27, 30–31, 34–36, 39–41, 69–70
urban renaissance 62–63, 69, 76
urban space
    constitution of 7
    contested 198–99
    and health 141–43
    and 'Irish' neighbourhoods 190
    and Irish towns 6
    isolation of 11, 146–47
    materiality of 5, 147
    as physical and ideological 165, 182
    and religion 193, 196, 198
    and rural space 7, 129
    and sites of power 165

Venice (Italy) 154
Vereker, Major John Prendergast 179
Vermeer, Johannes (artist) 162
Verner, Thomas 72–73
Vesey, Thomas (1st Viscount de Vesci) 14
Vesey, John (2nd Viscount de Vesci) 14, 16, 27, 29, 36
Vesey, Thomas (3rd Viscount de Vesci) 38, 39

Wakeman, W.F. (archaeologist) 41
Wakes 194
Walker, Anna 70
*Walkers Hibernian Magazine* 18–19

Warburton, J. 18, 23
Waterford 3, 42, 45, 46, 51, 53, 54, 56, 59
    Waterford Corporation 50, 55, 57
    Waterford Improved Dwellings Company 50
West, William (author) 168
White Linen Hall, Belfast 8, 61, 63, 64–68, 69, 71, 74–83
    Art and Industrial Exhibition held in (1895) 68–69, 81–82
    association with Irish Volunteers 67–68
    attempt to hold meeting in in 1797 68
    and Belfast Society for Promoting Knowledge 74–75
    construction of 64–65
    as a cultural space 74–75, 83
    as an exhibition space 80–82
    dismantled 64, 83
    foundation stone of 67
    interior of 78
    management of 79–80
    as a marketplace for linen 74, 77–79
    musical performances at 77
    as a recreational space 75–77, 83
    regulation of walkway surrounding 76–77
    subscription for 66
    and surrounding area as socially exclusive 70
Whitehand, J.W.R. (geographer) 13
Whitla, Captain (Master, Belfast Workhouse) 106
Whyte, Nicholas C., (Dublin City Coroner) 159
Wilde, Sir William (surgeon) 161
Wilkie, David (artist) 167
Wilson, Richard (artist) 173
women 12, 44, 76, 92–93, 109, 149, 168, 173, 185, 189, 190–94
    character 109–10
    migration 190
    religious 92–93
    unmarried 190
    in workhouse 109–10, 115, 117, 118, 122, 133

Wood, John (architect) 22
'workhouse test' 108
workhouses 9–10, 153
    absconding from 115
    administration of 106–07, 109, 117, 119, 121–23
    admissions to 108–12, 114, 116–19
    control 100–01, 104, 107, 111, 114, 118–23
    health 109, 111, 119–23
    overcrowding 108, 111, 119–21
    physical labour 103, 110, 118
    regulations 106–07, 111
    women 109–10, 115, 117–18, 122, 133
working class/classes 8, 43, 44, 45, 56, 57, 60, 77, 153, 168, 173, 192
    children 192
    Housing of the Working Classes Act (1890) 8
    Royal Commission on the Housing of the Working Classes 45, 46

Youghal Co. Cork 3